WRITING DISABILITY

Disability in Society

Ronald J. Berger, series editor

WRITING

DISABILITY

A Critical History

Sara Newman

FIRST**FORUM**PRESS

A DIVISION OF LYNNE RIENNER PUBLISHERS, INC. • BOULDER & LONDON

Published in the United States of America in 2013 by
FirstForumPress
A division of Lynne Rienner Publishers, Inc.
1800 30th Street, Boulder, Colorado 80301
www.firstforumpress.com

and in the United Kingdom by
FirstForumPress
A division of Lynne Rienner Publishers, Inc.
3 Henrietta Street, Covent Garden, London WC2E 8LU

Library of Congress Cataloging-in-Publication Data
Newman, Sara.
Writing disability: a critical history / Sara Newman.
Includes bibliographical references and index.
ISBN 978-1-935049-54-8 (hc: alk. paper)
1. People with disabilities—History. 2. Disability studies.
3. Sociology of disability. I. Title.
HV1568.N494 2013
305.9'08—dc23   2012030417

British Cataloguing in Publication Data
A Cataloguing in Publication record for this book
is available from the British Library.

This book was produced from digital files prepared by the author
using the FirstForumComposer.

Printed and bound in the United States of America

∞   The paper used in this publication meets the requirements
        of the American National Standard for Permanence of
        Paper for Printed Library Materials Z39.48-1992.

5 4 3 2 1

Contents

Acknowledgments

Many people and institutions have contributed to this study. My heartfelt thanks go to G. Thomas Couser for making the light bulb go off that led to this project. Other colleagues whose support is so greatly appreciated include Lewis Fried, Susanna Fein, Judy Smith, Sigrid Streit, Yvonne Stephens, and Patrick Thomas. Many thanks to Ronald Berger for having faith in this project and to Andrew Berzanskis, especially, for working with me with such enthusiasm and insight. Thanks also to the anonymous reviewers for their guidance. All of you have contributed in some irreplaceable manner to this effort.

Of the institutions that have supported me none has been more important than Kent State University: our English Department, our Ph.D. program in Literacy Rhetoric and Social Practice, and our Research and Graduate Studies program.

Beyond Kent State, my thanks go to Jonathon Erlen, curator of the History of Medicine, Health Sciences Library, University of Pittsburgh; to Elizabeth Ihrig at the Bakken Museum and Archive; to David Vancil at the Cordell Collection of the library at Indiana State University; and to Robert Hicks and Sofie Sereda at the Philadelphia College of Physicians for help with their collections, which contributed to this study.

To A.R. Morgenstern, my mostly companion, and Yoram Eckstein, my soul mate, my heartfelt gratitude for being such wonderful people.

Finally, to the two individuals who shaped my identity and self as well as my interests in only the most positive ways through their examples, I dedicate this book to my parents, Dr. Adele T. Lehrman, Ph.D. in English, and Dr. Harold B. Lehrman, M.D.

1

Disability and Life Writing

Google Search results: "About 3,220,000 results (0.18 seconds)."

How strange, I thought! What a high number of hits on "disability autobiography," search terms entered to investigate my working research assumption: that individuals with disabilities had long written about their worlds rather than only after such expression was made possible by cultural developments associated with Helen Keller, new technologies, and changing educational and civil rights laws.[1] The surprisingly high number of hits—3,220,000!—suggested that my instinct was not only utterly misguided but also that others had beaten me to my scholarly task. When I anxiously examined the results, they covered a range of issues associated with disabled individuals—disability history, writing by disabled authors, and analyses of these matters in scholarly and popular books, in college courses, lectures, blogs and the like. But, none of the references mentioned any autobiography or life writing by a disabled person before the twentieth century; of those mentioned, virtually all were written in its second half and few individuals were specifically identified other than Helen Keller.[2] My instinct, thus far, was upheld and leading me in a propitious direction.

Intrigued by these apparent imbalance and omissions, I conducted another search on "disability autobiography before 1900." This time, the response offered a "mere" 2,630,000 hits. The first 10 entries included coverage of Franklin Delano Roosevelt, Maria Montessori, Helen Keller, eugenics, "famous people with disabilities and dyslexia," and even Kaiser Wilhelm II. These were clearly less sources about life writing and disability than gauges of popular perceptions of life and disability.

As my initial search, then, this one located references to a history of disabled individuals as well as to life writing by and about disabled individuals, primarily the latter. But, none of the entries offered a single example of life writing by a disabled individual before Helen Keller.

As an academic, I am aware of the limitations of the Google search; it is not a scholarly site, to say the least. But, my search was not directed at finding scholarly materials. Because my purpose was to poll public interest in life writing about disability, Google was an appropriate choice. As it informed me, these interests were focused on recent writing, on disability history, and on analyzing others' efforts. Although it seemed reasonable that the public leaned in such directions, it still appeared odd that no individuals with disability wrote about their experiences before 1900.

Next, I conducted a scholarly search. This search confirmed the Google results: almost nothing emerged about life writing by disabled individuals before Helen Keller wrote. Thus, this study was born, a response to the following prompt: when, how, and under what circumstances have individuals with disabilities written from their own perspectives before 1900?

Although the Google results on life writing by disabled individuals was surprisingly limited, the number of hits was anything but unexpected. Life writing is an increasingly popular form of narrative non-fiction, both generally and within the context of writing about disabilities.[3] The genre's popularity is due, in part, to the increasingly globalized world exemplified by my Google search, one in which individuals connect and communicate by means of multiple media. Because life writing in particular allows authors to represent their own experiences, it has become a favorable medium for disability writing both for personal presentation as well as for educating the broader public about lives often spoken for by others (if at all). However, with assistive shifts in technology, accommodations, legislation, and education (and as my Google search confirmed), many contemporary readers assume that individuals with disabilities did not often write about themselves before the twentieth century, specifically before the publication of Helen Keller's classic text, *The Story of My Life* (1903).[4] This assumption is reinforced by the seeming scarcity of materials about disability life writing before Keller's work. Given these circumstances, this study questions that assumption by asking:

- what is disability life writing within the context of the Western tradition;
- how do we understand this genre; what changes has it undergone since its first recorded stories and what links its manifestations;

- what do we discover from those who speak for themselves within a history of marginalization and without the kinds of access and accommodations now increasingly available?

In responding to these questions, my investigation considers how individuals within the Western tradition have identified and represented themselves as disabled. To that end, I use a sociological and historical approach, an approach which considers the sources in their contexts and then relocates them in the present where they might inform current concerns about the body and its representation within disability studies, sociology, medical sociology, the history and rhetoric of disability, and related areas. In so doing, I trace a broad path within the socio-historical study of disability. Following that path reveals that many pre-twentieth century individuals with disabilities succeeded in representing their experiences but their texts have not yet been examined as life writing. When examined as such, these texts demonstrate that their authors were well aware of the stigmas they faced, offer an initial corpus of materials for further study, highlight a tradition of advocacy for the underserved, and contribute to understanding that tradition's contemporary manifestations. This introductory chapter lays out my plan for the investigation while preparing the way for individual chapters to discuss the specific relevant perspectives as well as the social and historical background.

Historical and Definitional Methodology

"Disability" is currently used and broadly accepted to frame a long history of perspectives on and practices involving human physical attributes and their many variations. While the term is but one of many (in many languages) within a complex history, I understood the concept against the backdrop of its very presence. Simply put, no two humans have the exact same physical attributes and conditions at birth nor do they experience the same physical fortunes over their life course. But, the presence of physical variations and societal perceptions of them are different issues. On the one hand, as current scholarship puts it, the percentage of problematic physical conditions or disabilities across recorded history ranges somewhere between 10% and 25%.[5] On the other hand, these statistics suggest a certainty about the numbers, categories, and people to whom they apply which closer scrutiny belies. First, the statistics conflate two key concepts, physical variation and disability. Through this elision, the statistics fail to acknowledge that only individuals whose physical attributes have been marked as different in their social context could be included in the historical documents from which they were culled. As a result, the statistics do not indicate how particular differences became marked as disabilities at any point within the millennia they document. What does it mean to fall into the range between 10% and 25% of individuals with physical differences? How do we account for the different ways in which cultures and individuals conceptualize such categories as disabilities and actualize them in social practices? And, how do we make sense of these ways of conceptualizing physical conditions, both looking back and forward?

Responding to these questions requires dealing with historical and cultural materials and, in turn, a methodology which examines these sources in their original social contexts and as they inform relevant contemporary concerns. Such a methodology also acknowledges the inherently socially constructive status of words, definitions in particular. As such, I look to the work of Edward Schiappa who advises investigators to examine historical documents by differentiating between two goals, historical reconstruction and rational reappropriation, each with its own tool set.[6] The former goal, historical reconstruction, attempts to understand cultural artifacts (printed texts, images, sculptures, and so forth) in their original contexts to the fullest extent possible; without such understandings, no study of society, social behaviors, and disability issues, within this, can or need be sought. Pursuing this task requires recourse to contemporaneous historical materials and attention to the use of language and ideas across them; to those ends, investigators should consider the frequency, resonance and density of key terms among other elements.[7] To study the health of the protagonist of Shakespeare's *Hamlet* in context, for instance, the investigator would need to investigate Elizabethan notions of melancholy, along with other historically appropriate concepts.

In contrast, rational appropriation seeks to understand how past principles and practices inform contemporary concerns. The appropriate tools for this task include the past texts and the current theories with which they might resonate. To discover this resonance, the investigator looks for themes, practices, and concepts which are evident on some level in both cultures. Because reappropriation brings the earlier concepts forward, so to speak, the investigator not only interprets past elements in light of current approaches but also acknowledges any anachronistic statements which the act of reappropriation might entail. Otherwise, the reappropriation could be misunderstood as a historical reconstruction and skew current understandings of the original historical context. Continuing with the Hamlet example, an investigator pursuing a rational reappropriation of his mental state, as Hamlet's condition might now be called, could diagnose him with an Oedipus complex but with the caveat that no Elizabethan had any familiarity with Freudian analysis (without recourse to a time machine); the diagnosis is an interpretation based on a reappropriation that might inform contemporary concerns with madness, critical theories, and the like, but neither Shakespeare's conceptualization of Hamlet's character nor his audience's reception of it.

As mentioned, this methodology also informs how I define key terms in this study. From this perspective, and again following Schiappa, definitions are socially constructed and hence serve argumentative or rhetorical purposes. That is, definitions are hardly universals inscribed in dictionaries but constructs whose various meanings are shaped by their use in social contexts and, accordingly, change over time and location. Students of disability studies are only too familiar with the argumentative force of definitions; each of disability's many historical and cultural definitions reflects its originating social context, and all manifestations make culturally specific arguments about the individuals thus identified, arguments which are open to analysis and interpretation.

Although this methodology embraces two different goals, the approach does not preclude conducting research to both ends within a single effort if the goals are pursued consistently and framed as such. With both goals in mind, then, this study analyzes life writing texts in conjunction with appropriate contemporaneous historical materials to determine how these individuals represented their identity as disabled. Based on these historical reconstructions (and when relevant), I reappropriate the historical representation into the contemporary context; by understanding the historical reconstructions in terms of recent theories and constructs involving class, gender, and the like, and acknowledging any changes or anachronisms such extension entails, my reappropriations of these concepts inform current work on disability issues. Maintaining these distinctions between past and present is not only critical to any study involving historical concepts and practices but also conforms with recent work in disability studies which addresses the complexities of assigning meaning, creating categories, and naming terms and concepts.[8]

To illustrate this approach while introducing the background necessary for the study, let me next sketch a history of the concepts and terms surrounding disability over the periods and locations my study covers (as indicated, individual chapters offer in depth detail where appropriate). It is against this history of Western cultural conceptions of disability—this history of assumptions associated with the concept regardless of the particular terms employed to name it—that my study examines and compares how individuals thus constrained have represented themselves as disabled. As that discussion makes clear, the term "disability" was only recently coined and is obviously an English term; nonetheless, I use it throughout the study for expository clarity and to trace an historical path for the concept associated with human physical variation.

Although the term "disability" is newly coined, the concept of disability has existed at least as long as recorded history. As many studies have discussed, the concept has by and large been understood in the Western tradition in terms of exclusion and deviance, understandings which separate "normal" individuals from those who are physically or mentally "deviant."[9] For ancient Greeks and Romans, problematic physical conditions were an everyday presence in a cultural landscape lacking, at the least, sanitation and antibiotics.[10] Based on the available humoral medical system, which was relatively abstract rather than categorical, those cultures judged humans and their physical variations in idealized terms of balance and proportion.[11] Against these canonical norms, individuals were typically characterized as beautiful, strong, virtuous, and superior or as ugly, weak, maimed and inferior.[12] Because these terms were also applied along lines associated with citizenship, they aligned disability issues with what we now call gender, race, and class. Throughout the middle ages, such matters of physical and intellectual/moral fitness were reframed within the scriptural guidelines of the Church.[13] In this context, the presence of problematic physical conditions was associated with spiritual matters, acquiring salvation especially. Within this model, imperfect, weak, and often womanly earthly bodies were obstacles, i.e. disabilities, to be removed from blocking the path to salvation, a goal which required perfect bodies and souls. In these ancient and medieval societies, then, disability had everything to do with the daily presence of physical variations in human lives and with the ways in which these variations aided or prevented individuals from living up to societal expectations.

From the sixteenth century forward—and obviously I am putting this broadly for now (see individual chapters for detailed discussions—social perspectives and practices as well as the notions of disability which they reflected were subject to standardization prompted by new technologies, especially print and medical technologies. The advent of mechanical printing is concurrent with the appearance of the actual word "disability" as well as with the ability to spread emerging categorical cultural conceptions of it more widely and systematically. In shaping these understandings, scientific and medical practices categorized how the body operated in mechanical terminology, contrasting the proper, effective, and smooth operation of body parts and systems with those that were defective, jerky, or convulsive.[14] At this time, the presence of physical problems, and their reconceptualization as disabilities, acquired an air of the automaton; one's body either operated correctly or was broken, disabling, and required repair. By the eighteenth century detailed medical taxonomies and associated practices named particular physical problems as disabling and framed them now as categorical illnesses to be cured.[15] With the medical model born and mass printing disseminating its sentiments, notions of impairment, diagnosis, and cure were more fully inculcated in cultural practices. During the nineteenth century, physical deviations from the norm were often understood as deformity, a term which focused on extreme bodily abnormality; disability had become spectacle.[16] To obscure (and yet enhance) their visibility, disabilities were categorized in the twentieth century along more medically specific lines, in some cases, explicitly including sexual orientation, class, and race; the fact that homosexuality appears as a mental pathology in the *Diagnostic Statistic Manual of Mental Disorders* (*DSM-III-R*), but not in subsequent editions, illustrates how concepts of disability shift in concert with socio-political issues. Although it retains its early associations with social issues, disability has also acquired an exceptional presence in the twentieth century which categorical naming seeks both to reveal and yet conceal.

Medical thinking still resonates in the public mind, but its normative understanding of disability has been complicated in the latter twentieth and early twenty-first centuries by the efforts of advocacy and academic communities to better understand and improve the lives of those marginalized for their perceived bodily differences. As an influential alternative to the medical model, the social model turns from the individual to society and from normalization to rehabilitation. "Unlike people who are ill, individuals with disabilities do not need to adopt the norms of the non-disabled majority or need to 'get well,' rather it is society that needs to accommodate their difference."[17] Further, the social model distinguishes between "impairment" and "disability." An impairment is a physical fact, but a disability is a social construction. For example, immobility impairs while a building without a ramp disables.[18]

As is generally the case with dichotomies, the binary on the social model is built, specifically between "impairment" and "disability," reifies the very categories it seeks to destabilize. Some scholars have replaced that binary with a spectrum which moves away from opposing impairments and disabilities to considering the reception and construction of such differences.[19] To populate this spectrum, disability has been considered in such transdisciplinary terms as embodiment, oppression, and identity.[20] Quite recently, sociological scholarship has explored how globalization and technology have affected contemporary disability issues by developing new models and concepts, among them: disability orientation and identification as they affect the life course; affirmation models which offer a "non-tragic" model; and aesthetization perspectives which pick up on recent concerns with designer bodies.[21] Such thinking publicly questions and challenges the ways in which the medical model continues to reconstitute itself in social norms and, in so doing, explicitly aligns disability issues with those of other marginalized groups.[22]

At present, contemporary theories and practices hold that physical disability has no universal inherent meaning; instead, disability is defined by a given community's understanding of member's roles within it. From this perspective, one which grounds my description above and my analysis below, social constraints impose notions of normality and ability on individuals within a range of mental and physical variations and differences.[23]

As the previous sketch also suggests, a "one-size fits all" approach to defining and understanding disability cannot embrace the fluidity within which social roles and associated notions of disability have been erected, maintained, and/or shifted over time. Such circumstances support my choice of approach, the socio-historical approach described above. Thus equipped, my study moves from its method and definitions to analyses based on the following assumptions. All humans deal with the brute facts of physical conditions. Lacking a social context, however, a particular physical condition is neither good nor bad. Something as simple as a spasm, for instance, has been characterized over time as anything from invisible to a sign of a violent and uncontrolled mind, of sin, or of involuntary neural function. To transform physical variation into disability, societies can be said to rely on values involving success; that is, when a society's values frame a condition as limiting an individual or group's ability to be successful (i.e. independent, flourishing, happy—these of course depend on the culture), than that individual is perceived as disabled.

But, an individual's perception of and response to his/her disability status may differ from its construction in her/his broader culture; marginalized individuals or groups may not accept how others define them. Thus, my study not only examines the social perceptions imposed on disability; it also distinguishes between those social perceptions and the ways in which the individuals themselves recognize and express that identity within their socio-historical contexts. In distinguishing between others' perspectives and the individuals' own, my study treats illness, impairments, and developmental differences in broad yet culturally specific ways within the Western tradition as well as the construction, recognition, and reception of that difference. For such a study of disability, life writing offers a distinctive perspective which other genres cannot provide.

Definitions: Life Writing

Although life writing is a new name, it is not a new practice. To acknowledge this circumstance while defining life writing in its past and present manifestations, I look to the work of Caroline Miller.[24] Miller rejects the conventional notion that genres are absolute categories identified by fixed features of form and content, as is the case with novels, poetry, plays, etc. Instead, Miller suggests that genres are kinds of social practices; this perspective recognizes that form and content change over time in response to writer and audience expectations (the novel is relatively recent form, for example). In contemporary business practice, for instance, a memo is a genre but so is, increasingly, a tweet.

Using Miller's perspective, I define life writing as writing by individuals about their own lives rather than writing by others about those individuals and their conditions. By extension, life writing about disability refers to texts by people who identify with their disabilities and write about their embodied conditions. Thus defined, life writing encompasses a range of formats in which individuals write about themselves, for example, autobiography, letters, diaries, pathography, visionary prophecies, poetry, and memoirs; fictional biography would not be a type of life writing.[25]

Autobiography is commonly used to designate texts which people write about themselves, but the form is a subset of life writing.[26] In fact, the term autobiography only appeared at the end of the eighteenth century first in German and then in English literature; no one knows who coined the terms.[27] I call life writing before that time "autobiographical." A similar relationship exists between life writing and pathography. The latter, which refers to narratives written about illness, is a recent term based on equally recent definitions of illness.[28] Because it does not pertain to my pre-twentieth century life writing texts, I use the term only to refer to recent examples of that form. Similarly, for consistency and acknowledging formal inconsistencies within the works I cover, I call them life writing as a whole and use historically appropriate terms in context.

The Data and Analysis

As any historical study, my corpus is limited to texts which survive and to the cultural and sociological comparanda now available with which to examine them. But, scarcity is another relative term, especially in the context of life writing about disability.[29] For one thing, historical materials are particularly hard to find if no one looks for them. To remedy that situation, I have recovered materials belonging to such traditional genres as history, epistolary writing, and sacred text, and relocated them according to my methodology and definitions within the genre and social practice of life writing about disability; this is the case with Seneca's letters regarding Stoic philosophy which appear in the upcoming chapter. In addition, I have acquired materials in archives and other locations which have not received much scholarly attention from a disability studies perspective, among them, the medieval and early modern women visionaries the study covers. Finally, survival issues also involve another matter. Scholarship currently favors print linguistic materials, and, so, I call attention to visual life writing, self-portraits, for instance, although they cannot be treated in this study except in some cases as historical comparanda.[30]

Despite my initial concerns, I found more materials than one study could cover. To select particular texts from this bounty, I relied on my methodological and definitional frameworks and sought interesting themes and patterns portrayed in complete texts. After collecting sources and contemporaneous historical materials, I examined the life writing texts in their contexts to determine if they were authentic instances of the genre and if they represented salient, recurrent, or diverging themes within their contexts and as they might inform a history of the genre. In so doing, I also attempted to present a coherent and compelling argument within an interesting narrative. Once my texts were selected, and keeping my criteria for historical reconstruction in mind, I divided and arranged the materials into chapters to reflect the broad historical periods with which readers are familiar. Because I could discuss only some of the documents I found, I challenge others to view these as exploratory case studies, to be extended, augmented, and changed through continued work.

I used a composite analysis to investigate the texts, or an approach incorporating two methodologies. In this way, I hope to provide a richer analysis than a single methodology alone can convey as well as to triangulate my research, especially since the works I treat are relatively diverse in several respects. Naturally, each period has different cultural conventions for writing and representation; at times, for example, experimentation is the norm and at others convention the more common practice.[31] These writing conventions intersect with those constraining concepts of disability; some individuals represent their identity as disabled in conformity with accepted writing conventions and some in contrast to them. Thus, the choices authors make in representing their experiences reflect individual responses to various cultural expectations and, in so doing, offer insights into the interplay between disability and normality as well as between individual in society in their contexts. To analyze the choices authors made, I first and primarily employed textual analysis; this approach allowed me to focus on content level issues, on the argumentative force of the texts, as it were. From close textual readings, interesting choices about word use, arrangement, and form, choices including metaphor and repetition, in particular, emerged.

At times, certain patterns appeared not only within individual texts but also across the texts in the particular historical periods under consideration. To investigate these patterns, I used corpus linguistics for two purposes: to determine how key words and phrases appeared and functioned in the text, primarily through forms of word repetition and collocation; and to provide context for the textual analysis of the life writing. For example, in Chapter Three, I examine the ways in which certain phrases associated with pain, suffering, and love appear across the chapter's corpus; this corpus analysis reveals broad patterns of transmission and usage which inform how these high medieval individuals came to represent themselves in the terms they did. As such, this more quantitative tier offers insights into how words and concepts were socially constructed and disseminated as well as quantitative evidence regarding validity and reliability, even in this admittedly qualitative study.

Despite its variations, all life writing relies on personal testimony and thus raises several methodological issues involving authenticity.[32] How can a story's content be verified and interpreted? Because my approach is sociological and historical, my interests lie in how the authors represent themselves as disabled to their audiences and what they are attempting to persuade those readers to think. This approach renders issues of precise historical accuracy regarding the events in the writers' lives less important than what writers choose to say and how they choose to present that material.

In sum, because each instance of life writing about disability is contingent on the context from which it emerges, this study examines the sources in their original cultural context; in particular, I focus on the ways in which the authors create arguments, implicit or otherwise, about their life experiences by means of metaphors, formal characteristics, and patterns of repetition which emerge from the text. In addition to investigating what these writers say and how they express themselves, I consider how they were viewed in their time period, especially in comparison with contemporaries who did not identify as disabled and against cultural conventions those contemporaries would value.

Book Overview

Based on the method outlined above, the body of the study moves chronologically between key periods and populations in the Western traditions, focusing on representative and/or provocative texts. Chapter Two examines ancient Greek and Roman representations of disability within what I call the civic model, a perspective associated with concepts of citizenship and belonging. Following the model from the time of Pericles to Hellenism reveals societal shifts from groups engaging in public debate concerning disability issues to crafting personal written reflections on such matters. Chapter Three connects the civic model with Wheatley's religious model of disability. From this Church based perspective, the texts of five women visionaries manifest as a form of life writing which shares and challenges cultural norms associated with their bodies by communicating about those very bodies. In contrast to the medieval women, the early modern visionary women described in Chapter Four enact their disabilities, one in public, with spiritual and political ends, practices associated with the appearance of the modern notion of the "self." During the long eighteenth century, as Chapter Five suggests, the concept of disability is increasingly subject to standardization, a circumstance enabled by the spread of printing and medical technologies; with these developments, the notion of personal identity begins to separate from a collective perspective, calling attention to disability in new ways. By the nineteenth century, as Chapter Six discusses, the force of new social standards attempts to remove disability from the public view. Those perceived as disabled are often hidden in asylums; institutionalized, they begin to identify and advocate in more radical ways. Given my goal of recovering pre-twentieth century life writing, Chapter Seven considers Helen Keller's story as a watershed in life writing about disability, especially since other life writing about disability was known and available at the time. Chapter Eight turns to a genre of life writing that is both underrepresented but representative of life writing about disability at the turn of the twenty-first century, the online stories of wounded American war veterans. The concluding chapter draws together what I have found and yet to know regarding such matters as the everyday and the extraordinary, form and function, writing and the body, and more.

At present, scholars have written about disability and disability writing from many perspectives but not from the socio-historical viewpoint on life writing my study takes. By focusing on self-representations of disability, I hope to place these texts and my discussions of them in dialogue with existing scholarship, all of which consider the ways in which marginalized groups experience difference. "Thus, far from being marginal to modern society, disabled people have been central to its most important intellectual projects—invisible but highly visible."[33]

---

[1] Because of the popular nature of Google, I used "autobiography" rather than "life writing" for my search.

[2] As Frank confirmed in 1993, "There are virtually no academic studies of nonfiction, first person, published illness narratives; the sole exception I know is Hawkins (1984). This omission is of sociological interest, given the number of publications on 'literature and Medicine.' 'Literature,' however, refers invariably to fiction and poetry. Contemporary nonfiction exists in a scholarly void. The journal *Literature and Medicine* has not even reviewed nonfiction illness narratives" ("The Rhetoric of Self-Change: Illness Experience as Narrative," p. 50, Note 1).

[3] See, for instance, Bauby, *The Diving Bell and the Butterfly*; Hockenberry, *Moving Violations. A Memoir. War Zones, Wheelchairs, and Declarations of Independence*; Jamison, *An Unquiet Mind: A Memoir of Moods and Madness*; Kuuisisto, *Planet of the Blind*; Mairs, *Waist-High in the World. A Life Among the Disabled*; Rapp, *Poster Child. A Memoir*.

[4] Oliver, *The Politics of Disablement: A Sociological Approach*, p. xi.

[5] Fine and Asch, "Disability Beyond Stigma: Social Interaction, Discrimination, and Activism," pp. 3-21; cf. Garland, *The Eye of the Beholder: Deformity and Disability on the Graeco-Roman World*, p. vii.

[6] Schiappa, *Protagoros and Logos: A Study in Greek Philosophy and Rhetoric*; Schiappa, *Defining Reality: Definitions and the Politics of Meaning*.

[7] Schiappa, *Protagoros and Logos: A Study in Greek Philosophy and Rhetoric*, pp. 32-35.

[8] Linton, *Claiming Disability: Knowledge and Identity*; Linton, "Reassigning Meaning," pp. 161-172; Siebers, *Disability Theory*; Wilson and Lewiecki-Wilson, *Embodied Rhetorics: Disability in Language and Culture*, pp. 1-24.

[9] Wilson and Lewiecki-Wilson, Embodied Rhetorics: Disability in Language and Culture, p. 4, for example.

[10] I am neither suggesting that subsequent medical and public health practices are simply better than ancient ones or that these practices always have positive consequences. But, developments in sanitation and antibiotics have improved the overall quality of human life.

[11] Majno, *The Healing Hand: Man and Wound in the Ancient World*.

[12] Rose (Edwards), *The Staff of Oedipus: Transforming Disability in Ancient Greece*, pp. 12-13.

[13] Wheatley, "Blindness, Discipline, and Reward: Louis IX and the Foundation of the Hospice des Quinze-Vingts," pp. 194-212; Wheatley, *Stumbling Blocks Before the Blind: Medieval Constructions of a Disability*.

[14] Newman, "Gestural Enthymemes: Delivering Movement in Eighteenth and Nineteenth Century Medical Images."

[15] Linton, *Claiming Disability: Knowledge and Identity*.

[16] Garland Thomson, *Extraordinary Bodies: Figuring Physical Disability in American Culture and Literature*.

[17] Darling and Heckert, "Orientations toward Disability: Difference over the Lifecourse," p. 133; cf. Oliver, *The Politics of Disablement: a Sociological Approach*.

[18] Shakespeare, "The Social Model of Disability."

[19] Davis, "Dr. Johnson, Amelia, and the Discourse of Disability in the Eighteenth Century," p. 56.

[20] Finkelstein, *Attitudes and Disabled People: Issues for Discussion*; Putnam, "Conceptualizing Disability: Developing a Framework for Disability Political Identity," pp. 188-198; Siebers, *Disability Theory*, for instance.

[21] Darling and Heckert, "Orientations toward Disability: Difference over the Lifecourse"; Swain and French, "Towards an Affirmation Model of Disability"; and Bill Hughes, "Medicine and the Aesthetic Validation of Disabled People."

[22] Siebers, *Disability Theory*.

[23] Siebers, "Disability Theory. From Social Constructionism to the New Realism of the Body," pp. 173-184; Snyder, Brueggemann and Garland-Thomson, Eds. *Disability Studies: Enabling the Humanities*.

[24] Miller, "Rhetoric as Social Action," pp. 23-43.

[25] See Couser, *Signifying Bodies: Disability in Contemporary Life Writing*; Smith and Watson. *Reading Autobiography: A Guide for Reading Life Narratives*.

[26] Ibid., pp. 6 ff.

[27] Ibid., p. 6.

[28] Hawkins, *Reconstructing Illness: Studies in Pathography*.

[29] Eyler, Ed., *Disability in the Middle Ages: Reconsiderations and Reverberations*; Metzler, *Disability in the Middle Ages: Thinking about Physical Impairment during the High Middle Ages, c. 1100-1400*; Stiker, *A History of Disability*.

[30] Stafford, *Artful Science: Enlightenment Entertainment and the Eclipse of Visual Education*.

[31] Smith, *Behind the Scenes, or, Life in an Insane Asylum*, p. 3.

[32] Barros and Smith, *Life-Writings by British Women 1660-1850: An Anthology*, p. 21 ff.; Smith, *Behind the Scenes, or, Life in an Insane Asylum*, pp. 3ff.

[33] Smith, "Foreword," in Husson, Thérèse-Adéle Husson, *Reflections. The Life and Writings of a Young Blind Woman in Post-Revolutionary France*, p. xiii.

2

Ancient Sources:
Outcasts, Oracles, and Old Age

As Chapter One discussed, all humans inevitably deal with physical conditions which, according to my framework, become disabilities when they are perceived in a given culture as limiting someone or some group's ability to prosper in that environment. Recovering past perceptions of disability in any period requires care; the individual who inquires about disability in antiquity must resist the impulse to apply more recent concepts to those earlier ancient understandings.[1] These recovery efforts have another significant constraint in terms of ancient sources.[2] While the overall number of extant ancient sources is limited, discussions of disability are further restricted to written documents and/or written and imagistic documents; imagistic documents (painted and sculpted works) alone do not indicate who is representing what kind of conditions in what light to the contemporary reader.

Certainly, these limitations are very real. Nonetheless, enough evidence exists to complicate Garland's claim that:

> no ancient author ever attempted to describe what it was like to be disabled. Rarely did he allude even in general terms to the physical, let alone psychological condition of that person. Nor did he ever ponder, in writing at least, upon what to do to make his or her life more tolerable.[3]

Following the methodology provided in Chapter One, this chapter begins to recover and reconstruct these ancient self-representations of disability by examining three texts, each of which addresses a different ancient disability at a different time and location: first, the plight of Greek war victims at the battle of Persepolis in 330 BCE; then, old age in Roman statesman Seneca's life (c. 4 BCE- 65 CE), when the Roman

Empire itself was aging; and, finally, the chronic pain of Hellenistic rhetor, Aelius Aristides (117-165 CE). Despite their textual, formal, and historical differences, the texts share certain values about citizenship and the body, values which underlie who was perceived as and who identified as disabled in antiquity, and values on which I can ground my recovery and reconstruction of these ideas. Thus shaped, and as this chapter details, disability was understood in ancient Greece and Rome as an inability to function in an individual or group's civic capacity, be it physically, morally, and/or mentally. Those who perceived themselves as disabled in those cultures represented that status in terms of their unactualized or broken membership within their broader communities; this status was typically associated with improper movement and shame. As such, the three examples of life writing that follow detail how occupational injuries prohibited soldiers from continuing to represent their country; how old age hindered a once active politician from living life to the fullest; and how chronic pain caused a hiatus in an orator's pursuit of his professional activities. I frame my reconstruction of these ancient understandings of ancient disability within broader disability studies work by extending Edward Wheatley's religious model of disability, itself an extension of the more recent medical model, and calling my perspective on ancient disability the civic model.

Ancient Disability and the Civic Model

Although neither the ancient Greeks nor Romans could have had an exact correlate to the contemporary term "disabled," they certainly had notions of how physical conditions complicated their lives, notions which emerged from the ways in which physical problems interacted with medical and civic standards of the day. Above all, in ancient cultures, physical problems were a pervasive presence, as in any culture; but these problems were also physically obvious in ways which differ from later societies where surgeries and medicines could remove or mask that physical presence.

Ancient written, imagistic, and epigraphic sources represent a wide range of physical conditions, among them, in contemporary parlance, arthritis, baldness, birth defects, blindness, cancers, clubfoot, deafness, epilepsy, heart problems, impotence, infertility, left-handedness, obesity, occupational wounds, old age, paralysis, polydactylism, rashes, and rickets.[4] "Though the evidence from antiquity is diffuse, we are certainly talking about a phenomenon which, if modern statistics can serve as an approximate guide, affected at least one-tenth of the population from a relatively early age."[5] These and other specific conditions—as well as the individuals in whom they are manifested—are described as disgraceful, imperfect, incomplete, maimed, ugly, and weak.[6] On the one hand, the terminology frames the problems as deficits in character or appearance. On the other hand, the accounts do not indicate if or how a condition was perceived in its culture as a disability (as opposed, for instance, to a cosmetic issue or no issue at all).

Such understandings and distinctions emerge not from the presence of the physical condition alone but from the condition's effect on an individual's or group's ability to actualize appropriate societal roles. These notions depend on ancient medical conceptualizations of the body.

In Greek and Roman medical discussions, those by Hippocrates and Aretaus, for example, convulsions, spasms, and inappropriate movements are said to be caused by various organic issues rather than the gods or the gods alone. Instead, these actions are considered signs of social shame and ignominy. When Hippocrates discusses epilepsy, a well known condition at the time, he characterizes its many manifestations as unseemly and shameful, and attributes their presence to organic causes. He mentions, for example, "convulsions," "a higher-pitched and louder cry," "pass[ing of] some faeces," "foam[ing] at the mouth," "attacks of fear and panic and madness and jump out of bed and rush out of doors."[7] Thus described, epilepsy and its shameful, public manifestations mark an individual of lowly civic status.

Areteus offers more detail in his Chapter IV, "On Epilepsy."

> Epilepsy is an illness of various shapes and *horrible*; in the paroxysm, *brutish*, very acute, and deadly.... Or if from habit the patient can endure it, her lives, indeed, enduring *shame, ignominy*, and sorrow.... and then, having rendered them more *deformed*, it destroys certain youth from envy, as it were, or by the *distortion of the countenance*, or by the *deprivation* of some sense.... And sometimes the disease is rendered painful by its *convulsions and distortions* of the limbs and of the face; and sometimes it turns the head distracted. The sight of the paroxysm is *disagreeable*, and its departure *disgusting* with spontaneous evacuations of the urine and the bowels. But also it is reckoned *a disgraceful form of disease*.... But if it become inveterate, the patients are not free from harm even in the intervals, but *are languid, spiritless, stupid, inhuman, unsociable*, and not disposed to hold intercourse, nor to be *sociable*, at any period of life...; the tongue is rolled about in the mouth *convulsively* in various ways. The disease also sometimes *disturbs* the understanding, so that the patient becomes altogether fatuous. The cause of these affections is coldness with humidity.[8]

Aretaus clearly associates epilepsy with shameful social status. Hippocrates, Aretaus and other ancient writers use similar terms to characterize other illnesses which manifest with unusual movements, among them, melancholy, paroxysm, phrenitis, apoplexy, paraplegia, paresis, paralysis, and tetanus. Consistently, inappropriate, public movements signify lowly civic status. Implicitly, ancient sources also constructed health in terms of a mind/body divide which separated the mind as logical and normative from the body as subjective and potentially deviant.

Broader ancient Greece and Roman perspectives on health and the body affected how those cultures perceived who belonged within their ranks and who, therefore, could be considered disabled. Developed by Greek physician Hippocrates (c. 460—c. 370 BCE) and extended by Roman anatomist Galen (129–199/217 CE), the humoral medical approach conceptualized the body as a whole rather than as a sum of its parts. Lacking the technology to directly observe the body's internal operations, this medical perspective relied on perceived correspondences between inner and outer states to evaluate bodily health and moral character. So conceived, the body was an abstract container comprised of four humors (choleric, melancholic, phlegmatic, and sanguine). The relative balance or imbalance of the humors within an individual's body reflected his/her corresponding mental and physical state; the association, for instance, between the melancholic humor and affect is still well-known.[9] Medical decision-making preceded deductively by applying established norms, in this context, humoral norms, to individual cases. Medicine was an art whose practitioners sought to diagnose by outward symptoms and appearances rather than to cure by systematic theory and practice.[10]

Such community, civic, thinking about physical problems depended as well on the structure of these ancient cultures, particularly their thinking about politics and communication. Politically, and at least in theory, the ancient Greek and Roman communities operated, respectively, as a participatory democracy and a representative republic. In such governments, citizens belonged as parts of the communal whole; non-citizens or outsiders (women, slaves, barbarians; see below) were duly prohibited from full membership. In turn, these democratic and republican forms constrained how particular communicative practices framed and disseminated particular kinds of information. As these cultures shifted from primary orality to print linguistic literacy, information was in large part mediated through oral communication.[11] Accordingly, civic decisions about laws, wars, court cases, and so forth emerged from public deliberation which was agonistic, public, and rhetorical (i.e., persuasive). In ancient Greece, all citizens were required to participate; significantly, slaves, foreigners, and women did not belong to these ranks. By the Roman era, elected representatives deliberated for constituents. In both contexts, and as medical decision-making, once consensus was reached on general principles, those broader premises were applied to particular situations on a case-by-case basis; often, as discussed below, these situations involved disability status, explicitly or otherwise.[12]

Ancient notions of the body also addressed its role in communication practices. Here, characterizations of improper movement, low status, and subjectivity are contrasted with proper civic behaviors. With respect to public discourse, Aristotle's (384 BCE – 322 BCE) early and influential discussion in the *Rhetoric* defines the delivery of speeches as comprised of gesture, facial expression, and voice.[13] Given these elements, he links gesture with acting, and describes it as a "vulgar matter when rightly understood" and notes that "[delivery] has great power... because of the corruption of the audience."[14] In so doing, he characterizes inappropriate rhetorical gestures, vis-à-vis bodily movements, as signs of ineffective, foolish, nonsensical, or garish behavior. This understanding of improper civic discourse is consistent with ancient medical classifications of improper bodily movements.

Elsewhere in the *Rhetoric*, Aristotle notes that improper movements are irrational and animalistic rather than logical and human; for "it is absurd to hold that a man ought to be ashamed of being unable to defend himself with his limbs but not of being unable to defend himself with rational speech, when the use of rational speech is more distinctive of a human being than the use of his limbs."[15] This sentiment is reflected in the language of Aristotle's older contemporary, logographer Isocrates (436–338 BC), who suggests that speech frees humans from animality.[16] Later, Roman statesman and orator, Cicero (106 BCE – December 18, 43 BCE) echoes these thoughts, separating humans from animals by virtue of their ability to speech; for him "eloquence" is the rational capacity which "transformed [humanity] from wild savages into a kind and gentle folk."[17]

Again, and like other ancient thinkers, Aristotle not only links improper, lowly, and brutish bodily movements with irrational, non-civic delivery but also characterizes elements of style as inherently irrational. In Book 3, chapter 11 of the *Rhetoric*, he discusses boorish behaviors, associating them with ornamental, subjective language uses. In particular, he locates riddles and puns within the context of style, *asteia*/urbanities, and metaphors, characterizing verbal humor, simply put for now, as ornamental and witty rather than expressly argumentative and substantive.[18] Such superficial language teaches but by means of clever word play instead of logical reasoning. As subsequent chapters demonstrate, the association between style, ornament, and subjectivity continues, even into current popular thinking about language.

In the extant book of the *Poetics*, Aristotle explains how bodily movements and civic status are reflected in communication practices, here different genres of poetry. He contrasts comedy with tragedy and epic as they contribute to the life of the *polis*/city.

> Since living persons are the objects of representation, these must necessarily be either good men or inferior—thus only are characters normally distinguished, since ethical differences depend upon vice and virtue—that is to say either better than ourselves or worse or much what we are. It is the same with painters…. it is just in this respect that tragedy differs from comedy. The latter sets out to represent people as worse than they are today, the former as better.[19]

In contrast to tragedy, which deals with humans who are better than ourselves, comedy deals with those who are lesser. Later, he adds that:

> comedy, as we have said, is a representation of inferior people, not indeed in the full sense of the word bad, but the laughable is a species of the base or ugly. It consists in some blunder or ugliness that does not cause pain or disaster, an obvious example being the comic mask which is ugly and distorted but not painful.[20]

Again evoking medical characterizations of improper bodily appearance, Aristotle indicates that comedy is about the shameful, lowly and brutish. Because these characteristics are identified in large part by means of bodily deportment, low civic status and disability are inextricably linked.

The body, its movement, and proper training were central to ancient notions of civic fitness to communicate. Seen this way, the healthy, rational, and ideal body was unmarked as the "norm;" proper physical behaviors reflected an individual's moral and mental status and literally embodied by the fully instantiated Greek or Roman citizen.[21] Deviations from the norm marked ill health or character, shameful non-civic, animalistic behaviors and, on some level, outsider status.[22] Hawhee demonstrates how the fittest Greeks were, accordingly, the fittest politicians; Corbeill underscores the degree to which disagreeable physical traits provided folder for Roman political bullying which aimed at denigrating a citizen's moral status. Baldness was considered a disability in ancient Rome when it prevented a man from succeeding in public pursuits and often the subject of public derision.[23] While a marked physical problem could simply be cosmetic, it could also represent disability. With respect to the latter, certain group's attributes came to embody aspects of its non-membership in the Greek or Roman community. Interestingly, the term "pygmy" originated in the Greek naming of a certain group of short and dark foreigners (or foreigners shorter and darker than Athenians) as outsiders because of perceived disabilities involving skin color and height.[24] Similarly, the proverbial barbarian was identified by a disabling, brutish physique, as it were, which defied ideals of proportion and balance.[25] In addition to groups perceived as outsiders by virtue of their race and/or class, gender affected an individual's status similarly. Women were non-citizens with a particular kind of outsiders' body. As Aristotle put it in the *Generation of Animals*, women's bodies were the inverse and hence defective, disabled version of male bodies; their physical condition mirrored their inherent political and social position.[26]

Together, these political, medical, and communicative values informed ancient notions of disability, providing criteria with which to evaluate those who did and did not belong as full, functioning, and virtuous citizens. Disability status reflected individuals with lowly social standing. Because of this communal approach, ancient Greeks and Romans perceived disability not necessarily in specific conditions but in a condition's effects on community and/or family roles.[27] This meant that disability was adjudicated on a case-by-case basis from a generalized norm.

Such a community perspective on disability is illustrated in a court speech by the sophist Lysias (c. 445 BCE–c. 380 BCE), "On the Refusal of a Pension," representing a lame man's case against a court action. Based on his apparent lack of disablement, the court was planning to revoke his pension. Although lameness could potentially prevent any individual from working, in this case, the man could ride his horse. With this ability intact, the court determined that he did not deserve the pension; in other words, this particular man's limp was deemed cosmetic rather than disabling.[28] Similarly, Demosthenes' stuttering did not seem to prevent his well-known career as orator/logographer since neither he nor any contemporary mentions the condition.[29] Finally, a gendered version of this perspective is illustrated in a story from historian Herodotus about Lahda, a lame Babylonian woman. Despite her withered limb, Lahda was not perceived as disabled because she was fertile and could fulfill her civic role as a woman.[30]

In his work on blindness in the middle ages, Edward Wheatley develops a religious model within which to frame the medieval perspective on disability in contemporary terms.[31] In developing this model, Wheatley extends Simi Linton's discussion of the medical and social models of disability.[32] According to the religious model, disability was measured against the institutional norms imposed by the Church. These norms, generally speaking and as discussed in Chapter Three, involved how an individual expressed piety. Contrary to conventional current thinking, disability was not simply considered God's punishment for sin; rather, physical conditions become disabilities when they prevented the individual from accepting and enacting God's role in his/her life and afterlife. As Wheatley also describes it, this model operates analogously to the medical model imposed by medical institutional practices on understandings of disability from the mid-nineteenth century to the present.

Building on Wheatley's work, I understand ancient perceptions of disability in terms of the civic model.[33] According to this model, ancient societies evaluated disability against the ideal, balanced body and the participatory practices expected of the Athenian or Roman citizen; that civic, institutional model permeated their cultural understanding of who was a full-fledged citizen. To make decisions about particular disabilities, a person's condition was evaluated on an individual basis against the group norm. In this way, an individual literally embodied his civic status.

The civic perspective implicitly underpins the existing scholarship on ancient disability. For that reason, these works support the previous discussion and my upcoming use of this model to understand ancient self-portraits of disability.[34] But, the model, of course, is untested against the ways in which individuals actually represented themselves as disabled and reflected on that status. Let the testing begin.

Ancient Life Writing: Persepolis 330 BCE

My first example is a quintessentially ancient Greek story, a narrative documenting what happened when Alexander the Great encountered war ravaged Greek soldiers in January 330 BCE on his way to Persepolis.[35] The episode is probably the earliest extant policy debate involving disabled people and a community reaction to them in the Western tradition.[36] From my perspective, the story offers perhaps the earliest instance of life writing by those who identify and represent themselves as disabled. Because the story offers that perspective within a debate, it also illustrates how the ancient Greek culture of Alexander's time used collective, embodied communicative practices to establish and apply civic norms, both generally and in association with disability, in this case occupational injury. As the story goes,

> when he was not far from the city, the king was met by a pitiful group of men whose misfortune has few parallels in history. They were Greek captives, some 4,000 in number, whom the Persians had subjected to various kinds of torture. Some had their feet cut off, some their hands and ears. They looked more like outlandish phantoms than men, with no recognizably human characteristic apart from their voices.[37]

Missing limbs and no doubt scarred, the men looked anything but human, a perception underscored by the only remaining trace of their humanity, the sound of their voices.[38] Represented by their embodied conditions, the men are less than the ideal and, implicitly, outside the embrace of their former Greek civic and familial statuses; but at present, they are only potentially disabled.

Moved by their situation, Alexander offers the men reparations and the opportunity of returning to their long abandoned families in Greece rather than remaining in Persia.[39] With two options available, the men engage in debate. As indicated, the discussion not only demonstrates the group's perspective as they identify collectively but also offers its take on how others, their families in particular, will feel about and react to them.

Representing the position to stay in Persia, Euctemon of Cyme, one of two otherwise unidentified men among the injured, begins the debate with a question:

> Do we now desire to parade these injuries of ours before all Greece, as if they provide a pleasing spectacle—injuries for which I'm not sure whether we feel more shame or bitterness? Yet people who hide their distress bear it best, and to those suffering misfortune no homeland is as welcome as solitude and being allowed to forget their former circumstances.[40]

Euctemon's rhetorical question presumes the group's communal response: because of their shameful injuries, they are better off forgetting their Greek homeland. If they were to return, it would be only to provide entertainment for former friends and family.[41] Advising against that option, Euctemon represents the soldiers as a group which has lost its home but not its memories of that land and its values. As

Euctemon sees the situation, their only decision is between the emotions of "shame or bitterness."

In another passage, Euctemon describes their lot; he calls them "we who but now were ashamed to come out from the darkness of a dungeon."[42] Referring to the underground prison which held them as captives, Euctemon associates their unsightliness with their shameful status as outcasts. Indeed, their condition is barely palatable to themselves, but it is all that binds them in any community.

> 'We are cut off far from Europe in the remotest areas of the East, old men and weak with most of our limbs mutilated.' … 'So shall we forthwith abandon those who are the moment dear to us when it is uncertain that we shall ever see those we seek? No, we shall hide among people who have become acquainted with us after out miseries began.'[43]

As outsiders unable to work as soldiers in Greece, their only option is to remain in Persia where, at the least, they have each other. Elsewhere, Euctemon reminds his fellow soldiers that "were we not sharing misfortune, we should long ago have found each other disgusting…. No one can maintain constant affection for what he finds repulsive."[44] Because the injured soldiers believe their families will mock them, they see themselves outsiders whose bodies reflect and embody their social standing.

Another member of the group, Theaetetus, offers an opposing position but one that is no less rooted in ancient Greek civic norms. Instead of focusing on their deplorable physical condition, Theaetetus turns to their families' feelings.

> No good man will judge his kin by their bodily condition, especially when the cause of their calamity has been an enemy's cruelty, not Nature. He deserves every misfortune who is ashamed of a misfortune due by chance; for he has a sinister opinion of humanity, and despairs of pity only because he himself would deny it to his fellow man.[45]

Suggesting that Euctemon is overly cynical, Theaetetus claims that their relatives in Greece value family above all. Certainly, they would realize that war rather than nature had damaged the soldiers and would thus offer them pity. Evoking community, family and civic virtues, Theaetetus deemphasizes their non-ideal bodily status and focuses on the misfortunes wrought by fighting for their country; yet, his position still speaks to the group norms that ground the ancient Greek notion of disability.

With the terms of the debate disclosed, the group deliberates. In the final analysis, their bodily condition is the critical issue. No longer feeling part of the Greek community, either in their minds or in those of their former families, they decide to stay in Persia.[46] Their status as disabled is actualized.

When Alexander learned of their decision, he "was moved to compassion not only for their misfortune *but also for their feelings about it.*"[47] Nonetheless, their decision was perhaps inevitable; now disabled by virtue of their bodies, neither recognized nor remembered, the men are incapable of fulfilling their civic and family roles, the roles that are central to understanding themselves as citizens of Greece.

Based on Alexander and the Persian's repatriation offers, Miles reads this incident as exemplifying a "charity model, a prequel to some elaborate modern classificatory systems on the medical model."[48] He also applies a kind of "social" model to Euctemon's argument that the soldiers' families would reject them. His thoughts are fitting as a reappropriation of the past story to inform current disability theory; from this perspective, all cultures are affected by and respond to injury. But, this perspective is not a historical reconstruction, and Miles' terms cannot capture how those involved conceptualized the experience in their own terms. From that perspective, the debate demonstrates how ancient perceptions of disabled are mediated through ancient communal, civic values involving body and belonging. In a culture lacking either an explicit medical or a charity system, the soldiers understood themselves not in subsequent taxonomic or charitable terms but as unable to function and belong because of their decidedly non-ideal bodies.

Lucius Annaeus Seneca

By the first century CE, written literacy had spread sufficiently in the ancient world for educated individuals to write and to do so, in certain cases, in the first person about themselves. One such author was Seneca, a Roman Stoic philosopher, statesman, and dramatist in the later years of the Roman Empire. Both tutor and advisor to Emperor Nero, he was forced to commit suicide in 65 CE because of his alleged involvement in an assassination plot. Typical of those times, his letters, dialogues, and plays reflect on the body, brutality, and death, often quite graphically. To that end, Seneca associates suffering with civic virtue, frequently referring to his own experiences.[49] In so doing, Seneca departs from the Greek veterans' collective debate, revealing an emerging, reflective sense of independent self that subsequently influenced St. Augustine's *Confessions.*[50]

Seneca most often addresses his personal suffering as a member of the Roman community within his collection of 124 letters.[51] Written as advice to a young friend, Lucilius, the letters represent Seneca's sense of himself as the elderly and aging Stoic man who values wisdom, learning and their guiding force, the soul, over merely bodily pursuits.[52] Although second to the soul and learning, Seneca notes, the body and its activities are natural parts of life. To fully manifest civic virtue and following humoral principles, the Stoic man must embrace the body both in health and illness.[53]

The aging process complicates the individual's ability to accept and embrace life to the fullest because, for one thing, illness *per se* and illness in old age are different. To clarify what is different and how to recognize and accept the difference, Seneca compares Lucilius' youthful illness to his now elderly state.

> That you are frequently troubled by the snuffling of catarrh and by short attacks of fever which follow after long and chronic catarrhal seizures, I am sorry to hear; particularly because I have experienced this sort of illness myself, and scorned it in its early stages. For when I was still young, I could put up with hardships and show a bold front to illness. But I finally succumbed, and arrived at such a state that I could do nothing but snuffle as I was to the extremity of thinness. I often entertained the impulse of ending my life then and there; but the thought of my kind old father kept me back.[54]

The youthful version of illness, Seneca explains, is neither overwhelming nor disabling. However, in old age, bodily balance is almost invariably lost; this imbalance prevents the elderly individual from living up to previous physical, civic expectations.[55] In his case, having always had poor health, he virtuously accepted the inconveniences of that pain rather than ending his life. Now elderly, the requirement to accept pain remains but the pain, now extreme, has changed. Seneca, still virtuous, accepts his illness, but it compromises, or disables, him as it did not in his youth.[56]

Elsewhere, Seneca explains the aging process in less bitter terms. He represents how old age disables him by comparing that bodily state to various structures and practices, both man-made and natural. Each metaphor frames his aging body in terms of its decreasing ability to function in the same capacity it once did.[57] For example, in his letter "On Old Age," he likens the physical breakdown of old age to the structural breakdown of an old building.

Wherever I turn, I see evidences of my advancing years. I visited lately
my country-place, and protested against the money which was spent
on the tumble-down building. My bailiff maintained that the flaws
were not due to his carelessness; 'he was doing everything possible,
but the house was old.' And this was the house which grew under my
own hands! What has the future in store for me, if stones of my own
age are already crumbling?... I owe it to my country-place that my old
age became apparent whithsoever I turned. Let us cherish and love old
age; for it is full of pleasure if one knows how to use it well.[58]

Old structures crumble not because they are either inherently flawed or
poorly constructed but because of the strain age places on their designs
and materials. So, too, does the human body decline over time in ways
which are unavoidable and irreparable. Still, older structures have a
certain beauty which, when properly appreciated, engage the all-
important soul.

Elsewhere, Seneca further characterizes wherein this appreciation
may be found. In his Letter III, he challenges Lucilius, now young, to
remain strong of mind and body.

Hold fast, then, to this sound and wholesome rule of life; that you
indulge the body only so far as is needful for good health. The body
should be treated more rigorously, that it may not be disobedient to the
mind.... Despise everything that useless toil creates as an ornament
and an object of beauty. And reflect that nothing except the soul is
worthy of wonder.[59]

In old age, the body is structurally unsound and operates ornamentally;
it can be seen but cannot necessarily be called on to act. Nonetheless, the
soul remains and compensates for what the body no longer provides.[60]
In this ornamental, useless state, moreover, his aging body is less
conducive to public spectacle. Now an ugly ornament, as it were, his
body no longer functions according to its youthful standards. As a result,
he desires not to be seen or active in the public realm. As he states in his
letter "On Crowds,"

Just as the sick man, who has been weak a long time, is in such a
condition that he cannot be taken out of the house without suffering a
relapse, so we ourselves are affected when our souls are recovering
from a lingering disease. To consort with crowds is harmful.[61]

Like the sick person who needs time alone to recuperate, the aging
individual needs space, out of sight, for the soul to recover. Here,
Seneca differentiates between youthful and elderly illness; he also

associates the health which the young experience with the fullness of the crowd. Because it is impossible to reverse the aging process and rejuvenate the body, it is better for the old and disabled to be alone, a state which allows them to mobilize what remains of the soul.

Finally, Seneca also compares the illness of old age with that of youth by means of natural imagery.

> If I may begin with a commonplace remark, spring is gradually disclosing itself; but though it is rounding into summer, when you expect hot weather, it has kept rather cool, and one cannot yet be sure of it. For it often slides back into winter weather. Do you wish to know how uncertain it still is? I do not yet trust myself to a bath which is absolutely cold; even at this time I break its chill. You may say that there is no way to show the endurance either of heat or of cold; very true, dear, Lucilius, but at my time of life one is at length contented with the natural chill of the body. I can scarcely thaw out in the middle of summer. Accordingly, I spend most of my time bundled up; and I thank old age for keeping me fastened to my bed. Why should I not thank old age on this account? That which I ought to not to wish to do, I lack the ability to do. Most of my universe is with books.[62]

Like the seasons that cool nature, old age inevitably chills the body, leaving the afflicted with limited options; the options do not include going back in time. But again, the soul provides learning and supreme solace when the body cannot function well. Elsewhere, Seneca indicates that without his learning, the bodily sickness associated with old age would lead to mental breakdown. At present and physically isolated, he compares his loss of physical ability to a devastating kind of seclusion, the opposite end of the spectrum than experiencing the crowd. His loss of learning with old age is the loss of life itself. At present, he retains his ability to write which provides a salve for himself and future sufferers.[63]

Seneca's attitude toward disability is reflected in comments he makes on the physical conditions of other individuals. Consistent with his views on himself, he discusses his wife's servant in terms of proper function. When his wife's attendant plays her usual role as a "clown," she is annoying but acceptable. She becomes disabled when she is blind and a burden.[64]

For Seneca, the mental imbalances brought on by old age are more serious than the physical but each form compromises his civic status. Old age, a process which compromises mind and body becomes, as the

> physicians call it 'practicing how to die.' For some day the breath will success in doing what it has so often essayed. Do you think I am writing this letter in a merry spirit, just because I have escaped? It

would be absurd to take delight in such supposed restoration to health, as it would be for a defendant to imagine that he had won his case when he had succeeded in postponing his trial. Yet in the midst of my difficult breathing I have never ceased to rest secure in cheerful and brave thoughts... death is non-existence as before we are born so this reassures him.[65]

Death is natural and inevitable and, so, the decline that belongs to it. Despite the pain, if he can still write than he can still access his soul and the resources it provides. Conversely, when he, as the Stoic man, can neither conduct his mental business nor maintain an appropriate balance of soul with body, he simply ceases to exist. Lacking any such balance, he is not in fact living. In his world as in that of the Greek soldiers at Persepolis, illness and the breakdown of age were inevitable. But in this less community-oriented context, this Stoic individual understandably found a perspective which allowed him to accept the inevitable degradation of the body.

Publicius Aelius Aristides

When Aristides composed *The Sacred Tales* and numerous orations in the second century CE, he had been influenced by the spread of written literacy and, as Seneca, wrote in the first person about his physical problems. In contrast to Seneca's reflective and personal Stoic sense of himself, Aristides' is a god-guided, mythological discussion, one which will resonate in high medieval life writing. But, both writers, along with the Greek war injured, share concerns about their bodies and embodying their civic roles which reflect their perceptions of themselves as disabled.

Recently, Aristides has been examined from a psychoanalytic perspective and labeled a neurotic with psychosomatic illnesses.[66] In addition to its anachronistic characterization of Aristides (who knew nothing of Freud), this interpretation neither acknowledges Aristides' actual pain nor attempts to reconstruct what he experienced in its particular social landscape. Others have illuminated his works to those ends by examining Aristides as an individual, typical of his times in his concern with his body, pain, and healing.[67] Given my purposes *The Sacred Tales* also offers an opportunity to consider how an ancient Hellenistic individual characterized his problematic chronic pain, as a disability, that is, as a condition which prevented him from working in his civic capacity as a rhetor.[68]

The facts about the some time orator and author are more or less these: Aristides was born at Hadriani in 117 CE to a wealthy Smyrnian family.[69] In 123 CE, when the family acquired Roman citizenship, Aristides was able to study with Roman philosophers and, through such contact, become an orator. In 141 BCE, he set out on a tour of Egypt, the traditional educational capstone.[70] After falling ill at the first Nile cataract in 142 CE, he returned to Smyrna. From then on, Aristides suffered from many physical conditions, among others, he names asthma, deafness, facial neuralgia, plague, rheumatism, spinal curvature, swollen organs, tumors, and general debility.[71] Presumably to help his situation, the healing god, Aesclepius, called Aristides to his Pergamon temple in 145 CE.[72] There, Aristides spent two years in incubation, a communal healing process during which he and other participants slept in the temple awaiting and responding to revelatory dreams.[73] In 147 CE, and rejuvenated, he set off as a part-time writer and lecturer. By 154 CE, he was well enough to resume his career full-time.[74] After many lecture tours in Greece and went to Rome, Aristides died in 165 CE of smallpox.

As the journal of his time in incubation, *The Sacred Tales*, reflects *post facto* on the 26 years when Aristides experienced his life as disabled, i.e. unable to work.[75] Although, as indicated, he suffered physical illness throughout his life, Aristides only writes about them as disabling when they keep him from pursuing his civic obligations. When he is able to work, even if he suffers a painful physical condition at that time, he no longer represents himself as disabled.

For example, Aristides associates illness with inability to work when he describes his first attack. "During approximately the first year of my sickness, I gave up the study of rhetoric, since I was in such great physical discomfort. And at the same time, I became despondent."[76] Here, Aristides explicitly associates the pain with his inability to study his profession. Similarly, he represents the failure of his body to function properly when he recalls that

> at the beginning of the tenth year of my illness, a vision came and said the following: "Sick with the same diseases, at the start of the tenth year, by the will of Asclepius, I went to the places where the disease began, and was rid of it."[77]

As the statement again indicates, Aristides identifies as disabled when he cannot function in his civic capacity as orator. Typical of ancient thinking, too, he does not associate his disability with the specific condition per se but with the inability to function in his civic capacity. Thus characterized, his perspective operates within the civic model.

In addition, Aristides characterizes his disability in terms of his outsider status, which is linked with his body. For instance, Aristides begins the text by comparing himself to a mythical Greek character whose bodily condition metaphorically represents her as an outsider.

> I believe that I shall speak like Homer's Helen. For she says that should would not tell all "the toils of stout hearted Odysseus." But she selects, I think, some one deed of his and narrates it to Telemachus and Menelaus. And I myself would not tell all the achievements of the Savior, which I have enjoyed to this very day. Nor at this point shall I add that Homeric phrase, "Not if I had ten plagues, ten mouths" (*Illiad* 2.489). [78]

As Aristides puts it, he "speaks like" Helen, the woman reviled for her body, whose beauty sparked a monumental war. Literally and figuratively, she is the archetypal ancient outsider. When Aristides compares himself to her, he identifies with her alienated body. Continuing, Aristides notes that his situation is "due to the tempests of my body. Therefore, in view of this, I have decided to submit truly to God, as to a doctor and to do in silence whatever he wishes." [79] Acknowledging the violent pains that he experienced at the first cataract, Aristides mentions that this condition necessitated the god's intervention, his own removal to the temple, and the subsequent healing process. By representing his condition in these terms, he actualizes his disability.

In identifying as disabled, Aristides evokes health and citizenship norms. For example, in Spring 144 BCE, he describes his initial illness at the cataract. He not only suffers from swollen intestines, cold, and choking, but "my other physical debilities were in proportion to these things." [80] As described, his pains correspond to a humoral imbalance which occasioned his incapacitation and trip to the temple. Similarly, two years later in Spring 146 BCE, he experiences various bouts of ill health and comments that "my sickness and the general weakness of my body and its purgation were in proportion to the circumstances." [81] Again, his sickness involves general imbalances rather than specific taxonomic conditions, imbalances which prevent him from pursuing his intended path. In turn, his trip to Pergamon becomes a means of regaining his ability to work, of relinquishing his state of disability, and of gaining his physical and civic balance.

The form and arrangement of the text, a text written to document his disability, embody Aristides' perspective on his condition and his disabled status. On first reading, the arrangement lacks structure, as it moves back and forth been time periods without an apparent pattern. On closer inspection, the organization reflects Aristides' own sense of his body's disabled condition at a given moment. When his ability to work as an orator is compromised, his writing is proportionately convoluted. Aristides frequently comments that he was commanded by the gods to record his dreams. On those occasions, Aristides also states that he composes his journal with difficulty because of the severity of his pain and weakness. In so doing, Aristides links writing and the healing process. When he describes his purpose for writing *The Sacred Tales* in these terms, he links this activity, the gods, and the task of healing his disabled bodily state.

> And this was the first of his commands. I made a copy of the dreams, dictating them, whenever I was unable to write myself. However I did not add in what circumstances took place nor what resulted after them. But I was satisfied, as it were, piously to fulfill my duty to the God, both because of the weakness, as I said, of my body, and because I have never expected that the God would be so providential.[82]

As Aristides explains, writing in the temple is arduous, and he has not always completed his entries punctually. He offers a guiding premise for the narrative structure: being out of balance affects his ability to function as well as to write. Once he can write, however difficult the activity might be, he begins to heal.

As Aristides makes clear in *The Sacred Tales*, his pain is disabling only when he is incapacitated. He counts on both the writing and healing process to return him to his proper civic life:

> I am myself one of those who have lived not twice but many varied lives through the power of the god, and consequently one of those who think that sickness for this reason is advantageous and who moreover have acquired precious gems in return for which I would not accept all that which is considered happiness among them.[83]

Here, Aristides indicates that his time in the temple was an opportunity to make him a more balanced, virtuous person. Whatever the causes or degrees of his illness, they measure his state of disability in terms of his career and life within the civic model.

Conclusions

Disability's everyday presence in antiquity contrasts with the general experience of late twentieth and early twenty-first century individuals. For us, disability is not simply "there." The rise of accommodations, education, and contemporary disability models highlight certain issues to the exclusion of others, marking disability at once now prominent and yet hidden. The disparity between the past and current experience of disability is reflected in Garland's thinking in the chapter's opening statement that individuals in antiquity did not life write about themselves as disabled. Of course, they did, but not in contemporary terms.

The ancient Greek and Roman cultures dealt with the presence of physical problems in ways which made sense in their worlds. To grasp that sense from the distance of several millennia, I have offered the civic model. That model depends on ancient values involving citizenship (community and family), bodily balance, and communication practices. These societies understood physical problems not by their mere presence but by their effect on an individual's ability to function within society at large. Any condition that potentially prevented the individual from being part of the group—regardless of its specific characteristics—could be actualized as a disability when that disruption occurred. Moreover, certain kinds of communication practices, inappropriate movements and/or the use of subjective stylistic elements, such as metaphor, were identified with disability.

Thus framed, as the three texts indicate, the collective ancient Greek and Roman cultures made specific decisions about who was disabled by moving deductively from group norms to individual applications. Calibrated along these lines, lines which linked disability with outsider status, that identity was associated with what we now call race, gender, and class. This insight conforms to contemporary perspectives on the accent world; these societies, the Greek especially, were transitioning from "orality" to "literacy" and, thus, they communicated publicly along lines of group norms. Finally, recognizing one's disability, as opposed to perceiving that status in others, was also associated with communicative acts that individuals literally embodied and were implicitly linked with style and ornament rather than reason and logic.

True, these examples are separated in time and place and as such exhibit differences and contradictions. The Greek soldiers communicate orally and agonistically; Seneca and Aristides wrote as individuals, but the former privately and the later by command of a god. In his response, which documents and embodies his disability in his writing, Aristides provides a segue to medieval disability.

---

[1] Garland, *The Eye of the Beholder: Deformity and Disability on the Graeco-Roman World*, p. xii; cf. Dasen, *Dwarfs in Ancient Egypt and Greece*, p. 166; and Rose (Edwards), *The Staff of Oedipus: Transforming Disability in Ancient Greece*, p. 6.

[2] I limit my understanding of antiquity to the Greek and Roman empires between the fourth century BCE and the second century CE. This encompasses the Western tradition from the time written culture emerged to Rome's fall.

[3] Garland, *The Eye of the Beholder: Deformity and Disability on the Graeco-Roman World*, p. xii.

[4] Majno, *The Healing Hand: Man and Wound in the Ancient World*, pp. 316-317.

[5] Garland, *The Eye of the Beholder*, p. xii. The numerous references to physical problems in myths—from Odysseus to Oedipus to Cyclops—testify to the importance of physical problems and their representation in ancient cultures (Ogden, *The Crooked Kings of Ancient Greece*). At present, there is evidence that in Middle Eastern antiquity blind musicians and eunuchs served as court servants; people with certain physical conditions, for example leprosy, were perceived as contagious or polluting (Miles, 'Segregated we stand? The mutilated Greeks' debate at Persepolis, 330 BC'," p. 867; prisoners of war were hobbled or blinded for security purposes (Garland, *The Eye of the Beholder: Deformity and Disability on the Graeco-Roman World*, pp, 22-23, 36, 38, 7). Contrary to common wisdom, however, the Greeks did not simply kill deformed babies (Dasen, *Dwarfs in Ancient Egypt and Greece*, p. 206; and Rose (Edwards), *The Staff of Oedipus: Transforming Disability in Ancient Greece,* p. 29), nor did they uniformly associate ill health with godly punishment. While it is true that "the evidence for physical disability is scattered, scant, and often contradictory" (Rose , Ibid., 6), there is plenty of information and no reason not to examine them.

[6] Rose (Edwards), *The Staff of Oedipus: Transforming Disability in Ancient Greece*, pp. 12-1.

[7] Hippocrates, in Longrigg, *Greek Medicine. From the Heroic to the Hellenistic Age: A Source Book* , p. 8.

[8] Aretaus, in Longrigg, Ibid., p. 296 (emphasis added).

[9] Hippocrates, *Hippocrates*, Vol II; Majno, *The Healing Hand*, p. 178.

[10] Garland, *The Eye of the Beholder*, pp. 141ff.

[11] On orality and literacy, see Schiappa, *Protagoros and Logos: A Study in Greek Philosophy and Rhetoric*

[12] See *Nicomachean Ethics* I.1-5, in Aristotle, *The Complete Works*, vol. 2.

[13] Aristotle, *On Rhetoric; A Theory of Civic Discourse*, 3.1.3.

[14] Ibid., 3.1.5-7.

[15] Aristotle, *The Complete Works*, Vol. 2, 1355b1.

[16] Isocrates, *Against the Sophists*.

[17] Cicero, *De Inventione* I.1-11.2-3.

[18] Aristotle, *The Complete Works*, Vol. 2, 1412a. On figurative language and subjectivity, see Fahnestock, *Rhetorical Figures in Science*.

[19] Ibid., 1448a.

[20] Ibid., 1449a.

[21] Garland, *The Eye of the Beholder*, p. viii. On studies which discuss the "Other" and the body in antiquity, see Foucault, *The History of Sexuality*; Lissarrague in Cohen, *Not the Classical Ideal: Athens and the Construction of the Other in Greek Art*; Vlahogiannis, "Disabling Bodies."

[22] Dasen, *Dwarfs in Ancient Egypt and Greece*, p. 166.

[23] Corbeill, *Controlling Laughter: Political Humor in the Late Roman Republic*; Hawhee, *Bodily Arts: Rhetoric and Athletics in Ancient Greece*.

[24] Ibid., pp. 63, 166.

[25] Ibid.; Garland, *The Eye of the Beholder*; Ogden, *The Crooked Kings of Ancient Greece*.

[26] Aristotle, *The Complete Works*, Vol. 1, 769a; see Rose (Edwards), *The Staff of Oedipus: Transforming Disability in Ancient Greece*, p.6.

[27] Ibid., p. 36 Rose (Edwards), "Construction of Physical Disability in the Ancient Greek World: The Community Concept," pp. 35-6.

[28] Rose (Edwards), *The Staff of Oedipus: Transforming Disability in Ancient Greece*, pp. 95-6.

[29] Ibid., p. 50.

[30] Ibid. p. 46.

[31] Wheatley, *Stumbling Blocks Before the Blind: Medieval Constructions of a Disability*, 2010. Wheatley, "Blindness, Discipline, and Reward: Louis IX and the Foundation of the Hospice des Quinze-Vingts."

[32] Wheatley, *Stumbling Blocks*.

[33] As models overall, I recognize that they cannot explain individual cases or ones outside those spheres (see Eyler, Ed. *Disability in the Middle Ages: Reconsiderations and Reverberations*, pp. 33 ff.).

[34] Dasen, *Dwarfs in Ancient Egypt and Greece*; Garland, *The Eye of the Beholder*; Miles, "Segregated We Stand?"; Ogden, *The Crooked Kings of Ancient Greece;* Rose (Edwards), "Construction of Physical Disability in the Ancient Greek World: The Community Concept"; Rose (Edwards), *The Staff of Oedipus: Transforming Disability in Ancient Greece*; and Stiker, *A History of Disability*.

[35] Both Quintus Curtius Rufus (active 41-54 BCE) and Diodorus of Sicily (345-323 BCE) document the story. As Miles shows, the specifics of the story cannot be confirmed, the overriding positions have been accepted as reflecting genuine and could well derive from those eye-witnesses. Thus, while they take certain liberties with historical matters, scholars indicate that the core of the matter is historically factual enough (Miles, "Segregated We Stand," p. 86). Accordingly, I take the speakers in the debate at face value.

[36] Ibid., p. 865.

[37] Curtius, *Quintus Curtius Rufus. The History of Alexander*, 1988, p. 103.

[38] Majno, *The Healing Hand: Man and Wound in the Ancient World*, pp. 316-317, 521 note 22, which notes the frequent reference to scars as a marker of trauma in literary and legal documents

[39] Curtius, *Quintus Curtius:History of Alexander,* 1962, p. 373.

[40] Curtius, *Quintus Curtius Rufus. The History of Alexander*, 1988, p. 103.

[41] Comedy and the body were often associated in Greek and Roman writing (Corbeill, *Controlling Laughter: Political Humor in the Late Roman Republic*;

Riu, *Dionysism and Comedy*; and Walters, "Making a Spectacle: Deviant Men, Invective, and Pleasure."

[42] Curtius, *Quintus Curtius: History of Alexander*, p. 373.

[43] Curtius, *Quintus Curtius Rufus. The History of Alexander*, 1988, p. 104.

[44] Ibid., 104.

[45] Curtius, *Quintus Curtius: History of Alexander*, 1962, pp. 375, 377.

[46] Curtius, *Quintus Curtius Rufus. The History of Alexander*, 1988, pp. 104-105.

[47] Ibid., p. 105; emphasis added.

[48] Ibid., p. 875.

[49] Edwards, "The Suffering Body: Philosophy and Pain in Seneca's Letters"; Griffin, *Seneca: A Philosopher in Politics*, p. 4.

[50] Ibid., p. 252. Many works are described as autobiographical which is fine for developing a history of influences (see Chapter One, p.). For example, see Butler, *Western Mysticism*, pp. 31-4) on the autobiographical nature of Augustine's confessions.

[51] Ruys, "Medieval Latin Meditations on Old Age: Rhetoric, Autobiography, and Experience," p. 171. Seneca also discusses personal feelings in some of his dialogues; for example, in *De Ira*/On Anger in his *Moral Essays*, Seneca discusses the frenzy and insanity he associates with anger. Perhaps significantly, Seneca wrote his letters around 63-64 CE, immediately before his enforced suicide.

[52] See Seneca, *Ad Lucilium. Epistulae Morales*. Vol. 1, Letter XLI.8-9.

[53] Ibid., Letter LXV.23.

[54] Ibid., Letter LX. 8.1.

[55] Ibid., Letter LXV.21 ff..

[56] This is not to say that physical conditions cannot disable youthful Romans; but it is a different issue than the chronic pain of old age Seneca is discussing here.

[57] Seneca, *Ad Lucilium. Epistulae Morales*. Vol. 1, Letter XXVI, for example.

[58] Ibid., Letter XII.1.

[59] Seneca, *Ad Lucilium. Epistulae Morales*. Vol. 1, Letter   III.5; cf. Seneca., Ad Lucilium. Epistulae Morales. Vol. 3, LXXVIII.11 ff.

[60] Seneca, *Ad Lucilium. Epistulae Morales*. Vol. 3, Letter LXXVIII.20 ff.

[61] Seneca, *Ad Lucilium. Epistulae Morales*. Vol. 1, Ibid., Letter VII.1.

[62] Seneca, *Ad Lucilium. Epistulae Morales*. Vol. 3, Letter LXVII.1.

[63] Seneca, *Ad Lucilium. Epistulae Morales*. Vol. 1, Letter VIII.2.

[64]Seneca, *Ad Lucilium. Epistulae Morales*. Vol. 2, Letter LIV.3 ff..

[65] Ibid., Letter L.2.

[66] Behr, *Aelius Aristides and The Sacred Tales*, p. 162.

[67] King, "Chronic Pain and the Creation of Narrative," p. 271.

[68] In addition to *The Sacred Tales*, his corpus consists of 53 works including: treatises; panegyrics; speeches on rhetoric; speeches to individuals; religious speeches and writings; and declamations.

[69] Aristides, *Aristides*, 1973, p. vii.

[70] Ibid., p. viii.

[71] Cf. Behr, *Aelius Aristides and The Sacred Tales*, pp. 18-19.

[72] Ibid., p. 21; Misch, *A History of Autobiography in Antiquity*, p. 498; Wickkiser, *Asklepios, Medicine, and the Politics of Healing in Fifth Century Greece: Between Craft and Cult*.

[73] What follows is a good example of dream and response:

"Feb 14 On the following day, fasting was enjoined, but enjoined in this way. I dreamed that I was in Smyrna, distrusting everything plain and visible, because I was not aware that I had made the journey. Figs were offered me. Next the prophet Corus was present and showed that the was a quick acting poison in them. After this, I was full of suspicion and eagerly vomited, and at the same time considered what if I should not have vomited completely? Next someone said that there was also some poison in some other figs. Therefore I was still more distressed and angry because I not hear it sooner. After these things were seen, I suspected that fasting was indicated, but if not, still I preferred it. But I asked the God to show more clearly what he meant, fasting or vomiting.

"I slept again and I thought that was in the Temple at Pergamum and that now the middle of the day had passed and I was fasting. And Theodotus came to me with friends, and having entered, he sat down beside me while I was lying thus upon a couch. I said to him I was fasting. But he indicated that he knew, and said that "after all the things which these men are doing, I have put off performing a phlebotomy on you. For there is an aggravation of the kidneys and fasting", he said, "is a sort of bastard outlet, which goes though the chest, for the inflammation". And while he said this, two sparks appeared before me. And in wonder I looked at Theodotus and felt it an omen of his words, and I asked him what there were. He said that they were from the inflammation, and he indicated what was troubling me. Then I awoke, and I found that it was that very hour, in which I thought Theodotus spoke to me, and friends had actually now come to visit me." Aristides, Aristides, p. 217 (emphasis in original).

[74] Behr, *Aelius Aristides and The Sacred Tales*, p. 285; Aristides, Aelius. Aristides, p. xiii.

[75] The 10 year gap from 155-165 CE suggests, according to my interpretation, either that he felt well or that he was too ill to write during that period; see Behr, *Aelius Aristides and The Sacred Tales*, pp. 23, 205.

[76] Ibid., p. 255.

[77] Ibid., p. 253, emphasis in original.

[78] Ibid., p. 206

[79] Ibid., p. 236.

[80] Ibid., p. 241.

[81] Ibid., p. 241.

[82] Ibid., p. 223.

[83] Ibid., p. 203.

3

Medieval Voices:
Sin, Salvation,
and the Female Body

The daily presence of disability was still very much the norm during the high medieval period. In this environment, however, success was no longer defined by civic status but by sacred Church doctrine. To better understand the ways in which this environment constrained notions of disability, this chapter examines life writing by five high medieval (c. 1100-1450) women visionaries (in chronological order): Hildegard of Bingen, Catherine of Siena, Mechthild of Magdeburg, Julian of Norwich, and Teresa de Cartagena.[1] As the upcoming analysis demonstrates, these women wrote from an identity as disabled not only to reflect on their own lives but also to communicate those experiences to others in their socio-religious context; using metaphors associating their bodies with sin, pain, love, sensory experiences, and self expression, they provided embodied models for achieving salvation and enacted how direct spiritual contact with God transformed disability into divinity. Understood as life writing, their descriptions of their spiritual lives demonstrate how they recognized and attempted to overcome disablement by using these bodies as the medium through which they sought loving unity with God. At the same time, they represent their identity with subjective, metaphorical language associated with deviant and feminine bodies.

In serving similar reflective and practical purposes, these writers also showed their readers how all too familiar disabilities could be used to clear obstacles blocking their path to salvation. And, by communicating about their lives through their bodies, the writers support recent research complicating the simple notion that the medieval "other" was the wild, possessed, sinful, and often female being.[2] Finally, by considering how medieval individuals identified with and represented themselves as disabled, this chapter extends efforts to better understand medieval perceptions on disability.[3]

Medieval Disability, Visionary Women, and Life Writing

At present, three related issues affect the study of medieval disability, issues akin to those facing inquiry into disability in the Greek and Roman periods: a deficit of sources has led to insufficient theoretical and methodological frameworks and, with this, to stereotypical contemporary interpretations of medieval conceptions of disability. To remedy the situation, scholars are recovering new materials and, thereby, embracing current understanding of medieval disability within more culturally and theoretically appropriate frameworks.[4] As mentioned, the sources now available support the understanding that medieval perceptions of disability arose from the prevalence of physical problems at the time along with the efforts of the Church to make sense of these problems.

As in the Greek and Roman periods, medieval individuals lived in a culture lacking germ theory, sanitary conditions, and antibiotic medications; this meant that most (if not all) of this medieval population experienced injuries, rashes, fevers, diseases, and infection. These conditions were persistent, publicly apparent, and were believed to be related to the afterlife.[5] To contend with these realities, medieval conceptions of the body were intertwined with those involving spirituality. Bodily concerns were located in an ideology that encompassed body and soul, as well as the present and the hereafter.[6]

From the prevailing (though more spiritualized) medieval humoral approach, external physical appearances, actions, and behaviors reflected internal spiritual and physical health. An imbalance in one realm corresponded to an equivalent symbolic imbalance in the other; for instance, a melancholic demeanor and facial structure reflected a downtrodden body and pessimistic soul.[7] But, of course, the presence of physical problems alone did not constitute disability, not when that presence was so common; perceptions of disability emerged from the ways in which medieval Church doctrine framed physical problems within their corresponding spiritual dimensions.

The medieval Church regulated the lives of all believing citizens.[8] According to Edward Wheatley's religious model of disability, mentioned in the previous chapter, the human experience of external, earthly physical problems is reflected in the imperfections of the earth-bound soul.[9] Achieving the life goal of salvation required perfection of body and soul. Because one of the Church's most significant tasks was to help believers heal through the mediation of Jesus, the ultimate physician, "the Church defined a disabled person as one who must first call upon the healer of souls before receiving treatment for bodily ills."[10] Understood this way, the Church itself did not simply conflate disability with God's punishment for earthly sin, as the common stereotype holds; instead, the imperfect states of body and soul were acknowledged as common among all humans' experiences, and attempting to perfect both body and soul was necessary for salvation.[11] Individuals who acknowledged these imperfections also acknowledged their earthly disablement. Because physical problems were common and generally undifferentiated by categories, the particular condition an individual manifested mattered less than the possibility of failure to be saved.

In defining the medieval human experience, scriptural, humoral, and cultural perspectives characterized disability along gendered lines.[12] While all humans were inherently imperfect and disabled in body and soul, medieval women were more so, so to speak, because of the subjective, emotional, and passive nature they inherited from Eve. According to scripture and medical theory, derived primarily from Hippocrates, Aristotle, and Galen, female bodies were inferior to the male version and fundamentally incomplete.[13] Yet that same scripture guaranteed that all souls were equal and deserved to be saved.[14] These constraints posed particular problems for high medieval women who sought salvation.

Reflecting this situation, spiritual practices developed gendered forms, based on a hierarchy rooted in Augustine's writings, male mystical experiences were intellectual, active, and superior while women's affective experiences were lesser and submissive to the male version.[15] Because of their presumably physical and sensual nature, women represented disability in ways more immediately engaging for their audiences than their more contemplative counterparts.

In the thirteenth century, a particularly influential type of affective piety emerged, one based on a Franciscan text, the *Meditations on the Life of Christ*.[16] This text, written in the vernacular, was widely read, imitated, and disseminated.

> Attuned to his cloistered female audience, the author of the *Meditationes* exploited sensory experience to make the story at once concrete and compelling, not only describing scenes rich in visual (and often homely) detail and dramatic in emotional context, but also exhorting his reader to imagine herself as though/actually present, as a

reverent eye-witness to, and even a vicarious participating, in the life and death of Christ.[17]

In general, the text and its imitations expressed a form of affective piety which called on worshippers to visualize themselves at the events in Christ's life.[18] In rejoicing with him in his happiness and suffering with him in his pain, they identified with Christ, and took a step towards realizing his perfection and gaining salvation. As indicated above, the corporeal character of the practice appealed especially to women who understood their experiences in sensory, affective terms. And as the previous chapter indicated, corporeal language, as the metaphorical words they chose, was implicitly associated with improper, disabled bodies and subjective experience.

As the chapter details, some women not only read or heard the texts but also wrote about their responses to them.[19] In discussing their participation in Jesus' life, in the painful crucifixion especially, they reenacted visionary prophecies about their way to salvation and called on their readers to share in the experience.[20] As described, felt, and enacted, the mediating point on which salvation depended was the body. As the visionaries represented their physical differences in writing, they participated in God's healing process. Using description filled with sensate detail, they were manifesting the norms allowed to women within a felt sense of their experience. By recognizing this process in writing, they were also identifying as disabled within the religious model.

According to Wheatley's religious model, Church doctrine defined disability in terms of the imperfect earthly body which corresponded to and symbolized the imperfect soul.[21] Disability blocked the pathway to salvation since that goal required bodily and spiritual perfection. Disability's presence was heightened for women not only because they, as everyone at that time, experienced public, physical impairment but also because women's lives were conceptualized and experienced in highly sensate terms which focused on their bodies. By discussing their physical problems along with the spiritual deficits to which they corresponded, the five women I examine in this chapter also explicitly identified as disabled within the religious model.

Each of the women wrote of her visions as moments of union with God; prompted by his presence in their lives, their writing set in motion a process whereby they identified with their physical conditions and recognized them as disabilities. By imitating Jesus—taking on his pain and joy, and, they hoped, his perfection—their human physical and spiritual problems would be healed, allowing them to arrive, no longer disabled, in heaven. In recognizing and expressing that experience, they characterized their physical problems as features of their inherent earthly disablement. More specifically, they described their physical and spiritual deficits in terms of extreme emotional and sensory experiences, often expressed in terms of love and pain, experiences which exposed their earthly, womanly weakness and opposed it to the healed state they sought in Jesus' model.

A Brief Statement on Method

Given the broader definitions on which this study rests as well as this chapter's particular context, I selected texts by five women who wrote from the position of disablement: Hildegard of Bingen, Catherine of Siena, Mechthild of Magdeburg, Julian of Norwich, and Teresa de Cartagena; Table 3.1 offers pertinent information about their lives.[22] These women not only referred directly to their physical problems but also characterized them as disabling obstacles on their path to heaven. Again, the particular physical problem with which each woman identified is not significant; rather it is her acknowledgement of physical problems that marked her identification as disabled and her manner of representing those differences that are interesting for the study. As such, the selected texts are diverse yet based on a shared practice of affective piety associated with disabling conditions at the time.

To examine this relatively large and diverse corpus, I applied a composite methodology to it, one embracing textual analysis as well as a corpus linguistics approach. As in this book's other chapters, the textual analysis allows me to examine how the authors represent their identity as disabled. As I detail below, their visionary writing depends on metaphors which demonstrate these women's understanding of their oppressed, earthly state and their hopes of healing through God's intervention so that, thus joined, they could enter heaven. Two groups of metaphors were salient. One group associated sins and physical deficits in terms which suggest ignorance – ignorance, that is, of disability on their audience's part; within this group, some metaphors highlight correspondences between certain sins and certain physical conditions while others represent those conditions as infectious. The second group of metaphors symbolizes the women's experiences of their physical problems as opportunities for communication and union with God; some metaphors focus on their womanly status—weak and especially disabled—and some look to the ways in which writing helps them overcome that condition.

Table 3.1: The High Medieval Life Writers

Name & Dates	Affiliations / Nationality	Physical Problem	Texts Examined
Hildegard of Bingen, 1098-1179	Benedictine, German	Migraines, synaesthesia;[23] sickly from birth; visions and periods of illness from early age 5 onward.[24]	Personal correspond-ence; *Scivias*[25]
Catherine of Siena, c. Nov. 8, 1347-1388	Italian, Dominican	Visions from age 5 or 6; first vision at 6 (Scudder 21); stigmatization in 1375 (Scudder 13); fasting	Personal correspond-ence; *The Dialogue of Divine Providence*[26]
Mechthild of Magde-burg, c. 1207 – c.1282 / 1294	Beguine, Flemish	Periods of sickness; mortification; ecstatic experience at 12; saw "all things in God and God in all things".	*The Flowing Light*[27]
Julian of Norwich, 1342-1416	English, Anglican (also venerated by Lutherans)	Suffered a serious illness at age 30; vision of Jesus Christ from deathbed	*Showings* (c. 1393)
Teresa de Carta-gena, c. 1425 and fell deaf between 1453–1459	Spanish	Deaf	*Arboleda de los enfermos* (Grove of the Infirm) and *Admiraçió noperum Dey* (Wonder at the Works of God).[28]

But the sources are relatively disparate, since they were written by women from different countries, time periods, and religious affiliations. To draw links between and across their representations of disability—to determine how and in what ways they constitute a coherent corpus—I investigated how words associated with physical difference ("desire," "pain," and "suffering," for example) were used within the visionary texts. Table 3.2 contains the words, their counts, some collocations, and their users.[29] This analysis, which follows the more lengthy textual reading, not only provides some quantitative data on the sources but also reveals that the particular discourse the women used was widely known and, as such, functioned as its own feminine form of normative language about disability within which the visionaries could operate.

Ignorance

As indicated, physical problems were everyday experiences for medieval people, and as such, conceived as earthly realities which blocked their path to heaven. Moved by their visions and the awareness gained from them, the five women wrote in part to inform others and to move them, too, to awareness. To that end, they wrote about those who did not yet recognize their own physical and spiritual obstacles by means of metaphors linking sins with corresponding physical illnesses. As such, the metaphors reflect the humoral perspective as well as the religious model of disability, which depended on recognition of one's earthly imperfect state, within which the model was constrained.

Blindness is perhaps the most common of these metaphors, no doubt because of its strong scriptural connections with light and knowledge.[30] As Hildegard writes to Hartwig, the Archbishop of Bremen, "be alert, for many shepherds are blind and halt nowadays, and they are seizing the lucre of death, choking out God's justice."[31] In advising Hartwig that blindness causes Church leaders to "[choke] out God's justice," she equates sinful injustice with unrecognized disability and quietly warns the Archbishop himself to be careful. Elsewhere, Hildegard equates blindness as well as other problematic sensory conditions with sinful behaviors which prevent the individual from seeing, hearing, or discussing his/her state of earthly imperfection: "Because of the foolishness of those who are too blind to see and too deaf to hear and too mute to speak, those whose treachery and thievery will lead to their own destruction."[32] Again, failure to "see" one's physical problems compromises one's ability to "look forward" to salvation.

Table 3.2: High Medieval Corpus Linguistics Data

Term	Frequency in Corpus	Some Collocations Appearing in the Corpus
Afflict	8	should it afflict you to endure a while
Affliction	104	
Ail	7	
Ailing	2	community of ailing and afflicted
Ailment	5	good and lasting ailment is a bridle to humble the proud neck; an ailment thus resists and curbs physical acts
Bliss	714	that in the supreme joys of bliss you may always live with God
Body	3854	
Bodily	582	
Chaste	21	
Chided	11	
Cried	98	
Death	2491	
Deceived	261	deceived by devil; so you see, the body's senses can be deceived, but not the soul's
Deception	40	...the wife. And let them not fall prey to that first deception, with the man accusing the woman, and the woman
Desire	4632	
Devil	2574	
Enemies	814	

Flesh	1540	...down by the devil's wiles, by the weakness of my flesh, by the world's allurements and deceit
Hurt	279	
Ill	324	
Illness	70	
Imperfect	293	I feel I am frail and weak and imperfect; it is a clear sign that your love is still imperfect; abandoning imperfect love for the knowledge; in what way, then, can the imperfect be made perfect?; I am imperfect and full of darkness
Infirmity	141	I therefore beg your holiness to bow to human infirmity and provide a physician; so that all justice was debilitated like to the infirmity of a woman; laments our insufficiency and deplores our infirmity
Insane	20	life, she makes healthy and hurts again. She makes insane and then again wise
Love	19252	
Lust	148	
Mad	69	
Madness	26	
Pain	1933	she dies through living, and dying feels the heavy pain of hell
Raving	26	
Reprove(d)	55	

Scorn	82	
Scorned	146	
Sick	359	that we had fallen sick because of our excessive longing for transitory; by the medicine of the blood that you gave to the sick human race in the person of your Son
Sickness	399	the medicine for our sickness is none other than this fire of love; a medicine against a hidden sickness that had not been recognized
Stench	191	alive each part of our body emits a stench... but a stench makes the whole world stink
Suffer	1159	suffer for the love of their God; the more they suffer the happier they are; [Christ] Who restored our life by suffering; my servants may suffer physically but their spirit is free
Suffered	554	your heart and body ought to suffer
Suffering	1388	
Ugly	40	flesh with ugly thoughts and sensations, the devil with his temptation, however, repulsive, filthy, and ugly it may be... ugly sins... ugly beasts
Vision	1574	
Weak	60	I am a women, weak, frail; we are all so weak and frail... for the devil is weak
Weakness	574	Christ's strength relieves us of our weakness

Like Hildegard, Catherine equates blindness with failure to recognize one's disabled earthly state. As she puts it in a letter to a priest in Asciano, "but when we are in deadly sin we do blindly sell ourselves to the devil."[33] Through blindness, humans trade with the devil and in sin. Elsewhere, she tells the Elders of Lucca that without God, people are blind. "In this dark life we are blind by ourselves. Now how can a blind person walk without a guide along so uncertain a road and not fall down?"[34] In so doing, she prompts sinners to recognize that their path to heaven is impassable without the guidance offered by God's light. Similarly, Julian of Norwich invokes blindness as a metaphor for spiritual weakness, suggesting that those who do not trust God are fearful and immodest: "And they take this fear for humility, but it is a reprehensible blindness and weakness; and we do not know how to despise it, as we should at once despise it, like any other sin which we recognize."[35] For Mechthild, too, blindness symbolizes a life lacking love for and from God; such a life has no hope for salvation and is manifested in suffering. "Alas, where have I been, wretched and blind, that I have lived for so long without powerful love."[36] For these women, blindness consistently represents sinful, painful ignorance of physical illnesses. A person without God is blind, cannot see his/her sin, cannot know and love God properly, and is not likely to be saved.

The women also represent other physical problems, corresponding sins, and denial in terms of infection. In so doing, the metaphor moves these characterizations of their earthly disabled state beyond individual illness, invoking a characteristic of many physical problems, their ability to spread and infect others. From the underlying humoral perspective, disease untreated spreads everywhere. Again sin and suffering are joined.

Hildegard, for instance, directs her reader to "let the sick sheep be cast out of the fold, lest it infect the entire flock."[37] Just as sickness can spread within an individual and beyond, so, too, can sin infect the individual and all those in proximity. As Catherine states, "correct vice and strengthen the virtuous in doing good. The failure to correct causes decay just as surely as does a gangrenous organ in the human body."[38] In other words, one sinner's misdeeds can spread to and damage the body of the Church as a whole. Elsewhere, Catherine frames that metaphor in terms of selfishness and leprosy. "We were like that when our foundation was in selfish self-centeredness, which is the most wicked wound and leprosy we can have. It is the leprosy that weakens and kills all the virtues, because it robs them of charity, their mother."[39] Given its biblical association with ostracism, leprosy was an apt metaphor to suggest how diseases of body and soul infect the healthy population and block all affected from community with God. Readers are thus warned against ignoring their spiritual and physical deficits, or, as the religious model puts it, ignoring their states of disablement.

Conversely, recognizing one's physical problems opens the door to the possibility of healing. To make this point, the women refer to God's role in their experiences. As Mechthild states,

> if one does not wish to kill the prisoners,
>
> One gives them bread and water.
>
> The medicine of which you speak
>
> Is nothing more than a protection for this moral life.
>
> But when your resurrection comes,
>
> When your body receives its fatal blow,
>
> I will be there to catch you
>
> To embrace you,
>
> I will be there to take your body from you,
>
> and to give you your love.[40]

Earthly sustenance is hardly medicine for the soul. Instead, she suggests that spiritual sustenance comes from God whose love heals one's sins and disabilities. It is not an easy task but better than the alternative. As she puts it elsewhere,

> God's true greeting, which springs from the heavenly flood of the flowing Trinity, has such great power that it robs the body of all its might, and by revealing the soul to itself causes it to see itself as being equal to the saints, to receive the divine glow, so that the soul departs from the body with all its might, wisdom, love and longing....
>
> With this greeting shall I die living;
>
> This the blind saints shall not take from me.
>
> They are those who love without knowing.[41]

Unlike those who remain blind, Mechthild suffers to see, to heal, and to leave this earthly world and her body to enter heaven. As the other visionaries, Mechthild uses metaphors to characterize physical problems as painful, infectious disabilities which, once recognized, can help one gain the love and wisdom needed for salvation.

Physical Problems as Communication and Union with God

The women not only attempt to make others aware of their disabilities; they also discuss how their own physical problems helped them recognize their disablement in both spiritual and physical forms. To that end, the women describe how their particular physical problems act as disabling obstacles blocking their path to salvation as well as how their identification with Jesus helps them to overcome those obstacles.

In one discussion of her personal suffering, Mechthild, who suffered from weakening of the eyes and limbs, notes

> my body is a long affliction, my soul intense joy, for she has beheld and embraced her loved one many times. It is because of/ Him that she has to suffer, poor creature/ if He seeks her, she flows to Him. She cannot contain herself, and He takes her to Himself.... 'Lord give me your blessing.' At that He looks at her, pulls her close to Him, and addresses her, saying what the body must never say. The body says to the soul:
>
> "Where have you been? I am tired."
>
> To that the soul replies: "Quiet, fool.
>
> I have been with my loved one;
>
> May you never recover.
>
> I am His joy; He is my suffering."
>
> This I her suffering from which she can never recover.
>
> This suffering you must endure.
>
> Never will you be free from it.[42]

As described, her body is the mediating point around which suffering and joy revolve to physical and spiritual balance; such balance wards off the spread of the affliction. More specifically, by imitating Jesus she attains union with God. With union and the love it brings, Mechthild recognizes her affliction and the disabled earthly state it entails, and thus can move beyond that inherently painful state.

Hildegard experiences bouts of illness and visions throughout her life. She describes the visions as flashes of light. "Heaven was opened and a fiery light of exceeding brilliance came and permeated my whole brain and inflamed my whole heart and my whole breast, not like a burning but like a warming flame, as the sun warms anything its rays touch".[43] For Hildegard, the visions involved all her senses, brought her in contact with God, and distanced her from the ignorant blind. By seeing and knowing him in these flashes, she could become more like him and stop the spread of sins within her which manifest her earthly state of disability.

Similarly, Catherine of Siena discusses her physical imperfections and the suffering they bring as disabling limitations that provide the point from which healing proceeds. She states that

> not all sufferings given in this life are given for punishment, but rather for correction, to chastise the child who offends. However, it is true that a soul's desire, that is, true contrition and sorrow for sin, can make satisfaction. True contrition satisfies for sin and its penalty not by virtue of any finite suffering you may bear, but by virtue of your infinite desire.[44]

While suffering is punishing for the individual, its essential purpose is to educate, prompt a person to desire regret and change, and initiate the healing process: as Father/God ministers to his Son/Jesus, so does Jesus tend to his children on Earth. Like Hildegard, Catherine demands that all people suffer in their flesh. "Mortify your body instead of delicately pampering it. Despise yourself, and do not pay attention to social standing or wealth."[45] For her part, Catherine practiced extreme fasting, calling the practice an *infermita*, illness. Instead of consuming earthly food, she only received Holy Communion (cf. Mechthild above). After enduring vomiting and stomachaches, she was ordered to stop. But, she refused because her practices allowed her to suffer pain with and through the body.[46] The task was difficult: "Perhaps the thought arises in our hearts: 'I can't pursue that sort of perfection; I feel that I am frail and weak and imperfect.'"[47] Yet, she succeeded by moving beyond her body to Jesus'. "Here I am, poor wretch, living in my body, yet in desire consistently outside my body."[48] Again, discipline and bodily suffering grants these women access to God; earthly pain and disability find their counterparts in heavenly pleasure and perfection.

Julian also endured pain while patiently following Jesus. As she puts it, "I wanted to have every kind of pain, bodily and spiritual... I intended this because I wanted to be purged by God's mercy, and afterwards live more to his glory because of that sickness."[49] To cure her earthly illness, Julian suffered and surmounted her earthly imperfections, that is, disabilities; through that recognition, she, as others, can accept God and the healing he brings. Julian writes,

> and for this little pain which we suffer here we shall have an exalted and eternal knowledge in God which we could never have without it. And the harder our pains have been with him on his cross, the greater will our glory be with him in his kingdom.[50]

Her physical suffering makes her aware of her spiritual state. Again, the body provides a means of educating and healing.

Teresa de Cartagena characterizes her mid-life deafness not as punishment but as gift from God to curb her gossiping; the cure thus corresponds to the physical imperfection with which she was advised to deal. As she puts it,

> but merciful God... knew how important it was to my health to have the chatter cease so that I would better understand what was necessary for my salvation, signaled me with his hand to be quiet. And one may well say that this suffering is given to me by His hand.[51]

Without access to the external world's sounds, she listened to her internal voice and heard God there.

> After much reflection in the prison of echoing sounds within the cloisters of her ears, Teresa reasons that her soul would have been purer if she had never been exposed to speech at all, which makes one turn to the outside material world and forget the inner spiritual world. Teresa's physical disability not only helps her make her way to salvation but also there acts remediation and educational purposes.[52]

Of course she suffers, but suffering brings her closer to God. "If by glorying in our sufferings we can bring to our soul such a good guest as the virtue of Christ, no invalid should be sad."[53] Suffering physically like Jesus helps her fight her sins and find salvation.[54]

In addition to characterizing their own sins and recognizing them in humoral terms, the women also represent their disabled conditions as those of the sensual and female; "woman" becomes a metaphor for their (and others') physical, mental, and spiritual weakness. In this vein, Theresa acknowledges her womanly disposition, noting that "the lowliness and grossness of my womanly mind do not allow me to rise higher, aspiring to the nobility and sanctity of the very virtuous king and Prophet David."[55] Hildegard frequently refers to herself and unjust circumstances as "womanish," for example, when she states, "O gentle father, poor little woman though I am."[56] Yet, she counters that sentiment by arguing that her feminine abilities can fix those situations. "This time is a womanish time, because the dispensation of God's justice is weak. But the strength of God's justice is exerting itself, a female warrior battling against injustice, so that it might fall defeated."[57] Thus, she accepts yet challenges the conventions imposed on her and makes a case for her womanly strength.

The women also manifest yet counter negative characterizations associated with their compromised female states through their writing. Indeed, Julian's *Showings* (c. 1393), is considered the first English language book written by a woman. Writing openly was a bold act in the middles ages, especially for women.[58] Still, these women wrote, and they did so to heal themselves and others. To those ends, the women represent writing as womanly yet essential to their recognition, identity, and healing, often in deferential language. For example, Catherine describes her command to write in weak female terms, "I Caterina, as useless servant, am in agony with desire as I search the depths of my soul.… I have written a letter to the holy father asking him, for the love of that most sweet blood, to give us permission to offer *our* bodies for every sort of torment."[59] By characterizing herself in these humble terms vis-à-vis the male authority, she opens a space for challenging the ban against writing.

As Teresa informs her readers, God told her to write about her visions, and she responded with *The Grove of the Infirm*, a book of consolations. Although this genre was typically written by and for men, Teresa co-opts the form. Still, she tempers her audacity by referring to "the lowliness and grossness of my womanly intellect."[60] Similarly, in *The Wonder at the Works of God*, she humbly notes that "any times, I have been informed that some prudent men and also discreet women have marveled at a treatise that, with divine grace directing my weak womanly understanding, was written by my hand."[61] Teresa colonizes the genre typically reserved for men yet acknowledges her inferiority, thereby walking a line between outright disobedience and humble silence.

Hildegard characterizes her writing as womanly and finds the task quite painful. As she explains, although she experienced visions throughout her life, she only wrote of them with great difficulty when instructed from God. That experience initiated a learning process.

> But I, though I saw and heard these things, refused to write for a long time through doubt and bad opinion and the diversity of human words, not with stubbornness but in the exercise of humility, until, laid low by the scourge of God, I fell upon a bed of sickness; then, compelled at last by many illnesses, and by the witness of a certain noble maiden of good conduct and of that man whom I had secretly sought and found, as mentioned above, I set my hand to the writing. While I was doing it, I sensed, as I mentioned before, the deep profundity of scriptural exposition; and, raising myself from illness by the strength I received, I brought this work to a close – though just barely – in ten years. [...] And I spoke and wrote these things not by the invention of my heart or that of any other person, but as by the secret mysteries of God I heard and received them in the heavenly places. And again I heard a voice from Heaven saying to me, 'Cry out therefore, and write thus!'[62]

God commanded her to write not to punish her but to promote her acquisition of spiritual knowledge. The command first produced illness, reflecting her weak state. But sensing God's encouragement, she recognized the need to write about the pain in order to obtain healing. Writing, then, prompted by God, led to spiritual and physical healing and growth.

Because Mechthild was warned against writing by her peers and elders, she often apologizes for having linguistic abilities and a "masculine" style.[63]

> I was warned about this book and was told by men
>
> That is should not be preserved
>
> But destroyed by fire.
>
> Then I did what I have done since childhood,
>
> And that is to pray when I am troubled.
>
> I leaned toward my loved one and said:
>
> "Alas, Lord, now I am very troubled.

For Your glory I must remain unconsoled away from You.

You have misled me

In making me write this book."[64]

Compelled to write, she is humble but persistent in struggling against her troubles by means of her words.[65]

Despite their ambiguity, words are the means by which these women could express a number of paradoxes involving the present and future conditions of their bodies. Writing about their physical differences, the women recognized their earthly, female disablement and initiated a process of healing. Reflecting the spiritual and medical values of the day, the five women characterized physical problems in their visions by means of corporeal, sensual metaphors evoking, at once, pain and love at once, emotions and weakness, and heaven and earth.

Because the body, sin, and disability are inextricably linked in the medieval world, the body becomes the obstacle and the medium through which humans must access God. By writing of that experience, these women recognize that their painful physical problems are not punishments but obstacles to move past; each of these women acknowledges that her disabled body leads her into sin and holds her back from achieving spiritual, loving oneness with God.

Corpus Analysis

As indicated, to provide a broader perspective on this diverse corpus as well as to determine how it held together as a group, I examined the texts by means of corpus linguistics. Based on the metaphors which emerged during the textual analysis, I selected 43 words associated with physical difference and disablement as they appeared individually and in collocations.[66] The highest counts belong to the following words: love (19,252!); desire (4,632), body (3,854), death (2941), pain (1,933), vision (1574), and suffering (1,399). As a group, these words and their frequent textual presence suggest that they had a certain cultural presence for these women. As various scholars have shown, repetition of key terms or phrases helps to shape cultural values.[67] Repeated frequently within the individual texts and throughout the corpus, the terms mentioned above belonged to and informed the social consciousness of the world within which the women lived—a consciousness which emphasized the extremes of love and pain thereby linking crucial high medieval notions of disability and redemption.

Moreover, the frequency of "love" and "desire" in the texts reflects the textual analyses above and, with them, the women's aim to overcome their painful earthly disabilities and find a proper loving union with God in the afterlife.

These observations are enhanced by the ways in which the words collocate with others; in so doing, they also support the textual analysis. For example, several collocations associating "weakness" and "imperfection" locate those terms in the woman's body and within the quest to achieve salvation, that is, to arrive at bodily perfection, though loving union with God. These notions are expressed in the following phrases:

- "I feel I am frail and weak and imperfect. It is a clear sign that your love is still imperfect"
- "Abandoning imperfect love for the knowledge"
- "In what way, then, can the imperfect be made perfect"
- "I am imperfect and full of darkness"

Each of these collocations associates weakness and imperfection with the earthly state of these women's bodies; they also link this imperfect worldly state with the perfect afterlife, an afterlife associated with love and wisdom, in heaven. In so doing, they again support the textual analyses, revealing how the religious model underpins their characterization of themselves as individuals who experience extreme emotions as they attempt to heal their imperfections.

Others collocations involving "pain" reveal the women's felt sense of their earthly body as mediating point for healing.

- "Christ and freeing us from pain"
- "Christ's pain for humans"
- "She dies through living, and dying feels the heavy pain of hell"
- "The soul has another way of love connected to much pain and misery"

Here, Christ's role in the healing process is made manifest in union with and through him and his body, a union both loving and painful. In linking the earthly disabled state with its heavenly goal in this way, the phrases reflect the overall operation of Wheatley's religious models in the texts.

So, too, does the content of other phrases support the textual analysis by rejecting current stereotypical thinking about how high medieval individuals conceptualized disability. For example, "devil" appeared relatively frequently (2,574) and always associated with sin, deception, and weakness rather than with punishment. The sentiment is captured in the following phrase: "down by the devil's wiles, by the weakness of my flesh, by the world's allurements and deceit." This and similar phrases indicate that disability or illness was not simply considered God's punishment at the time.

Significantly, the phrases cited above and others in Table 3.2 not only appear throughout the corpus but also in the works of all five women. In particular, these phrases are rooted in and variations on passages from *Meditations on the Life of Christ*, that significant source for forming medieval women's notions of affective piety.[68] By turning to these texts, which describe union with God, the visionaries articulated their own, embodied sense of self; by disseminating that text's notions of affective piety to others, they helped to instill those values in them. Clearly, these thoughts were widely known in Europe over the thirteenth through fifteenth centuries; indeed, I found the phrases in the works of other high Medieval women visionaries: Hadewjch of Brabant and Margery Kempe.[69] Through their embodied representations of the *Meditations*, the visionaries offered their own female version of living successfully and passed them on to others, women especially, who read or heard them. In this way, the women worked within cultural norms yet in their own feminine embodied terms.

In sum, the corpus linguistic analysis, the repetitive phrases especially, not only support the characterizations in the textual analyses but also offer some insights into the transmission of social norms at the time. Broadly speaking, these visionary texts demonstrate how these women who identified with their disablement offered embodied representations of their earthly female bodies; thereby, they helped to pass values on these to citizens of all socio-economic standings, the literate who read them and the non-literate who heard and saw them performed. Such practices remind contemporary individuals of the importance of oral performances, now lost, a point to which the next chapter returns. Despite later associations between the medieval world and "darkness," that period was not necessarily provincial or localized.

Conclusions

In the high medieval period, as in the earlier Greek and Roman cultures, physical problems were so common that their presence alone did not constitute disability; instead disability arose from abstract humoral notions of the body. In turn, those notions of body were linked with visible, embodied communication practices which included subjective figurative language. In contrast to those earlier cultures, where disability was associated with civic success, the high medieval centuries measured success by means of Church doctrine. Disability emerged when the individual recognized and discussed physical problems as barriers to achieving salvation and problems to be remedied.

Given such cultural conceptions, this understanding of disability placed particular constraints on the presumably weaker woman and her passive, subjective, corporeal body. Accordingly, the five women visionaries acknowledged their disability and wrote from this identity, reflecting on their ongoing efforts to arrive at salvation, healed and healthy in mind and body. To reveal that loving afterlife with God, they discussed their bodies, documented their extreme physical and spiritual responses to affective piety, and manifested those responses within a felt and highly metaphorical sense of their experiences. As such, this chapter validates the religious model of disability and offers one female position within that, a position which is sensate and passionate in its response to and experience of pain. Love and suffering in particular measured the range of these women's disablement.

Until recently, the communicative barriers have been higher for those who were poor and/or had visible physical impairments requiring accommodations. Unfortunately, this means we have at present very little of what the poor and illiterate thought and believed.[70] Nonetheless, in the medieval disability life writing recovered here, individuals write about the misperceptions they faced, and they advocate, explicitly or otherwise, for others. By representing their disabilities through their bodies, these writers also contributed to of spread of literacy in the medieval world.

---

[1] I locate the high medieval period between 1100 and 1450; typically, the cut-off is 1400 but given the dates of Teresa's life and the vague line between high medieval and the next time period, we feel the extra few decades are not problematic. Also, my thanks Susanna Fein for her help in preparing this study and especially to Yvonne Stephens who helped me in the preparation of a different version of this chapter.

[2] Newman, "Possessed by the Spirit." See also Turner, *Madness in Medieval Law and Custom*.

[3] Other high medieval individuals write from the identity of disabled, including males such as John the Blind Audelay and monk Opicinus de Canistri. Audelay, *The Poems*; Fein, ed., *My Wyl and My Wrytying: Essays on John the Blind Audelay*; Salomon, "A Newly Discovered Manuscript of Opicinus de Canistris: A Preliminary Report."

[4] Eyler, *Disability in the Middle Ages: Reconsiderations and Reverberations*, p. 2; Metzler, *Disability in the Middle Ages: Thinking about Physical Impairment during the High Middle Ages, c. 1100-1400*, pp. 16-18;

Stiker, *A History of Disability*, pp. 65-89. Accordingly, scholars have looked to the institutions which cared for medieval people with physical problems, for example, the Quinze-Vingts, the hospital for the blind founded in thirteenth century Paris. O'Toole, "Disability and the Suppression of Historical Identity: Rediscovering the Professional Backgrounds of the Blind Residents of the Hopital des Quinze-Vingts"; Wheatley, *Stumbling Blocks Before the Blind: Medieval Constructions of a Disability*. Still, the poor, with little opportunity "to represent themselves" left few records, few possessions, and few traces. Farmer, *Surviving Poverty in Medieval Paris: Gender, Ideology, and the Daily Lives of the Poor*, p. 2.

[5] Statistics suggest that at any given time the percentage of the population with physical conditions that problematized life was 15-25%. Garland, *The Eye of the Beholder: Deformity and Disability on the Graeco-Roman World*, p. xii.

[6] Lomperis and Stanbury, "Introduction: Feminist Theory and Medieval 'Body Politic,'" p. ix.

[7] Majno, *The Healing Hand: Man and Wound in the Ancient World*, p. 178.

[8] Wheatley, "Blindness, Discipline, and Reward: Louis IX and the Foundation of the Hospice des Quinze-Vingts," p. 194.

[9] Wheatley, *Stumbling Blocks*, p. 210.

[10] Pearman, "'O Sweete Venym Queynte!': Pregnancy and the Disabled Female Body in the *Merchant's Tale*," pp. 25 ff. In fact, "the Fourth Lateran Council of 1215 directly linked the cause of bodily illness to sin, explicitly asserting that divine intervention was important in the treatment such ailments." Ibid., 27.

[11] Eyler, *Disability in the Middle Ages*, p. 3; Metzler, *Disability in the Middle Ages*, p. 13.

[12] Robertson, "Medieval Views of Women and Female Spirituality in the Ancrene Wisse and Julian of Norwich's Showings," p. 143.

[13] Ibid., p. 145.

[14] Voaden, *God's Words, Women's Voices: The Discernment of Spirits in the Writing of Late-Medieval Women Visionaries*, p. 8.

[15] Augustine, *The Confessions of St. Augustine*, p. xvii. See also I *Timothy* 2.11-12 and I *Corinthians* 14.34-5 as well as Thomas Aquinas, thirteenth century Scholastic theologian, in his *Summa theologiae* (*2a2ae, qu.171-8*) who reinforces prohibition against women speaking or teaching in public. Voaden, *God's Words, Women's Voices*, pp. 8 ff. The two extreme characterizations existed within a spectrum—some men practiced relatively affective pieties and some women manifested more intellectual practices.

[16] Phillips, "The Meditations on the Life of Christ: An Illuminated Fourteenth-Century Italian Manuscript at the University of Notre Dame." The text was written ca. 1300 by a Franciscan friar. See Phillips for issues of dating, attribution, distribution ("it enjoyed immediate success as a medieval bestseller"), and illuminations. Ibid., p. 237.

[17] Ibid., pp. 239-240.

[18] This kind of piety also affected high medieval painting, illumination, and sculpture, especially in Northern Europe. In works by such artists as Jan van Eyck, Hans Memling, and Hugo van der Goes, donors appear as part of the scenes depicting scenes from scripture. Panofsky, *Early Netherlandish Painting*, vol. 1, p. 333.

[19] Some women wrote for themselves, others had their visions dictated by others. Mechthild's confessor, Heinrich of Halle, convinced her to write down her ongoing mystical visions. As she put is in Book 6.43, "This Book Has Flowed from God ... and has been faithfully recorded as it was given by God and written down by her hands." Mechthild of Magdeburg, *Flowing Light of Divinity*, p. 206. Mechthild's images of Hell in that work may have influenced Dante's *The Divine Comedy*, and Mechthild may have been represented as that book's character Matelda. Often assumed to be illiterate, Catherine could read Latin and Italian, and Tommaso Caffarini, a hagiographer, claimed that although she could write, most her written work was dictated. Hildegard's *Vita* was begun by Godfrey of Disibodenberg under Hildegard's supervision.

[20] Voaden, *God's Words, Women's Voices*, pp. 12-15.

[21] Wheatley, "Blindness, Discipline, and Reward."

[22] See p. 63.

[23] Maddocks, *Hildegard of Bingen: The Woman of Her Age*, pp. 63-4.

[24] Ibid., pp. 213-14; 229.

[25] Hildegard has also attracted contemporary interest because of her music, her plays, her illuminations, and her holistic and natural view of healing. Hildegard of Bingen, *Scivias*.

[26] Catherine of Siena, *The Letters of St. Catherine*; Catherine of Siena, *The Dialogue*.

[27] Mechthild of Magdeburg, *Flowing Light of Divinity*.

[28] Teresa de Cartagena, *The Writings of Teresa*.

[29] See pp. 64-66.

[30] Singer examines how blindness could also be used to characterize some individuals as gifted in the fourteenth century in particular. Singer, "Playing by Ear: Compensation, Reclamation, and Prosthesis in Fourteenth-Century Song."

[31] Hildegard of Bingen, *The Letters of Hildegard of Bingen*, p. 48.

[32] Ibid., p. 34.

[33] Catherine of Siena, *The Letters of St. Catherine of Siena*, p. 58.

[34] Ibid., pp. 162-163.

[35] Julian of Norwich, *Showings*, p. 168.

[36] Mechthild of Magdeburg, *Flowing Light of Divinity*, p. 49.

[37] Hildegard of Bingen, *The Letters of Hildegard*, p. 28.

[38] Catherine of Siena, *The Letters of St. Catherine*, p. 57; cf. pp. 17, 70.

[39] Ibid., p. 171.

[40] Mechthild of Magdeburg, *Flowing Light of Divinity*, Book 1.3, pp. 8-9.

[41] Ibid., Book, pp. 1.2, p. 7.

[42] Ibid., Book 1.5, pp. 9-10. For other examples from Mechthild, see: Books 1.25, pp. 6-17; 1.26, p. 17; 4.8, pp. 106-107; 4.12, pp. 110-111; and 7.65, pp. 269-270. See Book 7.64 on her weak eyes and limbs.

[43] Hildegard of Bingen, *Scivias*, p. 59. cf. Hildegard of Bingen, *The Letters of Hildegard*, p. 171.

[44] Catherine of Siena, *The Dialogue*, p. 28.

[45] Catherine of Siena, *The Letters of St. Catherine*, p. 34.

[46] As Bynum has shown, extreme fasting practices had little to do with contemporary eating disorders and everything to do with establishing a relationship with God. Bynum, *Holy Feast and Holy Fast: the Religious Significance of Food to Medieval Women*.

[47] Catherine of Siena, *The Letters*, p. 28.

[48] Ibid., pp. 71, 21.

[49] Julian of Norwich, *Showings*, p. 178.

[50] Ibid., p. 215.

[51] Teresa de Cartagena, *The Writings of Teresa de Cartagena*, p. 26.

[52] Ibid., p. 20.

[53] Ibid., p. 42; cf. pp. 34, 36.

[54] Ibid., pp. 73-76.

[55] Ibid., p. 24.

[56] Hildegard of Bingen, *The Letters*, p. 21.

[57] Hildegard of Bingen, *The Letters of Hildegard*, p. 88; cf. p. 32.

[58] Clark notes that many Beguines had a "'sickness' that afflicted many women in orders who broke conventions in order to speak in their own languages, although hampered by a language written, controlled and passed on by men" (Mechthild of Magdeburg, *Flowing Light of Divinity*, p. xvi).

[59] Catherine of Siena, *The Letters of St. Catherine*, pp. 80-81.

[60] Teresa de Cartagena, *The Writings of Teresa*, p. 74; cf. p. 80.

[61] Ibid., p, 87.

[62] Hildegard of Bingen, *Scivias*, pp. 60-61; cf. p. 59.

[63] See Mechthild, of Magdeburg *Flowing Light of Divinity*, Books 2.23; 3.5; 6.38; Book 2.3; 3.1; and Book 5.12; p. 140.

[64] Ibid., Book 2.26, pp. 55-56.

[65] Ibid., Books 4.2; 5.12; 3.1.

[66] See Table 3.2.

[67] Fahnestock, *Rhetorical Figures in Science*, provides an excellent discussion of the persuasive character of repetition by means of figures of speech and thought.

[68] It would be interesting to examine the particular contexts from which these repeated phrases were culled; but that effort is beyond the scope of this chapter.

[69] Hadewijch, *Hadewijch. The Complete Works*; Margery Kempe, *The Book of Margery Kempe.*

[70] Eyler, *Disability in the Middle Ages*; Metzler, *Disability in the Middle Ages*; Pearman, "'O Sweete Venym Queynte!'"; Stiker, *A History of Disability*; Wheatley, "Blindness, Discipline, and Reward"; Wheatley, *Stumbling Blocks Before the Blind: Medieval Constructions of a Disability*.

4

Early Modern Era:
Reenacting Reform

In general, life writing began its ascent to public popularity in the early modern period. At that time, the printing industry expanded, producing abundant and inexpensive texts, thus increasing the numbers of writers, the kinds of issues they treated, and the forms and venues in which they appeared. In association, the concepts of the autonomous self and individual identity, so vital to life writing, emerged.[1] That vitality and freshness resonates in the popularity life writing now enjoys.

Given these circumstances, scholars have examined early modern life writing in the context of the publishing industry. These efforts have shown that early modern women took particular advantage of the opportunity to write and publish in impressive numbers. According to Elaine Hobby, over 200 mid-seventeenth century women writers published works which allowed them to tell their stories in such life writing forms as spiritual autobiographies, conversion narratives, diaries, and prophecies.[2] Prophecies comprise perhaps the highest number of texts by women (although some men wrote them, too). Between 1649-1688, more than half the texts published by women were prophecies.[3] By examining these works in terms of gender, embodiment, prophecy, and genre and self-formation, scholars have demonstrated how such publications helped early modern women to address public issues through reference to private matters.[4] These efforts have also differentiated early modern life writing from contemporary forms such as autobiography; while the latter typically tell unique stories of personal growth, the former link personal experience with public affairs through reference to scripture. But, these scholarly efforts have not examined the influence of developments in printing and conceptions of self on issues of identity and disability.

This chapter examines the writing of two mid-seventeenth century, British women as individuals who identify as disabled and write about their lives in that capacity, English Puritan Lady Margaret Hoby (1571– 4 September 1633) and Protestant prophet Anna Trapnel (b. 1630s-fl. 1654).[5] On the one hand, they were affected by the same cultural changes as their contemporaries who did not identify as disabled; on the other hand, they gave life to these changes in two narrative forms which were linked to and represented through their bodies. In representing bodily issues as a fundamental part of their identities as disabled, they speak to the ways in which disability informed the political, spiritual, and everyday life of early modern citizens. In particular, these early modern women writers not only challenged cultural norms by referring to their bodies but also by enacting their disabilities through their writing. In enacting their disabilities, these women continue the medieval tradition associated with highly metaphorical prophecy discussed in the previous chapter; and, yet, they changed critical aspects of these representations to reflect various social concerns of their time.[6]

When Hoby journals about her physical problems, she writes for healing purposes, as the medieval women before her; but she does so in a private, reflective matter and with a more individual style and arrangement. With that, she demonstrates an emergent individual sense of self, one associated with the Church's diminishing cultural power and the spread of associated perspectives through new printing practices. Similarly, Trapnel's visions give life (in some senses quite literally) to cultural changes involving printing and the emerging sense of the individual self. In this manifestation of life writing, Trapnel's approach continues the high medieval women's visionary tradition of using their bodies to convince others to follow their spiritual example; yet, by enacting her disabilities and message publicly, Trapnel moves beyond that tradition, as she addresses spiritual as well as political issues. Thus, Trapnel advocates for herself and her fellow citizens in ways which challenge cultural norms by fusing body, identity, and disability with text, content, style, and delivery. She implicitly calls attention to the performative element in disability life writing about disability which has not appeared in this study since the disabled Greek soldiers at Persepolis. Yet, her highly metaphorical language choice, reaffirm the associated between subjective, irrationality, and the disabled body.

Early Modern Disability and Life Writing

As this study holds, physical, bodily conditions, in all their varied forms, are the brute facts with which all humans must deal. Those conditions become disabilities when they are perceived within a given culture's value system as hindering individuals or groups from flourishing; as Chapter Two mentioned, baldness was disabling in ancient Rome by hindering men from being persuasive in civic matters. While early modern individuals do not mention baldness, they did experience the expected range of conditions which, then as now, effected nearly everyone in her/his life course; these conditions involved senses (blindness and deafness), thought and movement (hearing and seeing unverified phenomena), mobility (lameness, paralysis, convulsions), and birth defects (missing limb, cleft palette). From the early modern perspective, these conditions became disabilities within a framework which reflected prevailing values regarding medicine, spiritually, and gender.

According to early modern medicine, a more diagnostic, less religious version of the humoral perspective, external physical conditions and behaviors reflect internal correlates. Another early modern woman life writer, Hannah Allen (b. around 1638; fl. before 1670-1683), expresses this relationship in her *Narrative*.

> The Soul of Man hath a singular affection for its own Body, rejoicing in its Prosperity, and sympathizing with it in all its Maladies, Miseries, and Necessities. Hence if the Body be out of frame and tune, the Soul cannot be well at ease. As the most skilled Musician cannot make any pleasing melody upon an unstringed the broken down Instrument. The blood and humours are the Souls Organs, by which it doth exert its actions. If these be well temper'd and kept in a balance, ordinarily there is an inward calm serenity upon the Spirit. Ordinarily, I say: For in some cases the most cheerful Temper may be broken down and overwhelmed either by the immediate impressions of God's wrath upon the Soul, or the letting loose of those Bandogs of Hell to affright and terrifie it.[7]

As Allen describes, outward unbalanced conditions and associated behaviors are out of tune elements which reflect similarly broken down interior parts and their operations; a parallel correspondence exists between pleasing external bodily conditions and interior harmonies. By noting how these manifestations of health, both ill and good, also reflect God's wrath or approval, Allen associates this conception of the individual's physical state with that person's character and morals.

Like high medieval societies, spirituality was not only a significant part of the lives of every early modern believer's life but also of the way physical conditions were understood as disabilities.[8] God was the supreme judge of each person's earthly actions and the arbitrator of appropriate consequences as he guided that individual past earthly sin and physical disability towards salvation.[9] From this perspective, a legacy of medieval thinking, reaching that ultimate life-goal required perfection of soul and body. As Allen suggests above (and Hoby and Trapnel echo below) individuals should seek God's approval and support to fight sinful temptations; only through such union with God can individuals acquire the perfection of body and soul necessary to be saved.

Despite the possibility of divine support, women's efforts to acquire salvation were further constrained by early modern perceptions of their gendered condition. As Chapter One discussed, since at least Aristotle's time (see *Generation of Animals* 769a), women were considered the bodily inverse of men and, with this, morally, intellectually, and physically inferior to them.[10] Defective bodies rendered women disabled by their very embodied nature. The early Church fathers also characterized women as inherently irrational and defective (i.e. disabled) on the basis of their body, and augmented this understanding through reference to scripture, above all, to Eve's actions in *Genesis* as well as the events they foreshadowed in the *New Testament* (for example, I *Timothy* 2.11-12 and I *Corinthians* 14.34-5). It followed that women's spiritual ideas and exercises were also inferior to men's. Augustine conceptualized this inferiority by creating a hierarchy of spiritual practices; the highest, or intellectual, was practiced by men and the lowest, the corporeal, by women.[11]

In the high medieval visionary tradition described in Chapter Three, authors such as Catherine of Siena and Hildegard of Bingen manifested this spiritual hierarchy by practicing a corporeal affective piety; in contrast to the prevailing male intellectual transcendent experience, these visionaries identified with Christ and expressed that association in the physical and emotional terms available to and characteristic of women.[12] By expressing their nature and faith in these terms, they sought union with God and his help in entering heaven. As part of these efforts, these visionaries wrote about their bodies and perceived earthly and gendered disabilities. Through such documentation, they also attempted to involve their audience in similar corporeal practices. Although these practices affirmed these women's disabled status, their writings challenged cultural norms, at least those which relegated women to silence and inaction.[13]

Early modern women writers such as Allen, Hoby, and Trapnel also wrote from a sense of exclusion and inherent disability as women by documenting their embodied, affective, visionary practices in metaphorical language.[14] "Fueled by the belief that the bodies of the

godly were the truest iconic, made by God himself in his own image …
[they] reproduced in many diverse bodily practices which used the
believer's body as a sign for divine workings."[15] By referring to their
own bodies in their writing, these early modern women linked
themselves to the divine as well as to the cultural norms which
characterized female bodies in general as passive, private entities, and as
physical forms which should not be seen, let alone participate in public
affairs.

Unlike the high medieval women visionaries, Hoby and Trapnel
incorporate public, historical events within their life writing. Moreover,
when Trapnel enacts her disability in public before her audience, she
moves beyond the practices of the earlier female life writers who simply
documented their visions. She deploys her disability to be political as
well as spiritual; making her deficits visible helps her advocate
politically for herself and for her country. As Trapnel gave life to her
values and her identity by reference to and representation of her body,
her disability narrative becomes a kind of embodied prophecy and
political message through which she advocates for herself and others, in
the here and now.

Hoby and Trapnel speak to the ways in which disability informed
the political, spiritual, and everyday life of early modern citizens,
particularly Protestant women. Their work demonstrates how a new
sense of self and individual identity, enhanced by new developments in
printing, was taking shape in their self-representations.

Lady Margaret Hoby

The earlier writer of the two women, Lady Hoby, a first-generation,
Puritan woman, lived most of her adult life at Hackness, her estate in
north-east Yorkshire.[16] In her personal five year diary (1599-1605),
Hoby neatly and concisely documents her daily activities—affairs of the
house and grounds, trips to London, interactions with guests, neighbors,
and staff, and spiritual exercises of various kinds. As captured in these
records, hers is a world of routine whose center is her spiritual link to
God. Typical of her time, that relationship involves her health, or in
Hoby's case, her poor health, since she experiences a continuing variety
of problems; she mentions, in her rote manner, headaches, weariness,
sore feet, toothaches, coughs and colds, indigestion, and a kidney stone.
By documenting her world in this way, she assuages her self-doubts as
she looks to God to help her overcome both her sinfulness and its
external manifestations. Following the prevailing perspective, then, her
disability lies in her identification of herself through her infirmities.

As described, her outward physical conditions are a measure of her relative sinfulness during the five year course of her diary. In describing her physical problems in this way, she identifies as disabled.

> Satweday 18 [1599] After I was readie I praied privately, and, because I was weak and had paine in my head, I wet little but wound yearne and walked tell dinner: after which I went about the house, and did walke abroad, workinge little all that day because of me weaknes, lest I should be *disabled* to keepe the Lordes day as I desired and am bound: before supper I praied and examined my selfe, not so pertecularly as I ought to have don, which I beseech the Lord to pardon for his christs sack, and giue me grace after to be more carefull.[17]

As Hoby explicitly indicates—she uses the actual word "disabled" for the first time in this study (or elsewhere that I have found)—disability is an unavoidable issue, one linked to her spiritual identity. Clearly, Hoby knows no contemporary medical model of disability which mandates that disabilities are abnormal conditions to categorize and cure. Neither could Hoby countenance any social model of disability which recognizes such issues as constructed within their broader cultural context. Instead, as disability measures Hoby's relationship with God, it is an essential part of her world, as it would be for others at this time whether or not they identified explicitly as disabled.

More specifically, Hoby measures disability through this relationship by enacting it. Thus understood, the waxing and waning of Hoby's disabilities manifest her state of body and soul at a given time and, in so doing, reflect both her struggles with Satan as well as God's reactions to those temptations. For example, in 1602, when she often experiences the harshest aspect of her disabilities, she mentions the following event.

> Munday 10... after that I wrought a little, and neglected my custom of praier, for which, as for many other sinnes, it pleased the Lord to punishe me with an Inward assalte: But I know the Lord hath pardoned it because he is true of his promise, and, if I had n taken this course of examenation I think I had for gotten itt.[18]

Following humoral theory, the state of her external disability measures her internal spiritual state. On the one hand, she experiences self-doubt, anxiety and guilt, and, on the other, feels satisfaction at any positive response from God. As she notes elsewhere, God is the ultimate doctor, and so attends to her spiritual health which is made manifest on her body.[19] By working to be a better person, she can enter heaven. Her aspirations are similar to the high medieval life visionaries; but her focus is the present world of disablement.

In addition to the content of her narrative, Hoby's style reflects the state of her relationship with temptation and with God. Her style is plain, each entry typically consisting of a series of simple often repetitive sentences. Yet, her consistency wavers when she discusses her physical struggles. It would be interesting to know more about her, to know, for example, why she wrote for these five years only and if she always suffered so dearly. Her concern about her redemption may be associated with her barren reproductive state. [20] It also seems significant that she seems to write in the most disabling times of her life. From what remains this much seems clear. For Hoby, writing belongs to the physical and spiritual process of coping. As David Mitchell and Sharon Snyder might put it in their contemporary terminology, Hoby's life writing is a disability coping mechanism of sorts—like her very own textual "prosthetic."[21]

At any moment in this private work, the state of Hoby's disabilities embodies the state of God's presence in her life. In reflecting her personal sense of self, her identity, and her relationship to God, hers is a most simple yet bold manifestation of early modern life writing about disability. On the one hand, she still looks to a spiritual end. On the other hand, her journal is rooted in the present, in the early modern sense of individual self, and in a more categorical notion of physical difference. After all, she recognizes explicitly that because of her physical problems, she is disabled.

Trapnel's Body and Identity

Trapnel identifies as disabled not by explicit use of the term but by enacting that status by means of her body. In contrast to Hoby, Trapnel is a member of the Fifth Monarchists. For such radical Protestant sectarian groups, prophecy served political purposes. In this case and in contrast with the high medieval visionaries, prophecy served political purposes.[22] Using prophetic statements, early modern radical women (and some men) described an imminent fifth eternal kingdom which followed the four earthly ones thus far sequentially established.[23] To that end, they adopted the apocalyptic Biblical tone and language, of *Daniel* and *Revelations* especially, to address political and religious concerns.[24] As a member of the Fifth Monarchists, Trapnel wrote four of her six prophecies in 1654, marking a significant time for herself and that group.

Her fame began when she traveled to Whitehall on behalf of the Fifth Monarchists. There, she experienced a 12 day trance which prophesized, among other things, Cromwell's demise. That event is recorded in two documents, *Strange and Wonderfull Newes from White-Hall* and *The Cry of the Stone*, a more detailed pamphlet intended for publication. Following her experiences in Whitehall, Trapnel traveled to Cornwall and later imprisoned in London for her actions. Those events are described in her *Report and Plea*. The last of the 1654 works, *A Legacy for Saints*, is a published account of her childhood conversion. Because her detailed discussion of her trance best enacts her understanding of herself as disabled, I focus on *The Cry of the Stone* (*The Cry*).

In publishing her work, Trapnel exhibits the hallmark early modern characteristic, a sense of personal self, authorship, and identity, traits associated with the expansion of the printing industry and the diminishment of the Church's control over secular matters. As an intentionally published work, unlike Hoby's, *The Cry* begins with a preface which testifies to the text's validity (an element also evident in comparable medieval texts). That purpose is also evident in the text proper when Trapnel speaks directly against the accusation that she is possessed or a witch.[25] In defending herself as a divinely inspired individual, Trapnel speaks much like the female high medieval visionaries. Yet, by calling on fellow citizens to witness her prophecy, Trapnel engages in spiritual matters as well as in public discourse. To increase authenticity as well as immediacy (since Trapnel was in a trance when she uttered them), her prophecy was actually transcribed *in situ* by a "relator." Nonetheless, *The Cry* is published in her name. Because such review suggests she had reviewed its content, the work is considered authentic life writing.[26] Her text becomes a script of her actions which contains a new, creative, participatory element, one consistent with her spiritual and political goals.

Trapnel identifies her outward physical conditions as manifestations of her disabilities. Accordingly, her disabilities have many forms.

> From this time [1642], for a whole year after, the Lord made use of me for the refreshing of afflicted and tempted ones, inwardly and outwardly.... Oh let simmers admire free grace with me, that hath freed me from as stony, as feared, as benumbed, senseless a condition, as any could or can be in hearing or reading, or Saints speaking to me as to one deaf; I still concluded my condition to be like theirs the Scripture speaks of, that were given up by the Lord to blindness or mind, and hardness of heart.[27]

As humoral theory dictates, the state of her external disabilities reflects her internal spiritual state. Thus, she experiences many physical problems, problems of hearing, sight, and sensation, which reflect her defective gendered nature, her spiritual state as well as her link with God. Because God is the ultimate doctor, he attends to her spiritual health and mind so that she may one day enter heaven healed.

Trapnel discusses at length and in various places how disabilities reflect God's purpose for humans. In one prayer, for instance, she describes how God will one day make his children honorable in heaven but, in their present earthly condition, they are not ready. "The reason is, because of the infirmities of the flesh, and because of a stammering heart, and of stuttering tongue, but thou hast promised that the time will come that there shall not be a people of a deeper speech than thy now have, and they shall not be of a stammering tongue [Isaiah 33.19]."[28] Because of their many disabilities, most humans are not yet ready for salvation but eventually, through Christ's model, can attain that goal.

In another prayer, Trapnel compares true believers with those who are not. As to the latter, she assets, "they pamper their bellies.... Have not their fullness brought blindness on them."[29] Again reflecting humoral theory and the perspective of her high medieval predecessors, the prayer indicates that those who are not yet saved are individuals who manifest disabilities such as blindness and sins such as gluttony; these problems block their path to heaven. It follows that healing those problems through one's relationship with God reveals the true, untarnished believer.

In contrast to those earlier women writers, when Trapnel speaks and acts through God in a trance, she is experiencing this believer's sense of union with God and its associated perfection. At those times, the

> way the soul is raised that is indeed wrapped up in thee; there are raptures in the tongue, and in the brain, but the raptures of the heart no floods can drown, no fire can quench [Song of Songs 8.7]; the tongue, and the fancy, and the natural life may be taken away, but the spiritual sense, that returns into the sun. Oh what is the carcass, the vessel ... I am made perfect in thy self.[30]

Again, God heals disabilities. In her world, disabilities measure an individual's location on the path to salvation. By documenting the world in this way, Trapnel assuages her self-doubts as she looks to God to help her overcome both her inner sinfulness and its external manifestations, and arrive at perfection.

As described, Trapnel's outward physical condition is a specific measure of her relative sinfulness during her spiritual journey. For example, she describes a moment of temptation, stating that

> the Lord suffered Satan to buffet me, yet I questioned not the truth of my visions and revelations.... I was tortured in my body, as he had full possession of thereof ... though he had power over my body, and natural life ... temptations of a sorts were violent to me. And at the end of those seven days, my body was freed from the torture caused by Satan.[31]

Thus understood, the waxing and waning of Trapnel's disabilities manifest her state of body and soul at a given time and, in so doing, reflect both her struggles with sin as well as God's reactions to those struggles. Trapnel measures her relationship with God, and the relative state of her disabilities, by enacting them. As such, "the Lord as he had cured my spirit, so by faith he restored my body."[32]

Trapnel explicitly identifies the link between her disabled state and the divinity to which she aspires through her body; she writes prophetically and as a model for others.

> They say they are convulsion-fits, and sickness, and diseases that make thy handmaid to be in weakness. But oh they know not the pouring forth of thy spirit, for that makes the body to crumble, and weakens nature. In these extraordinary workings thou intended to show what is coming hereafter.[33]

Elsewhere, she describes her call to prophecy in similar terms, an event which happened after she experiences her first illness at age seven.[34] As she puts it, "then I was taken weak in my outward man ... and then broke forth in prophecy."[35] She offers that prophecy to her fellow believers through her embodied writing. Interestingly, too, she uses a standard phrase in medieval visionary writing, "outward man," to describe her disability. This imagery suggests that to explicitly think of herself as strong and manly is beyond the realm of early modern femininity.

Like her medieval visionary predecessors, Trapnel writes to convince others to follow her spiritual example, and so she prompts her audience to identify directly with her physical and emotional conditions and her spiritual aspirations. But unlike these earlier writers, whose purpose was neither expressly political nor concerned with present public issues, Trapnel makes her political intentions public—both by publishing her work as well as by linking her spiritual utterances with current political ones.

> The Lord filled me with many spiritual hymns, as to my temptations, promising me that my joy should abundantly outpass my sorrow. And while I was thus singing and triumphing over Satan, challenging now a battle, and seeing the Lord so glorious before me, I was drawn into my visions, as the calling in of the Jews, the overthrowing and shaking all the nations.... And a vision I had concerning the dissolution of the Parliament.[36]

Through her rapturous visions, Trapnel advocates for herself and others on spiritual and political levels; as she puts it, as God defeated Satan, an event reflected in her personal situation and in biblical the overthrowing of the Jews, so England must now dissolve Parliament. As such, her prophecy models her spiritual encounters with God; and, these manifestations of sin and salvation also measure the ways in which the biblical and historical past inform her country's political present and future.[37] Reflecting her mission of prophetic advocacy and the conventions of the genre, Trapnel repeatedly uses biblical quotations to ground her efforts in God's words and works, to describe past events, and to link those events to England's present and future; pointing out these links, she hopes, will compel others to heed her words and take political action.[38]

Trapnel also makes her political intentions explicit in the complete title of the other account of her prophecy in *Whitehall: Strange and Wonderful News from Whitehall: or the Mighty Visions ... to diverse Colonels, Ladies and gentlewomen, concerning the government of the common wealth of England, Scotland, and Ireland; and her revelations touching his highness the Lord Protector, and the army. With her Declaration touching the state affairs of Great Britain even from the death of the late King Charles, to the dissolution of the late King Charles.* Advocating openly, Trapnel's visions connect her female body, the body of Christ, and the body politic; the female prophetic body becomes a way of reading "sectarian subjectivity."[39]

The high medieval visionaries in the previous chapter wrote or dictated their visions after the fact with subsequent salvation in mind. By recording hers within a live performance and by publishing it in a manner that captures that performance, Trapnel not only represents her body as a divinely sanctioned spiritual model, but she also links that purpose with present, political ones.

To enhance the persuasive effect of her prophetic advocacy, Trapnel's style and delivery reflect and make tangible the state of her relationship with God. With respect to style, the experience is represented in process, through the use of the active present tense, rather than as an event long since passed. This active element appears in other aspects of her style. For example, Trapnel represents the intensity of her physical and spiritual struggles within the shifting of tone, genre (poetry, prose, free writing), grammar, and syntax. Some of that sense is incorporated in the following part of a prayer, a three page verbal rampage embedded within poetry and song of various forms, meters, and rhythms.

> They come forth in sheep's clothing [Matthew 7.15]. You council, you think you have done well in this, but surely the passing bell shall ring for you. This is the saddest day that ever poor England had; formerly their children had black patches, and naked necks, and so do they now. What David! Thou whom I have raised up from the lowest of men from the dust [Psalm 113.7-8; 1 Samuel 2.8], wilt thou do this?[40]

Here, Trapnel gives life to prophecy in free form incorporating biblical references, vehement and varied punctuation, and changes in voice, person, and tone. The resulting language is forceful and determined, yet mercurial; it calls on the audience to pay attention to what Trapnel says along with how she expresses her message. Thus engaged with the words on several levels, the audience is engaged in the text.

Trapnel also delivers her vision in a manner which offers her affective piety directly to her audience—and it was a broad public rather than expressly religious group she addressed. Trapnel's embodied writing prompts the reader to react in kind. Not only did I read the text in this responsive manner but the redactor's narrative of Trapnel's actual audience suggests that they, too, reacted sympathetically to her delivery. An aside (written in third person to distance the presence of the realtor) notes, for example, that

> after she had breathed forth this song with more enlargement than could be noted by the relator, she proceeded in prayer which for the press of people crowding and darkening the chamber could not be taken.[41]

As the comment suggests, this is a performance delivered live. Trapnel has been described as a passive vessel through which God works.[42] Understood as a living prophetic advocate, Trapnel is an active presence in *The Cry*. Reflecting the state of her personal struggles, Trapnel's text is unorthodox in form, content, and purpose. Through this live reenactment, she prophecies to her audience; thus warned and informed, they can react accordingly—both spiritually and politically.

Like Hoby's, Trapnel's text embodies at any moment the relationship between her disabilities, her earthly, gendered condition, and the state of God's healing presence in her life. But, writing as a radical, Trapnel offers a more extreme manifestation: her disability is represented in process for expressly political, active prophetic purposes. Put another way, Trapnel not only represents herself and her identity in an embodied form; writing as a radical Protestant, Trapnel also characterizes her disability in a creative, participatory process for expressly political, active prophetic purposes in a public venue. For Hoby and Trapnel, writing functions like a narrative prosthetic, a story which attempts to resolve a cultural conundrum about disability.[43]

Conclusions

I have offered snapshots of two early modern British women who wrote about their lives through their identification as disabled; one identified privately and one for others with present political purposes. By writing about their personal identities, both reflect conventional early modern values.

When Hoby identifies herself in her personal diary as "disabled," she demonstrates the notion of the individual self has emerged. In using the term within a narrative of coping, she also represents that identity as felt, felt in both content and style. Doing so conforms with existing patterns, patterns evident since the ancient soldiers at Persepolis, which link disability, subjectivity, body, and communication practices.

Trapnel's writing also confirms these associations. Moreover, by writing about her enacting her identity publicly, and publishing it, Trapnel makes visible the daily presence of disability in her world and its ability to influence public events. In their individual ways, then, their work bridges the gap between the more mediated sacred medieval worlds and the Enlightenment period when emerging notions of the individual self and disability meet the new scientific method and concerns with categorization and logic.

We may never know how many other early modern individuals explicitly identified disability. Nonetheless, Hoby and Trapnel demonstrate that the disabled participated quite actively in the early modern world. Through writing, they give their experiences vibrant, physical shape. Trapnel in particular recalls the performative aspect of the ancient Greek notion of disability, an aspect that reminds us of the fundamentally embodied character of all human experience. As I indicate in subsequent chapters, I believe that this practice, physically manifesting oneself in the text, first diminished significantly as mass publishing led to standardized ways to present the printed word; more recently, with the advent of cinematography and the internet, this performative aspect is returning. As twenty-first century scholars have noted, and Chapter Nine discusses, disability is an increasing presence for all world citizens as accommodations and education are more readily available, people live longer, and various media disseminate materials on these and other issues globally.

[1] Coleman, "Introduction: Life-Writing and the Legitimation of the Modern Self," p. 1; Smith and Watson, *Reading Autobiography: A Guide for Reading Life Narratives,* pp. 5-6.

[2] Hoby, *The Private Life of an Elizabeth Lady: The Diary of Lady Margaret Hobby. 1599-1605,* p. 1.

[3] See Hoby, *The Private Life of an Elizabeth Lady,* p. 126; cf. Purkiss, "Producing the Voice, Consuming the Body: Women Prophet of the Seventeenth Century," p. 223 note 5; Hinds, *God's Englishwomen: Seventeenth-Century Radical Sectarian Writing and Feminist Criticism,* pp. 1-3.

[4] Chedgzoy, "Introduction" in Anna Trapnel, *Strange and Wonderfull Newes from White-Hall*; Coleman, "Introduction: Life-Writing and the Legitimation of the Modern Self"; Hoby, *The Private Life of an Elizabeth Lady*; Hobby, "The Politics of Women's Prophecy in The English Revolution," pp. 295-306; Mack, "The Prophet and Her Audience: Gender and Knowledge in the World Turned University Pressside Down," pp. 139-152; Purkiss, "Producing the Voice, Consuming the Body: Women Prophet of the Seventeenth Century".

[5] Hoby, *The Private Life of an Elizabeth Lady: The Diary of Lady Margaret Hoby. 1599-1605.*

[6] The works of many other early modern British women writers could be included in a broader study of life writing about disability for example, those written by Hannah Allen, Elinor Channel, Eleanor Davies, and Margaret Hobby. A broader study of early modern life writing about disability might also include several men, for example, François Malaval and Jean de Samson, both blind.

[7] pp. iii-iv. In discussing all three writers, I retain the original spelling and punctuation of the texts.

[8] Hinds, *God's Englishwomen, Seventeenth-Century Radical Sectarian Writing and Feminist Criticism,* p. 7.

[9] Metzler, *Disability in the Middle Ages: Thinking about Physical Impairment during the High Middle Ages, c. 1100-1400,* p. 60.

[10] See Chapter Two, p. 21.

[11] *The Literal Meaning of Genesis: Books 7-12,* vol. XLII, 186; Voaden, *God's Words, Women's Voices: The Discernment of Spirits in the Writing of Late-Medieval Women Visionaries,* p. 8.

[12] Bynum, *Holy Feast and Holy Fast: the Religious Significance of Food to Medieval Women;* Voaden, *God's Words, Women's Voices: The Discernment of Spirits in the Writing of Late-Medieval Women Visionaries.*

[13] For example, thirteenth century Scholastic theologian Thomas Aquinas wrote in his *Summa theologiae* (*2a2ae, qu.171-8*) that women should be silent.

[14] Bynum, *Holy Feast and Holy Fast*.

[15] Purkiss, "Producing the Voice, Consuming the Body: Women Prophet of the Seventeenth Century," pp. 140-2.

[16] Hinds, "Introduction," in Hoby, *The Private Life of an Elizabeth Lady: The Diary of Lady Margaret Hobby. 1599-1605*, pp. xv ff.

[17] Ibid., p. 7; emphasis added. See also pp. 180, 183.

[18] Hoby. *The Private Life of an Elizabeth Lady*, p. 16; cf. pp. 17, 20, 168, 180, 182, 186, and 214.

[19] Ibid., p. 13.

[20] Hinds, "Introduction," Ibid., p. xxvi.

[21] Mitchell and Snyder, Narrative Prosthesis: Disability and the Dependencies of Discourse.

[22] This use differs from the contemporary sense of prophecy which suggests forecasting future events.

[23] Hobby, "The Politics of Women's Prophecy in The English Revolution."

[24] Ibid., pp. 295-6; K. Chedgzoy, "Introduction" in Trapnel, *Strange and Wonderfull Newes from White-Hall*, p. 238.

[25] (see 3, 29, for example).

[26] Hinds, "Introduction," in Trapnel, *The Cry of a Stone*, pp. xxi-xxii, 3, 4.

[27] Ibid., pp. 6-7.

[28] Ibid., p. 40.

[29] Ibid., p. 48.

[30] Ibid., p. 47

[31] Ibid., p. 10.

[32] Ibid., p. 11.

[33] Ibid., p. 29.

[34] Ibid., p. 6.

[35] Ibid., p. 9.

[36] Ibid., p. 12.

[37] Ibid., p. 45.

[38] Ibid., pp. 10, 67, and 74.

[39] Hinds, "Introduction," in Trapnel. *The Cry of a Stone*, p. xlvi (italics in original).

[40] Ibid., p. 71.

[41] Ibid., p. 21; emphasis in original.

[42] Hobby, "The Politics of Women's Prophecy in The English Revolution," p. 24.

[43] Mitchell and Snyder, *Narrative Prosthesis: Disability and the Dependencies of Discourse*.

5

The Long Eighteenth Century: Reason and Logic in an Enlightened Age

In 1835, John Burnett commented on his experience as a deaf individual in a manner that differs significantly from the manners in which ear moderns Lady Hoby and Anna Trapnel discussed their disablement. Instead of speaking to an afterlife, Burnett addresses only the present by reversing the conventional logic of those who do not share his particular sensory situation. As he puts it,

> Of all the long catalogue of infirmities which flesh is heir to, deafness is the one which is least apparent at first sight, and which least affects, directly, the vigor of the bodily or mental faculties, and yet there is no other infirmity, short of the deprivation of reason, which so completely shuts its unfortunate subject out of Society of his fellows. Yet this is not because the deaf are deprived of a single sense; but because the language of the hearing world is a language of sounds. Their misfortune is not that *they* are deaf and dumb, but that *others* hear and speak.[1]

Deafness, he notes, is but one infirmity in the many humans may experience; typically unnoticed, it is also considered quite isolating. On the contrary, Burnett adds, it is not his silent world but the world of those who hear that is impoverished. The silence he inhabits is a complete and comfortable residence, one without undue deprivation; although it lacks sound, it also lacks the need to engage in it.

In identifying himself in this manner, a characterization unfamiliar to his intended audience, Burnett's thinking is antithetical on various intersecting levels: in his formal use of words and wit, his creation of an argument that counters cultural assumptions, and his direct assertion of an unspoken perspective on disability.[2] To present his antithetical statements, Burnet also relies on testimony, that is, on reference to conventional cultural values and to his own informed experience. In so doing, he overturns that conventional thinking 180 degrees, creating in its wake a sometimes contradictory mirror image of the one it replaces. At once, he offers a new standard on deafness and affirms the norm he refutes. These characteristics, antithetical and referential reasoning, reversal and reaffirmation, inform the eighteenth century life writing this chapter covers, as these works inform and are informed by the shifting literary, political, and scientific impulses of a period whose citizens considered their age to be both revolutionary and rational.[3]

In responding to these shifts and, in this respect, like the high medieval and early modern writers in previous chapters, eighteenth century disabled individuals make the invisible visible as they speak to their identities as disabled. By using ironic or antithetical turns of speech, their language implicitly draws on the link between irrational language and the improper body. However, these eighteenth century individuals do not embody and enact their disability through reference to the church, nor do they advocate for themselves, others, and country as they seek salvation. Instead, they write at a time when earlier notions of sacred authority and pervasive disability had been replaced by secular sources and selves, and by particular infirmities. No longer part of the fabric of everyday life, disability is marked as something to cure in this life rather than to heal in preparation for the next. As such, the eighteenth century life writers I discuss in this chapter address their individual disabilities by means of the disembodied written reason and logic of their Enlightened Age. In so doing, they inform an uninformed audience about their experiences as disabled. Thus engaged, eighteenth century life writers depend on developing theories and practices in science, printing, and literacy which value categorization, standardization, and reference to those standards. With the rise of objectivity and rational logic, came the fall of subjective, embodied representation.

To demonstrate these shifting sensibilities and practices, I focus on texts by two writers, William Hay (November 16, 1695-June 22, 1765) and Thérèse-Adéle Husson (Feb 4, 1803-1830), each of whom represents one of the two new major categories of disability that are named at this time, "deformity" and "disability," respectively. Both Hay's *Deformity: An Essay* (1754) and Husson's *Reflections* (1825) have received attention as exceptional works; they are in the sense that they manifest new directions in disability life writing and concepts of self. Seen in conjunction with Burnet and other writers, however, they are not alone in their time, or as they belong to the longer history of disability life writing to which this books speaks.[4]

Both Hay and Husson were active citizens rather than outsiders in their worlds. Hay was born with a hunchback in Sussex, orphaned at five, and attended Christ Church, Oxford, from 1712 to 1715. Between 1715 and 1718, he had smallpox which impaired his vision. After touring Britain and the Continent between 1718 and 1720, he returned to Sussex, became a country magistrate, married, and was elected to Parliament for Seaford. In these capacities, he wrote extensively to overturn perspectives on deformity as well as to improve living conditions for the poor.[5] Similarly productive, Husson lost her sight at age nine after a bout with smallpox.[6] Based in part on her difficult childhood, she wrote *Reflections* as an educational manual for raising the blind from the blind individual's perspective. The manual also captures the flavor of Husson's life, which was certainly unconventional.[7] Politically, she lobbied and alienated many; socially, she married a blind man with whom she had two children (contradicting her own advice), and publicly, she died tragically in a mysterious fire. Although Hay lived more conventionally than Husson and tended to understatement as she toward the bold, both wrote to inform others about their lives as individuals with particular disabilities.

The Short on the Long Eighteenth Century

The shifts in conceptions and representations of self and disability which Hay and Husson manifest reflect concurrent shifts in late seventeenth and eighteenth century scientific and literate theory and practice. During this period, the presumably objective Scientific Method displaced earlier concepts of and practices in natural history. While Francis Bacon contributed inductive reasoning and observation to the new perspective, René Descartes insisted on separating the mind, and logic, from the body, and subjectivity.[8] The resulting method and mentality sought to induce universal truths by objectively observing, measuring, and documenting the world's myriad phenomenon.

One of the phenomena scientists examined was the body.[9] With the new interest in demonstration and data, the abstract humoral perspective lost its explanatory power. Equipped instead with their new method, scientists characterized the body in mechanical and taxonomic terms. Accordingly, the noseologies of Sauvage and Cullen labeled and organized the body's parts and its diseases, while the writings of Burton and Cheyne subjected mental problems, located in the brain, to similar systemization.[10] These taxonomic pursuits were aligned with interests in separating the normal from the abnormal.[11] Under these circumstances, the medical model of disability, described in Chapter One, emerged with clarity within which disabilities were the visible signs of organic disorders; these abnormalities were to be treated through scientific means without any spiritual intervention. Thus, science sought to tame all subjective impulses in the body, impulses previously felt and embodied in medieval and early modern life writing.[12] These efforts, as discussed below, affected how individuals with proper bodies and minds were encouraged to communicate, although the results were not necessarily as clean cut as they aspired to be.

From this approach came the two broad categories of bodily abnormality previously mentioned, disability and deformity. The former referred to deviant sensate experiences such as blindness, deafness, and lameness, which were acquired congenitally or post birth. In contrast, deformity was inherited rather than acquired, and often associated with the mother's thinking or activities during pregnancy.[13] Reflecting this understanding, Hay attributes his spinal deformity to undue shock to his mother during his gestation.[14] As Burnet's opening quotation suggested, disabilities were less visible than deformities although each category was subject to logical scientific observation and categorization.[15]

Categorization and documentation also characterize the revolution in printing already underway in the early modern period. Enabled by new mass-production print technologies, eighteenth century thinkers launched early efforts to standardize spelling, paragraphing, and dialects as well as to develop consistent notations for dance, music, and public speech, among other artistic pursuits.[16] In conjunction with these efforts to standardize literate practices, new writers, subjects, readers, and genres emerged; printers strove to disseminate these materials and writers to demonstrate their knowledge of standard works. A man of his time, Hay refers to more than thirty sources in his essay.[17] All are classical, historical or contemporary. Although Husson refers to God, her purpose is in no way spiritual. Because her text is "an Educational Plan Suitable for People Blind from Birth," she depends on an existing genre of educational texts, written by the sighted, but changes their standard content to offer her own more informed perspective.

In turn, literate practices influenced attitudes toward self-expression in writing. In addition to more references to disabled individuals in fiction and non-fiction alike, more individuals wrote autobiographies in such forms as family histories, conversion narratives, scandalous memoirs, defenses, and travel writing.[18] These varied forms allowed individuals to talk about themselves in more direct, unmediated ways than earlier life writers. Through these efforts, individuals, those who identified as disabled and those who did not, "negotiated cultural conflicts" in a world of sometimes revolutionary change.[19]

Hay and Husson wrote from these influences. By speaking to their specific disabilities in purportedly reasoned words, they challenged as well as validated the disembodied scientific model that drew attention to them. In particular, they use antithesis and testimonial to identify as disabled, based on their own experiences; to characterize that identity as fortunate; and to separate themselves into groups which ironically reinforce the norms they have rejected. Again, such an approach deviated from the spiritual paths the early moderns Hoby and Trapnel followed but still depended in some measure on subjective turns of style.

Disability Identity from a Disabled Perspective: Ugliness and Dependence

Both writers address their purported abnormalities by means of antithetical, often ironic, reasoning to inform the uninformed about their personal experiences of their particular disabilities. For Hay, deformity is about ugliness, while the key feature of blindness for Husson is dependence.

When Hay dedicates his essay "*Detur Pulchriori*/To the Greatest Beauty," he refers to the inscription on Venus' golden apple and thus to the Judgment of Paris and the Trojan War.[20] By linking his essay with a story in which beauty begets horror, his opening indicates that ugliness is not what it seems. Developing this reversal through another classical reference, he turns to *The Sublime*, Longinus' first century AD treatise on aesthetics. In this work, Hay notes, Longinus criticizes Gaius Plinius Cecilius Secundius (230-168 BC) for describing the sublime by means of dull exemplification. As Longinus attempted to better Cecilius by writing well about the sublime, Hay continues, so he intends "to write of Deformity with beauty: and by a finished Piece to attone [sic] for an ill-turned Person."[21] In words that link as well as contrast beauty, deformity, his out of tune body and its atonement, Hay announces his plan to reverse what Cecilus and Longinus each in turn accomplished by writing beautifully about deformity. In so doing, his beautiful writing makes up for his own inherent ugliness. In content, reasoning, and figure of speech, Hay is antithetical.

To emphasize the essence of his identity, its ugliness, Hay next refers to Ovid. "Just as Thersite's ugliness prevented him from hiding his appearance, so Nireus was conspicuous on account of his beauty (4.13.16-17)."[22] Continuing to reverse notions of beauty and ugliness, Hay notes that Ovid not only compares Nireus and Thersite's respective appearances but also his own writing to Carus's as deeply inferior. True to his opening statement of purpose, Hay continues to oppose beauty and ugliness as well as the state of one's writing and body. Thereby, he prompts his readers to question standard thinking about ugliness.

Hay next notes antithetically that although deformity is highly visible, the non-deformed have no idea of what it is like to inhabit such a body.[23] To explain what that experience is like, Hay dismisses the efforts of 12 Oxford colleagues who formed "The Ugly Club" based on their outward physical attributes.[24] As *the Spectator* indicates, their organization is meant to mock superficial social behaviors, behaviors involving appearance associated with fashion and grooming. From Hay's perspective, such a target misses the point. First, this club draws attention to the "similitude" of the members and thus evokes "ridicule."[25] The deformed hardly need such attention. Thus, and more to the point, Hay overturns their inaccurate uniformed efforts through reference to his own experience.

Having demonstrated what deformity is not, Hay turns to what it is, naming several deformed people, Aesop and Socrates, among them, as "Members of our Society."[26] Given his prior discussion, they are ugly because of their misshaped bodies rather than their faulty fashion sense. Yet, Hay rescues others from the grips of membership. "I will not (on this occasion) accept of *Richard's* Statue from the Hand of any Historian, or even of *Shakespeare* himself; but only from that of his own Biographer, who tells us (and he ought to know) that *Richard* was a handsome man."[27] Hay continues to overturn the conventional expectations and untested assumptions on which polite society bases its opinion of the ugly deformed individual; in this way, he suggests that its essence is neither an ill sense of fashion nor any associated fame.

For much of the essay, Hay counters Bacon's uninformed essay "On Deformity" (1635). Ironically adopting the logic of the contemporary he rejects, Hay offers a methodical step by step refutation of each of Bacon's points. Their guiding premise is that the person with a deformed body has a deformed mind. Arguing thus, Bacon ironically relies on the humoral perspective that his own scientific method rejects. To Bacon's premise, Hay asserts that if the deformed are "void of natural affection."[28] (35), than every deformed person would be "a complete monster" (35). Presuming that is not the case, Hay asks "if Lord *Bacon's* Position is verified in me" (35). Clearly, Hay has feelings and, accordingly, uses his direct experience to trump Bacon's uninformed assumptions.

Hay makes that sentiment explicit elsewhere in the refutation. He notes, for example, that Bacon believes that deformed people are "extremely bold" (38; a statement that seems to contradict the affective void Bacon attributes to them, at least positive ones). This cannot be correct Hay points out, since, he himself is bashful.[29] In regard to the feelings of the deformed, Hay makes another cogent point. "Deformed Persons are despised, ridiculed, and ill-treated by others; are seldom Favourites, and most commonly neglected by Parents, Guardians, and Relations: and therefore, as they are not indebted for much Fondness, it is no wonder, if they replay little."[30] In explaining that the deformed individual may at times respond boldly to abuse, he also asks ironically why anyone would wish to be treated as the deformed. Hay then indicates that Bacon's argument is not based on direct experience of deformity; how ironic since Bacon advocates close observation.[31]

When closing the essay, Hay reiterates the central reversal with which his essay opened and twice validates the reversals he has used throughout in association with his personal experience of deformity. First, in the postscript, Hay refers to his 1753 work on Hogarth. "Since I finished this Essay, I am in Doubt whether I ought not to change the Title. For I have heard of a very ingenious Performance, called *The Analysis of Beauty* which proves incontestably, that it exists in Curve and Lines; I congratulate my fraternity; and hope for the future the ladies will esteem *Des Beaux Garcons.*"[32] Here, Hay refers to Hogarth's own ironic treatment of beauty, a treatment which mocks superficial fashion statements. And, as Hay has argued through the essay, his curved, deformed frame is not what it seems but a frame which the ladies might "esteem."

In his "Post-Postscript," Hay speaks poignantly and antithetically with respect to his postscript.[33] As he states ironically, he has neglected to mention some "inconveniences" associated with his deformity. For example, when he is seated in a coach with a fair lady whose view of his deformity is obstructed, "I am in Purgatory in the Confines of Paradise. I therefore beg one Favour, and which she may grant with Honour; that (since I despair of supplanting her Lap-dog) she will allow me a Cushion to raise me above such Misfortunes."[34] In fact, the ladies only offer esteem when his body is not visible. Visibility is the bane of Hay's deformed identity. His contrasting reversals reveal his perspective; the ironies of his situation are quite real—his world is hardly "void of affection" but fraught with uninformed opinions of ugliness.

Hay offers his experiences to correct what the non-deformed think of his ilk. In the end, ugliness is not what the unacquainted and/or fashionable set think. Ideally, Hay does not want his body to be noticed. Because that is not possible, he urges tolerance.

On the whole, I could wish, that Mankind would be more candid and friendly with us: and instead of ridiculing the distorted person, would rally the Irregularities of the Mind: which generally are as visible as those of the Person ... but go unnoticed."[35]

In his typically ironic fashion, Hay states that normal stupidity is as visible as abnormal deformity.

As Hay, Husson presents her direct experience with disability to overturn what the uninformed think about it. Rather than an essay depending on and referring to the testimonials of classical and contemporary authors, Husson writes an educational manual based on existing standards in that genre. Significantly, Husson adopts the form used by sighted manual writers but changes the content to reveal her perspective.[36] In this overturning, she offers what those sighted writers could not know—the experience from her own blind perspective. In particular, those writers misunderstand the nature of the dependence on which that disability depends.

For the blind, dependence is inevitable and should be cultivated to proper ends. To demonstrate how and why dependence is something to foster rather than forgo, Husson points out, for example, that it may seem absurd to teach the blind to do needlework. After all, that activity not only requires considerable guidance from the sighted but also creates products the blind cannot see. Husson experiences the situation quite differently. "That which one looks upon as vanity among those who see should be encouraged as a noble form of self-esteem among the blind."[37] In antithetical contrast to conventional teaching, needlework is hardly a useless or even self-defeating activity for the blind. Instead, learning needlework builds healthy relationships between sighted and blind; the latter feel good not for producing something they cannot see but simply for creating. And, in enhancing self-esteem, needlework reduces dependence. Similarly, dressing oneself reduces dependence but increases creativity, self-esteem, and confidence.[38] Besides, a little "luxury" brings with it well deserved "pleasure."[39] What seems undesirable vanity from a sighted perspective is positive and pleasing for the blind.

Addressing other issues of dependence from her own direct experience, Husson turns to child rearing practices. Because sighted parents misperceive their blind children's needs, they raise them inappropriately. Even if well intended, cautious parents "inspire in us suspicion, even terror that is impossible to overcome;" these fears, moreover, "so often are only imaginary."[40] This was Husson's situation; when her sighted parents overprotected her, they instilled "unrelenting fear" in her as well as the feeling that she was "an insignificant being whose needs had to be provided for."[41] While the sighted think erroneously "that blind people should always remain in a complete state of immobility," such thinking does more to encourage than discourage that state.[42] Thus, Husson asks the sighted parents of blind children to turn the tables on traditional thinking.

In addition to overprotecting their blind children, sighted parents "think they are providing a great service to a child deprived of sight by satisfying all his wishes and caving in to his tiniest whims."[43] But what if the parents of a blind child die? In such cases, the orphan will be taken in by others; and previously indulged blind children are unprepared to adapt to any new dependences they encounter. Rather than being indulged, the blind must learn the opposite, "how to practice the humble submissions that is extremely necessary for his status."[44] As Husson states, "without resignation, there is no calm, without calm, no satisfaction, no bliss."[45] Using two figures of speech, repetition and *cumulatio* to suggest inevitability, Husson indicates that for the blind, happiness and independence involves a counterintuitive kind of resignation to the will of others.

Throughout, Husson overturns conventional wisdom about the blind and the dependence on which it depends. Despite her concern with developing dependence with humility, she reverses standard logic by dissuading the blind from marrying. In particular, if a blind man marries a woman, she serves simply as "a protector."[46] "If this portrait is horrifying, that of a young woman marrying a sighted man is even worse, for if she has any money, she shouldn't deny the fact that this would be the only motive for seeking marriage... keep hold of your freedom." [47] Finally and worst of all is the marriage between two blind people. Each individual would be limited by the other and neither could tend to their children.[48] Laying aside the apparent irony that Husson married a blind musician with whom she had two children, for Husson, dependence is unavoidable and, as such, to be used to develop the particular kinds of virtues and experiences the blind need (see below). Although the sighted may not be familiar with nor trust Husson's characterization, her experience confirms its accuracy and reasonability.

Both Hay and Husson identify directly with their respective infirmities while reversing Enlightenment thinking about them. Clearly, theirs is not the earlier embodied, felt experience of pervasive disability based on spiritual concerns but an experience of specific problems imbued by and based on logical thinking; such thinking prevents them from enacting their disabilities subjectively. In their reliance on conventional sources and reasoning, they are on some levels, and ironically, still encumbered by those assumptions.

Disability Identity as Fortune

Again recalling Burnet's opening reasoning, Hay and Husson use antithetical statements to characterize their identities as fortunate rather than pitiable. Much as Hay overturned Bacon's propositions, he uses carefully reasoned antithetical statements to characterize his deformity in fortunate terms. True, he acknowledges, "it is certain, that the Human frame, being warped and disproportionate, is lessened in Strength and Activity; and rendered less fit for it functions."[49] But, again (and referring to Bacon's inductive method), this common belief is not true to "the Facts: and in this Case the Instances are too few, or unobserved, to draw a general conclusion from them."[50] For one thing, "bodily Deformity is very rare; and therefore a Person so distinguished must naturally think, that he has had ill Luck in a Lottery, where there are above a thousand Prizes to the Blank."[51] No doubt aware of the irony in his statement, Hay reasons that because something rare is valuable, deformity is a great treasure. Moreover, deformed individuals get used to the "inconveniences continually attending a Figure like mine;" they hardly destroy happiness, as his life certainly demonstrates.[52]

And although external deformity suggests internal malfunction, as Bacon argued, health is the responsibility of the individual. Relying once more on his own experience, he notes he is healthier and has already lived to a greater age than either of his parents; yet, "my father was not deformed, but active, and my Mother a celebrated Beauty."[53] And, he reasons syllogistically, since temperance is surely significant to health and since deformed people, who have less strength than the non-deformed, tend to moderation, they are in fact often very healthy and equally fortunate.[54] To illustrate, he offers numerous examples of temperance by means of maxims which reverse conventional thinking and thus

> to the World will seem Paradoxes; as certain true Geological Theorems do to those, who are unacquainted with the Globe: the smallest Liquors are best... The best Dinner is one Dish.... A Fast is better than a Lord Mayor's feast ... [and] also moderate exercise. As a deformed person is not formed for violent Exercise, he is less liable to such Disorders as are the natural Consequence of it.... On the whole I conclude, that Deformity is a Protection to a Man's Health and Person; which (strange as it may appear) are better defended by Feebleness than Strength.[55]

Very moderate by nature, the deformed, Hay indicates, are healthier than the non-deformed and, in this, more fortunate.

In addition to addressing how the physical aspects of deformity are fortunate, Hay discusses mental capacities in like manner. He presents a series of parallel antithetical statements. Underlying each statement is a central argument: what the deformed lack in ability to build bodily strength is compensated for by capacities to strengthen the mind.[56] And so, "if he cannot be a Dancing-master to adjust the heels [that's him mentioned earlier]; he may be a School-master to instruct the Head. He cannot be a graceful actor on the Stage; but he may produce a good Play."[57] Throughout, Hay practices what he preaches when he observes fortune in his condition. "Ridicule and Contempt are a certain Consequence of Deformity: and therefore what a person cannot avoid, he should learn not to regard ... and triumph is complete if you exceed the other in wit and pleasantries."[58] His glass is certainly half-full. No need to pity him or anyone in his club, quite the opposite.

For Husson, the fact that she cannot see is no loss; the blind cannot miss what they never knew.[59] "The blind are pitied yet have no idea what light and seeing are."[60] While the sighted "admire everything that catches their eye ... the blind do not have the power to contemplate the attractiveness of nature, but they rejoice in the capacity to small. Their souls can receive the most vivid and most profound impressions."[61] Thus, Husson feels fortunate in her life. As she also puts it, her "reasoning" tells her that if she is in a way "unhappy," it is but for "the sad exclamations of people who see me."[62] Because she has no regrets, it angers Husson that her sisters felt she envied them, wishing she could see.[63] Instead, they do not understand her perspective. As she puts it antithetically, "an ancient writer noted judiciously, one can do good without seeing but eyes are indispensable for doing evil."[64]

If the blind cannot see, they have strength and good fortune in their other senses.[65] In fact, she notes ironically, their sense of touch is so powerful that some sighted may even be jealous of them.[66] Yet, she would never trade senses.[67] Moreover, what the blind share in their sense of touch is not what the sighted think. Among its other virtues, this sense helps them establish the strong and unique bonds which characterize their group.[68]

The blind are also fortunate to have superior hearing, hearing which works in ways which make them happier than the sighted's experience of that same sense. Because of their fine hearing, the blind enjoy music, value what they hear, and participate in conversation to a far greater extent than the sighted.[69] True, lacking vision, the blind do not read facial expressions. Instead, they use their hearing physiognometrically, to "judge the face to be extremely sweet ... We make a mistake ... only rarely."[70] In overturning the thinking of the sighted and pointing out her good fortunate, Husson also overturns conventional eighteenth century physiognometric medical theory.

Given their particular experiences, the blind have a "distinctive character" which serves them in necessary, appropriate, and fortunate ways. [71] Because they must deal with dependence humbly, they are intelligent, enthusiastic, proud, patient, and noble, as well as "fearful, defiant, sweet but impassioned."[72]

As indicated, the blind are fortunate to share a kind of friendship, one that depends in part on the dependence which is central to their lives. Thus, the blind are not likely to alienate those upon whom they depend.[73] Moreover, their relationships are strong and reliable rather "superficial" or "banal" as are those of the sighted.[74] Indeed, with the "better judgment" their experiences give them, the blind learn that "external charms fade rapidly, but such is not the case for those that adorn the soul. Ugliness follows attractiveness, but goodness, beauty, and sweetness united with piety, spirit, and reason survive as long as the one who can hears them."[75] In expressing these thoughts, Husson suggests that these characteristics are different than what the sighted assume the blind possess but also beyond the possession of the sighted. How unfortunate for the sighted.

In example after example, Husson overturns conventional, established thinking about the blind, demonstrating from her lived experience how fortunate they are. "When I started this work by saying that blindness offered an incalculable number of charms, I was not deceiving my readers, who must have already noticed them, for I seek to prove to my readers that far from imposing on them, I have only dimly painted the advantage that we enjoy."[76] Like Burnet, who discusses his completely silent residence, her non-visual world is complete despite the dependence it bears.

For Husson as for Hay, pity makes no sense. When Husson reveals how the sighted misunderstand the unsteady gait of the blind, she speaks for many disabled and deformed individuals. "Forgive me, dear reader, if I dare to say frankly that this is less our fault than it is that of those who surround us."[77]

Disabilities as Separate Categories

In representing their disability experiences as antithetical to common wisdom, Hay and Husson rely on Enlightenment penchants for categorization and logic. Thus, they ironically work within the conventional practices of the day.

As various statements have demonstrated, Hay groups himself with other deformed individuals in ways which maintain the prevailing cultural distinction between disability and deformity. He states that "it is not easy to say why one Species of Deformity should be more ridiculous than another, or why the Mob should be more merry with a crooked Man, than one that is deaf, lame, squinting, or purblind."[78] Elsewhere, he mentions that "even if deformed people lament that their soul doesn't have a nice place to live at least it is habitable.... he is in a state to be envied by the Deaf, Dumb, the Lame, and the Blind."[79] Not only does Hay separate himself from disabled individuals such as Husson, but he is, ironically, not entirely sympathetic to other marginalized individuals. Similarly, when Hay rejects public attention, he implicitly separates his experience (or ideal experience) of deformity from the so-called freaks that became cultural spectacles at that time.[80]

As his references to the disabled and deformed also indicate, Hay makes distinctions across categories involving class. When Hay separates himself as deformed from other kinds of disabled, he denigrates the "mob" who would find his form more ridiculous than other disabilities. Elsewhere, Hay associates his particular deformity with the superior intelligence and education of the cultural elite (though ironically he was a poor orphan who never finished his Oxford degree). For example, Hay claims that one of the greatest advantages to deformity is its tendency to "the improvement of the Mind" for those of the privileged classes.[81] Indeed, "among 558 Gentlemen in the House of Commons I am the only one so. Thanks to my worthy Constituents, who never objected to my Person; and I hope I never gave them cause to object to my behavior."[82] Although he is the only deformed individual in Parliament, his educated peers accept him without qualification; and despite his deformity, he characterizes himself with educated peers as superior.

Conversely, Hay associates the poor with an unenlightened identity. When Hay states, "he's never been insulted by a gentleman, but he has with the "Mob; where Insolence grows in Proportion, as the man sinks in Condition," he again belittles the virtue of the lower class and uneducated.[83] And finally, Hay comments, "fine Cloaths attract the Eyes of the Vulgar; and therefore a deformed person should not assume those borrowed Feathers, which will render him double ridiculous."[84] Echoing his statement about the Ugly Club, he notes here that the deformed should not draw attention from the low class by donning fancy clothes.

With regard to these low types who offer the ugly contempt and ridicule, Hay notes that

> men naturally despise what appears less beautiful or useful: and their Pride is gratified, when see such Foils to their own Persons. It is this Sense of Superiority, which is testified by Laughter in the lower sorts: while their Betters, who know how little any Man whatsoever hath to boast of, are restrained by good Sense and good breeding from such an Insult.[85]

The lower class has not been bred to respond to the deformed appropriately. Instead of withholding judgment based on superficial elements, these "lower sorts" laugh at those they can find reason to belittle. As such, Hay distinguishes between himself and the lower, uneducated class. Presumably, his work for the poor would provide them with the education that would improve their lot.

In identifying as he does, Hay reveals his status as literate and deformed while using the language of his oppressor to overturn it; in so doing, he oppresses others on the basis of class. On one level, Hay's essay perpetuates norms in ways which a later contemporary audience may easily see through.[86] Given his honesty, honor, and pain, his is also a sympathetic story. It is sad though not pitiable that "he doesn't care upon his death about his contemptible carcass."[87]

When Husson groups the blind together on the basis of their many fortunes, she separates them from the sighted. Besides maintaining this conventional cultural category, she also draws a line between the blind and individuals with other disabilities, particularly the deaf. For example, she compares the blind to the deaf "who are embarrassed and distrustful in gatherings because they cannot hear."[88] Because Husson can hear, she feels superior to the deaf. As far as she is concerned, deafness leaves an individual less sympathetic to others and in a sense less human since "these people can't know if they have a heart, for unlike ours, that of the deaf-mute is not animated with a thousand delicious sensations; being unable to judge feelings, they can feel neither sympathy nor friendship.... We know how to cherish because we can hear."[89] It is understandable but ironic that she elevates herself in this manner above individuals with a different disability. Like Hay, the hurt she has experienced prevents her from perceiving the perspectives of others at the same time that she perpetuates conventional categories and values by drawing these distinctions.

Conclusions

Both authors use particular verbal strategies to reverse yet reify conventional thinking about disabilities and deformity. On the one hand, they overtly identify with their disabilities in ways which overturn the thinking of those who do not share their experiences. On the other hand, they erect their own categories which depend on the categories, method, and sources they reject. Still, to avoid representing their experience in unacceptable, subjective, embodied terms, they speak in the logical, categorical language of their opponents. Antithesis especially allows these authors to express their personal feelings more directly than earlier writers and thus reverse prevailing opinion that their bodies are subjective and illogical. Yet, ironically again, antithesis is a figure of speech traditionally considered a subjective linguistic element of style, but no more so than by Bacon and Sprat, proponents of logic in science. Using this figure renders them, therefore, not as logical as they presume. Another irony is evident in their use of genres. Although they may employ forms different than those characteristic of the early modern era, each genre was based on standards set by the presumably "non-deformed" writers against whom they railed.

These ironies depend in part on new print technologies which allowed more people to read, to become familiar with new forms and content, and to offer their own perspectives at the same time that their thinking was affected by the increasing standardization therein.

In contrast to the life writers before them, neither Hay nor Husson was a visionary; neither enacted her/his infirmity to cope; neither advocated for spiritual guidance; and, neither hoped for ultimate perfection. Instead, both wrote reasoned responses to prevailing logic, advocated on behalf of their specific conditions, and asked for some tolerance if not outright acceptance. Despite their differences, each attempts to inform others what it is like to live in their world as individuals who now explicitly identify with particular categories of disability.

With the emergence of the overt medical model, disability is no longer a pervasive everyday presence but noteworthy and noticed.[90] By focusing on their experiences and making them topics of discussion and debate, Hay and Husson ask for acceptance rather than cure; as such, they look forward to nineteenth century disability life writing which advocates and speaks directly to reform.

[1] John Burnett in Krentz, A Mighty Change. *An Anthology of Deaf American Writing, 1816-1864*, p. 40; emphasis in original.

[2] Antithesis is a figure of speech which features parallel clauses with contrasting meaning, for example, as stated by Abraham Lincoln in "The Gettsyburg Address": "The world will little note, nor long remember, what we say here, but it can never forget what they did here."

[3] Although no explicit dividing line separates the Early Modern World from the Modern, or the "long" eighteenth century, I draw the standard line between 1688 and 1815, from the Glorious Revolution to the Battle of Waterloo.

[4] In addition to Hay, Husson, and Burnett's text, other individuals who wrote about their world as disabled, specifically as deaf, during this period include Pougens, Saboureux De Fontenay (in Lane, *The Deaf Experience Classics in Language and Education*, pp. 14-27); Pierre Desloges. *A Deaf Person's Observations about an Elementary Course of Education for the Deaf* (in ibid., pp. 28-48); and Laurent Clerc (in Krentz *A Mighty Change. An Anthology of Deaf American Writing, 1816-1864*, pp. 1-31).

[5] Davis, "Dr. Johnson, Amelia, and the Discourse of Disability in the Eighteenth Century," criticizes Hay's essay for "reiterating (although humanizing and questioning to a degree) stereotypes about people with disabilities," p. 60.

[6] Kudlick and Weyland "Introduction" to Husson, *Reflections. The Life and Writings of a Young Blind Woman in Post-Revolutionary France*, p. 95.

[7] Ibid., p. 135.

[8] Bacon, *The Advancement of Learning*; Descartes, *Discours de la Méthode et Première Méditation*. These characterizations are, of course, generalizations but nonetheless accurate snapshots of the sentiments of the time.

[9] Foucault, *Madness and Civilization: a History of Insanity in the Age of Reason*; Foucault, *The Birth of the Clinic: An Archaeology of Medical Perception*.

[10] De Sauvages, *Nosologie méthodique: ou distribution des maladies en classes, engenres et en espèces, suivant l'esprit de Sydenham, & la methode des botaniste*; Cullen, *First Lines of the Practice of Physic*; Cullen, *A Synopsis of Methodical Nosology: In Which the Genera of Disorders are Particularly Defined, and the Species Added with the Synonimous of those from Sauvages*; Burton, *The Anatomy of Melancholy*; Cheyne, *The English Malady*.

[11] Davis, "Constructing Normalcy: The Bell Curve, the Novel, and the Invention of the Disabled Body in the Nineteenth Century."

[12] Sprat, *The History of the Royal-Society of London for the Improving of Natural Knowledge*.

[13] Deutsch and Nussbaum "Introduction" in Hay, *Deformity: An Essay*, pp. 2-3; Boaistuau, *Histoires Prodigeuses*; Epstein, *Altered Conditions: Disease, Medicine, and Storytelling*; Gould and Pyle, *Anomalies and Curiosities of Medicine*; Paré, *Des Monstres et Prodiges*.

[14] Hay, *Deformity: An Essay*, pp. 24. This was also a time of interest in various categories of freakishness including feral children; see Chapter Seven, p. and Garland Thomson, *Extraordinary Bodies: Figuring Physical Disability in American Culture and Literature*.

[15] Statistical records about disability and deformity for this period remain scant. Nonetheless, anecdotal evidence and common sense indicate that numbers of disabled and deformed people were significant and many were poor; see Husson, *Reflections. The Life and Writings of a Young Blind Woman in Post-Revolutionary France*, p. 5.

[16] Goring, *The Rhetoric of Sensibility in Eighteenth-Century Culture*.

[17] These include *The Spectator*, Hogarth, Homer, Ovid, Bacon, Spartans, Longinus, Dryden, Pope, Montaigne, Greek Myth, Shakespeare, among them, as well as maxims.

[18] Barros and Smith, *Life-Writings by British Women 1660-1850: An Anthology*; Husson, *Reflections. The Life and Writings of a Young Blind Woman in Post-Revolutionary France*, pp. 24-33; Smith, *A Poetics of Women's Autobiography*; Smith and Watson, *Reading Autobiography: A Guide for Reading Life Narratives*.

[19] Barros, and Smith, *Life-Writings by British Women 1660-1850: An Anthology*, p. 24. The novel appeared at this time. Excellent scholarship discusses the presence and characterization of the disabled in literary works of this time. See Goring, *The Rhetoric of Sensibility in Eighteenth-Century Culture*; Smith in "Foreword" to Husson, *Reflections. The Life and Writings of a Young Blind Woman in Post-Revolutionary France*.

[20] Hay, *Deformity: An Essay*, p. 23. Apparently, Hays insisted on this dedication over the wishes of his publisher who had a contemporary person in mind; Ibid., p. 48.

[21] Ibid., p. 24.

[22] Ibid., p. 24, note 12.

[23] Ibid., p. 24.

[24] *The Spectator* of March 20, 1711, #17.

[25] Hay, *Deformity: An Essay*, p. 27.

[26] Ibid., p. 24 and 33.

[27] Ibid., p. 25.

[28] Ibid., p. 35.

[29] Bacon also compares the deformed to eunuchs because they possess envy ("Of Deformity," pp. 426-427; apparently, envy is not an emotion for Bacon; it not at least not a good one).

[30] Hay, *Deformity: An Essay*, pp. 426-427.

[31] Ironically, Hay also comments that he is both bashful and a public figure and, thus, a "perfect Riddle" (*Deformity: An Essay*, p. 39) to himself. Being bold and bashful, Hay acknowledges his own antithetical nature.

[32] Ibid., p. 46.

[33] Ibid., p. 47.

[34] Ibid., p. 47

[35] Ibid., p. 34.

[36] Rodenbach, *Lettre sur les aveugles faisant suite à celle de Diderot, ou Considérations sure leur état moral, comment on les instruit, comment ile jusent des couleurs, de la beauté, ainsi que leur méthode pur conserser avec les sourd-muets, suivies de notices biographiques sure les aveugles les plus remarquables*.

[37] Husson, *Reflections. The Life and Writings of a Young Blind Woman in Post-Revolutionary France*, p. 47.

[38] Ibid., p. 47.

[39] Ibid., p. 47
[40] Ibid., p. 20.
[41] Ibid., p. 20.
[42] Ibid., p. 20
[43] Ibid., p. 45.
[44] Ibid., p. 45.
[45] Ibid., p. 45.
[46] Ibid., p. 53.
[47] Ibid., p. 54.
[48] Ibid., p. 53.
[49] Hay, *Deformity: An Essay*, p. 28.
[50] Ibid., p. 28
[51] Ibid., p. 27.
[52] Ibid., p. 29.
[53] Ibid., p. 29.
[54] Ibid., pp. 29-30.
[55] Ibid., pp. 30-31.
[56] Ibid., p. 42.
[57] Ibid., p. 31.
[58] Ibid., p. 40.
[59] Husson, *Reflections. The Life and Writings of a Young Blind Woman in Post-Revolutionary France*, p. 16.
[60] Ibid., p. 25.
[61] Ibid., p. 29.
[62] Ibid., p. 16.
[63] Ibid., p. 18.
[64] Ibid., p. 22.
[65] Ibid., p. 24.
[66] Ibid., p. 22.
[67] Ibid., p. 23.
[68] Ibid., pp. 22-24.
[69] Ibid., p. 34.
[70] Ibid., p. 37.
[71] Ibid., p. 25.
[72] Ibid., pp. 24-26.
[73] Ibid., p. 26.
[74] Ibid., p. 260.
[75] Ibid., p. 60
[76] Ibid., p. 32
[77] Ibid., p. 20.
[78] Hay, *Deformity: An Essay*, p. 34.
[79] Ibid., p. 44.
[80] Davis, "Dr. Johnson, Amelia, and the Discourse of Disability in the Eighteenth Century"; Garland Thomson, *Extraordinary Bodies*.
[81] Hay, *Deformity: An Essay*, p. 42.
[82] Ibid., p. 27.
[83] Ibid., pp. 25-26.
[84] Ibid., p. 42.
[85] Ibid., p. 33.

[86] It is neither uncommon nor inconsistent for a marginalized group to perpetuate, on some level, the norms it overturns. Various works on feminist and racial perspectives address this issue; see Wilson Logan, *We Are Coming: The Persuasive Discourse of Nineteenth-Century Black Women*, pp. 139-40, 150, for example.

[87] Ibid., p. 38.

[88] Ibid., p. 33.

[89] Ibid., pp. 33-34.

[90] Davis, "Dr. Johnson, Amelia, and the Discourse of Disability in the Eighteenth Century," discusses another irony at the time, that while certain deformities are noted others are not discussed such as Samuel Johnson's tics and behaviors, or at least they are not discussed by the individual him or herself. Others, of course do discuss these issues (Boswell most notably). It seems to me that the fact that Johnson and others do not discuss their physical issues at length does not contradict the fact that their presence was noted and categorized.

6

The Nineteenth Century: Insanity and Asylums

In the course of the nineteenth century, medical and cultural concerns with categorizing and standardizing the phenomena of the world increased. Reflecting this trend, the numbers and kinds of mental disability swelled.[1] This chapter examines seven mid-to-late nineteenth century white, middle-class American life writers, individuals with mental and physical differences who were classed as insane and institutionalized on that basis: Phebe Davis (1855; 1860), Hiram Chase (1865), Robert Fuller (1833), Sophia Olsen (1871), E. P.W. Packard (1871, 1874), Amos Swan (1874), and Anna Agnew (1887).[2] Writing after their release and from their own experiences, these individuals recount how they were held by the "system" because of their perceived disabilities; having gained freedom of body and voice, they advocate for reforming that system while challenging the cultural misconceptions about mental, physical, and cognitive disabilities on which they are based.

Speaking implicitly for the group and others similarly held, the writers often articulated ironic awareness that they were institutionalized for allegedly thinking and behaving inappropriately by those who, they feel, thought and acted in inhumane ways. As Davis describes her personal ordeal,

> it is now twenty-one years since people found out that I was crazy, and all because I could not fall in with every vulgar belief that was fashionable. I never could be led by everything and everybody, simply because they all told me their arguments were right, and at the same time they were all in direct opposition to each other, and I knew that all truths harmonized.[3]

For Packard, the problem takes on institutional proportions.

> The legalized usurpation of human rights is the great evil underlying
> our social fabric. From this corrupt center spring the evils of our social
> system. This corruption has culminated in the Insane Asylums of the
> nineteenth century. Let the Government but remove the cause of this
> insanity, and the need of such Institutions would be greatly lessened.[4]

It is against such systematic hypocrisy and mistreatment that they now
write. The authors also speak to the cultural construction of disability as
a threat and crime.[5] Through their narratives, these life writers turn the
tables on their oppressors and portray the system, as Packard notes in the
epigraph, as the cause of their legal, medical, and personal misfortune.
Using irony, the legacy of Hay's subversive satires, these individuals
now directly expose the system's hypocrisy; in particular, they advocate
against a mechanism that removed them from public view on the basis
of bogus legal and medical categories.

To demonstrate such advocacy, I focus on two broad but related
themes which the narratives share; all characterize their
institutionalization in terms of medical and legal abuses, abuses
manifested on social, emotional, and physical levels. Before turning to
the stories, I begin with some background on life writing about
disability, on nineteenth century American asylums, and on these seven
individuals held within them.

Nineteenth Century Asylums

Packard's comment and other sources affirm that the nineteenth-century
can be characterized as an era of asylums in the United States.[6] Various
medical and legal factors combined to make this the case. As previous
chapters discussed, pre-modern physicians and natural scientists could
not directly observe internal bodily operations. As they understood it,
bodily health and character were reflected in outer manifestations and
behaviors and depended, in turn, on a balance of humors within the body
as a whole.[7] Conversely, internal humoral imbalance was evident in
unhealthy, inappropriate outward display; when this imbalance was
perceived to be a mental problem, it was associated with the
melancholic humor especially.[8]

From the mid-sixteenth century onward, scientists continued to
identify inner health and character in terms of outer features and
movements. But, they attempted to make this identification even more
systematic and less spiritual by linking particular organs with particular

illnesses.[9] In the eighteenth and nineteenth centuries, attempts to link specific organs with specific outward signs were aided by emerging technologies, technologies involving electricity and photography, for example, which allowed scientists to look more directly into the body.[10] From this more empirical perspective, mental illness was a matter of faulty brain operation.

Following the categorical approach, insanity could be traced to parts of the brain, each associated with a particular physical or mental attribute; identifying that outward sign thereby pinpointed the corresponding internal location and cause.[11] This condition not only resulted from faulty brain function but such problems also rendered the afflicted developmentally deficient. Deficits were placed on a spectrum, depending on the degree of insanity and its originating source, which located each disabled person somewhere between fully mature adult humans, at one end, and savages, children, old people, and brutes, at the other. According to nineteenth century medical student William Horner, such brain "impressions in Brutes instead of falling quickly on the mind, fall on their limbs."[12] The insane brain was not only a brutish entity but one manifested in strange leg movements.[13] Detecting, diagnosing, and treating such an ill-defined condition required expertise, a situation which empowered physicians.

Insanity, now the catch-all term for mental, social, and cognitive differences, was applied to a range of behaviors and symptoms from fever to delirium, melancholy, nervous movements, speech, and excitability.[14] Reflecting the breadth of the diagnosis, treatment was universal and aimed at improving character and health since, according to the prevailing correspondence approach, these elements were linked. As framed in medical manuals of the period, such universal treatments included herbal remedies, rest, fresh air, and therapeutic baths. Perhaps because of insanity's broad scope, these practices often seemed to have missed their therapeutic marks.

Also given the breadth of this term, the numbers of people considered insane increased dramatically during this period and to deal with them more asylums were built.[15] With the upsurge in reported cases, the State, or states were empowered to evaluate and manage those individuals judged insane. Conceived on humane grounds, asylums were intended to provide appropriate protection and treatment for those they held. According to the 1774 Madhouse Act in England, confinement was legal only when a medical practitioner certified that the individual in question was insane. In the United States, similar strictures were put in place on a state-by-state basis.[16] Presumably, too, this approach protected the patient against arbitrary confinement by family, although, as we shall see, this was not always the case. Isaac Ray's *A Treatise on the Medical Jurisprudence of Insanity (*1838) provides early categories for determining legal insanity. He divided his subject into two groups, one with "defective development of faculties" (idiocy and imbecility) and the other with "lesion[s] of the faculties subsequent to their development" (mania and dementia); typically, these categories embrace a wide range of issues involving "defective" intellectual and affective capacities.[17] Medically and legally, then, insanity characterized individuals considered outside the norm and incapable of managing their own lives. Institutionalizing these individuals prevented them from harming themselves or others and presumably helped them return to normal functioning.

To accommodate individuals of different economic means, a tiered asylum system emerged. Often, poor, disabled individuals went to prison or were left homeless.[18] Otherwise, poor, middle-class, and wealthy were sent to asylums with accommodations fitting the individuals' assets.[19] The individuals in this study all appear to be middle-class citizens and all are white. Although nineteenth century asylums for the wealthy encouraged them to write poetry and fiction, inmates did not write about their disability in that setting.[20] After release, however, they wrote of the abuse, isolation, and ironies they experienced within a system that was purportedly designed to heal their insanity.[21]

In sum, insanity characterized individuals considered outside the norm and incapable of managing their own lives. With insanity so broadly defined, its numbers increased significantly during the nineteenth century as did the numbers of asylums. Institutionalizing these individuals presumably prevented them from harming anyone and helped them to function more normally.

Complementary Corpus Analysis

To enrich this background and support my analysis, I again used corpus linguistics. In Chapter Three, I did so to consider the demographically diverse corpus of visionary texts both as a unified group and as part of the broader societal context. Although less temporally and geographically diverse than the high medieval corpus, the asylum reports examined in this chapter are no less a product of their social context. In this case, I looked beyond the life writing texts on which the chapter is based to case history reports about institutionalized individuals much like those who wrote those texts, specifically, to case histories in "The Insane Hospital Reports." Housed in the University of

Pittsburgh Health Sciences Library, the collection contains volumes of reports from American asylums from the same mid to late nineteenth century time period as the life writing I analyze below.[22] Examining these doctors' reports as a corpus thus provided an interesting complement to the seven life writing texts analyzed belong.

From this rich resource, I picked 15 case histories in the collection (itself randomly bound by state). These histories originated from asylums in four states, 11 from New York, two from the same institution in Connecticut and one each from Massachusetts and Ohio.[23] Coincidentally, one case history is from the same institution in Utica, New York at which Phebe Davis was held, although there is no way to determine who the observed individual is in the case history.

To ensure that these reports were representative of the time, I examined other documents throughout the collection; they shared similar structures and content, in particular, sections devoted to the asylums' operating practices and procedures; the typical report addresses budgets, purchases, visitors, deaths, particular local funding or legal issues (the use of restraints, for example, in Case 1), and, of course, patient case histories. Similarly representative of the collection and medical thinking of the time, the reports consistently categorize the patients' insanity in terms such as acute, sub-acute, chronic mania, melancholia dementia, epilepsy, and paresis, each associated with a particular brain/body malfunction.

Within this corpus, I counted the occurrence of 69 terms individually and in collocations.[24] To select terminology, I relied on medical dictionaries and encyclopedias from the seventeenth through the twentieth centuries.[25] These sources identified conventional nineteenth century medical terminology associated with individuals considered insane.

Of the 69 words, the highest counts belong to the following words: feeble (1238), attack (1163), maniacal (1020), habits (838), restless (599), insanity (524), depressed (523), violent (518), mental (571), talkative (478), incoherent (475), paralysis (415), irritable (328), muscular (309), destructive (299), mania (293), excitable (247), excited (229), nervous (220), and disturbance (204). Generally, these highest counts involve inappropriate movements, behaviors, and habits. While the corpus in Chapter Three provided a surprising number of hits on "love," at least from a contemporary perspective, in this corpus, and equally appropriate for the context, "feeble" appears the most often of all words counted. By the late nineteenth century, this word not only suggested infirmity and weakness but, like notions of "defective," was associated with a particular set of negative physical and moral

Table 6.1: Nineteenth Century Asylums: Institutional Information

Case Number & Page Numbers	State / Institution	Year	Report form
1, 18 (pp. 1-19)	Resident Physician Kings County Lunatic Asylum, NY	1872	Annual report
2, 8 (pp. 19-27)	CT	1871	Pathologist's report
3, 41 (pp. 42-83)		1861	Annual Report of the Managers of the State Lunatic Asylum
4, 3 (pp. 10-13)	Longview Asylum Cincinnati, OH	1862	14th Annual Report, section on insane epileptics
5, 10 (pp. 49-52)	State Lunatic Asylum	1873 or after	Annual Report of Managers, State Lunatic Asylum
6, 3 (pp. 40-43)	Lunatic Asylum of Northampton, MA	Oct., 1874	Public Document No. 21
7, 26 (pp. 29-55)	NY	1875	State Senate No. 17 Post-mortems and histories of cases
8, 16 (pp. 37-53)	NY	1875	Annual Report of Managers, State Lunatic Asylum
9, 22 (pp. 30-52)		1875	Post-mortems and histories of cases
10, 21 (pp. 33-54)	NY	1879	13th Annual Report of the Managers of the State Lunatic Asylum. Pathological report

11, 5 (pp. 72-77)	NY	1878	36th Annual Report of the Managers of the State Lunatic Asylum. Regulations, Conditions, and Forms
12, 36 (pp. 49-85)	NY	1877	35th Annual Report of the Managers pf the State Lunatic Asylum.
13, 2 (pp.23-25)	Danvers Lunatic Asylum, CT	Oct., 1880	Pathologist's Report
14, 3 (pp. 30-33)	NY	1868	25th Annual Report of the Managers of the State Lunatic Asylum (deaths)
15 (pp. 42-44)	NY	1867	24th Annual Report of the Managers of the State Lunatic Asylum

characteristics involving intellect, appearance, and heredity. For example, "feebleness" was used to evaluate children and place those perceived as innately intellectually disabled in schools for the retarded where they learned by rote the basic life skills which befitted their feeble, brutish, underdeveloped nature.[26]

Reflecting its appearance in the life writing texts, "feeble" appears within the concurrent nineteenth-century Ugly Laws, regulations which outlawed anyone "diseased, maimed, and deformed"[27] and "feeble" from begging in public.[28] At the time, "feeble" had strong negative connotations and distinct associations with disability issues. Its frequency in the case histories locates them in this broader context and within a typical pattern of characterizing individuals who do not look and act in acceptable ways as deficient. Its legacy is evident in Hay's earlier discussion of his deformity.

Other frequently appearing words characterize the patients' movements and behaviors in explicitly violent terms: "abusive," "attack," "destructive," "disturbance," "maniacal," "vicious." In other cases, words associate the patients with habits and behaviors which locate them beyond the realm of polite company: "excitable," "incoherent," "irritable," "nervous," and "restless." "Habit" is used

Table 6.2: Nineteenth Century Asylums: Words and Collocations
(Column B = Number of Times the Word Appears)

Word	B	Files	In Collocation with
Abnormal	81	1-15	abnormal pigmentation; mental action; appearance; accumulation of fat in the; at the base of the brain no abnormal conditions were detected
Abusive	122	1,3-15	threatening and violent; to his family, and finally assaulted his wife; noisy, incoherent, talkative, irritable
Agitated	19	1, 6-15	tithing the patient from the agitated congregation, constitutes no agreeable or desirable
Attack	1163	1-15	pneumonia, rheumatism, insanity, mental disturbance, paralysis, mania, convulsions, phlegmonous erysipelas,
Bile	19	2,7-15	liver substance
Blind	30	1, 3-15	became totally blind; periods of excitement, and gradual mental; had been blind, and was led for five years
Convulsions	124	1, 3-15	After a time she was seized with convulsions, and had frequent fits for five; uttered word. A few days afterward be had convulsions; indicated his wants by signs and occasionally; later he had paralytic attacks, with convulsions, followed by; he had several well marked. epileptiform convulsions
Countenance	83	1, 3-15	countenance, the tremulousness; countenance; said she was well; bore a marked cachectic look; there was considerable; expressed pain and anxiety
Crazy	20	1,	labored ill six months before

		6-15	admission; crazy, harsh and disagreeable
Defective	10	7-15	very defective. Though his countenance
Delusion	156	1-15	that he was a telegraph operator; that she was wealthy, but that her property; before his committal to jail; What delusion ordinarily possessed the mind; delusion that the house was on fire, and tried to throw
Depressed	523	1,3-15	somewhat depressed and gloomy, seemed thoughtful and gave; and gloomy; cried much of the time; irritable; melancholic; restless
Destructive	299	1,3-15	maniacal and filthy; and incoherent in speech. The paroxysm lasted some; of clothing, broke the glass in the car window a; posed care; endeavored to get away
Disturbance	204	1,3-15	of speech, unsteadiness of gait and tremulousness; and violence. After some fifteen months, and with; but more extensive paralysis; he exhibited mental disturbance. Ten days ago while in chapel in
Epilepsy	57	1,3-15	man age nineteen, good habits. Had epilepsy for nine; Fifteen were from general Paresis, three from epilepsy; meningitis, six from exhaustion, four from epilepsy, two from cerebral
Excesses	25	2,7-15	point of a series of extravagant notions and excesses. which manifested them; is the circulatory movements consecutive upon excesses in the use; indulged in sexual excesses; was vicious and ugly when under the influence
Excited	229	1-15	and talkative, and wanted to address the; refused food or drink, threw himself about; and incoherent in speech; should be

			restrained in a prostrate position,
Excitable	247	1,3-15	talkative and excitable, but continued his work; some light work, but was excitable and talkative. In spring he became melancholic; emotional and irregular in feeling person, and considered eccentric, resided alone; talkative, restless and sleepless. At periods; and restless, walked the floor rapidly,
Feeble	1238	1-15	and maniacal; and irregular; in both mind and body; a diarrhea supervened; emaciated; and sleepless; in health; slow; dull
Frenzy	47	1,3-15	attacks of frenzy, during which she often threatened to take; he slept poorly and of late had periods of frenzy
Gait	194	1,3-15	unsteady; tremulous
Gesticulating	33	1,3-15	almost constantly in motion, gesticulating wildly; gesticulating, shaking his fists in a threatening manner
Habits	838	1,3-15	had been insane; hoarded articles; strong hereditary tendency; had an attack of acute mania; had epilepsy for nine; no hereditary tendency to insanity
Hectic	50	1,3-15	flush, twitching of muscles
Hereditary	154	1,3-15	patient was unwell for about six years; tendency to insanity, but was of a highly, nervous; patient had a strong hereditary taint, his grandfather, mother and
Hysteria	25	1,3-15	while suffering from hysteria
Hysterical	57	1,3-15	it was followed by an attack; laughing and crying alternately
Incoherent	475	1,3-	in speech; and violent; lost power of writing; neglected care

		15	of person; a year from time of admission; had hallucinations of hearing; and had exalted delusions of wealth; opposed care, wandered about; in speech, made foolish gestures and laughed immoderately; the paroxysm lasted some six weeks
Insane			nervous, excitable
Insanity	524	1,3-15	symptoms of insanity developed about two mouths before coming; to insanity. Patient was said to have been insane for; Insanity not hereditary. Patient was unwell for about six; of insanity. Patient had been a healthy, hard-working man; first manifested insanity; became irritable and faultfinding; hereditary tendency to. insanity; but was of a highly, nervous; manifested first symptoms of insanity, was jealous of his wife
Intemperate	107	1-15	man, aged twenty-five, intemperate in his habits. Father (4,7,8..); man, age seventy-four, of intemperate habits ; had been in (in 7 and 8); intemperate in habits; was first married twenty-four years
Irritable	328	1,3-15	was cross and irritable, became profane, obscene, noisy; and willful, tongue was tremulous, pupils; abusive to his family, and finally assaulted; and seclusive for sonic years afterward; petulant, fault-finding; almost constantly in motion, gesticulating wild
Mania	293	1-15	she left the asylum, recovered; that time her father was also in the asylum; but recovered in a short time; when fifteen years of age, which her mother; was talkative
Maniacal	1020	1,3-15	and talkative; and filthy; and destructive of clothing; and violent; took nourishment

			sparingly; pressed his hand to his head; paroxysm
Melancholic	153	1,3-15	restless and silent, lost in strength and became; and depressed, and remained in the; and again elated, till a few days; state, was reticent; inclined to be by herself
Melancholy	61	1,3-15	seemed to realize that she was; though at times was more; this condition continued until
Mental	571	1-15	disturbance have occurred since, at intervals of; disturbance; state, in that she became; abnormal mental state; very disturbed mental state; suspicions and fearful, and remained in this mental state up to the time of his death
Muscular	309	1-15	in August last had a fit; rheumatism, characterized by great pain; increased impairment of speech, muscular tremors, short; the pricking sensation occasioned by muscular activity
Muscle	25	1,3-15	muscle. Dura mater adherent to calvarium. A large clot
Nervous	220	1-15	hysterical, excitable
Nice	20	2,7-15	eyes in same condition
Noisy	734	1,3-15	nervous
Obscene	34	1,3-15	was obscene and abusive in speech; obscene and incoherent in speech. The following month she; as cross and irritable, became profane, obscene, noisy and; as maniacal, noisy, profane, obscene in speech and resisted; talkative, restless, profane and obscene, and pulled her hair
Paresis	263	1-	was fully marked, in the

		15	tremulousness; existed to a marked degree when he was brought; in five months he had become quiet; twitchings; in the uncertainty of gait
Paralysis	415	1-15	lost control of the movements of right side, which continued; fourteen months the paralysis had become general, and so complete
Paralytic	106	1,3-15	seizures; attacks
Possessed	19	1,7-15	believed herself possessed of great riches, and spent; what delusion ordinarily possessed the mind
Profane	195	1,3-15	obscene in speech and resisted everything that; and obscene, and pulled her hair out; and very abusive language!; expressed delusions; this was, her condition when admitted
Restless	599	1,3-15	he rapidly grew; and silent, lost in strength and became; talkative and; sleepless and at times turbulent; and sleepless; was out of bed at night and; profane and obscene, and pulled her hair; inclined to go from home without purpose; throwing herself about, bored head in pillow; lost flesh and died apoplectic; incoherent and had exalted delusions of wealth; movements, worked the straw into her hair
Reticent	19	1,5-15	without interest in himself or surroundings; thin, anemic and feeble; inclined to be by her self, and would turn her; and dangerous, and a few days before
Sexual	117	1-15	normal; excesses
Silent	38	1,3-15	melancholic, restless and silent, lost in strength and became; at times considerably depressed,

			silent and seclusive, an
Spasm	25	1,3-15	breathing, spasm of the glottis, globus-hystericus, crying, and
Spasmodic	34	1,3-15	spasmodic twitchings of muscles of face and
Steady	15	9-15	amid correct in habits until two; movement of the
Sympathy	12	2,7-15	care of the insane here, is made lighter by your sympathy and care. It is our highest aim
Talkative	478	1,3-15	[see excited, incoherent, restless]
Threatening	58	1, 3-15	his fists in a threatening manner, often using profane and very abusive; threatening in speech and dangerous. Notwithstanding; became abusive, threatening and violent
Tic	119	1,3-15	tic attack affecting the entire right side; the grey substance of the convolutions
Tremulous	95	1-15	and hands tremulous, and golf very unsteady; when admitted, tongue and hands were tremulous and gait unsteady ;was exalted and dictatorial
Twitching	45	1,3-15	of muscles of face. There was no loss of consciousness; of the muscles of the face
Ugly	16	8-15	indulged in sexual excesses; was vicious and ugly when under the influence; hands to his face, was reticent, [ ] ugly, and continued to lose
Unclean	13	1,5-15	unclean. Soon became restless
Unsteadiness	88	1, 3-15	there was marked hesitancy of speech and unsteadiness; and unsteadiness of gait; the disturbance of speech, unsteadiness of gait; was too incoherent; and tremulousness indicating

Unsteady	118	1, 3- 15	gait unsteady , was exalted and dictatorial, refused to; and there was twitching of the muscles of the face; and feeble; gait unsteady; so that he could not move about the ward without
Vicious	20	1,7- 15	habits; indulgences continued after a period of service; was vicious and ugly
Violent	518	1- 15	toward his brother; attacked and threatened to kill; had exalted delusions of wealth; and opposing care; tore off her clothing; was abusive; from this time she gradually failed; and manifesting so much excitement
Wild	42	1,3- 15	wild boy, though never much given to drink; on admission, was wild arid maniacal, talked incoherently, and; she continued wild and excited
Willful	25	1, 3- 15	he was irritable and willful, tongue was tremulous, pupils

frequently, as the collocations indicate, to evaluate the patients as inferior with respect to normal adults. Another group of terms, "hysteria," "muscular," and "paralysis" applies clinical nomenclature involving abnormality.

Through corpus-side word repetition, the case histories consistently characterize the asylum patients in terms of inappropriate movement and habits. Following then current thinking about those deemed disabled by insanity, physical health had a moral component; all patients exhibited habits, thoughts, movements, and/or expressions which do not conform to cultural norms, characteristics equated with underdevelopment and unsoundness of mind and body, with weak impulse control, and, therefore, with brutish behavior. Such descriptions apparently justified institutionalizing these individuals rather than allowing them to be publicly visible.

The collocations extend the associations between movements and inappropriate, uncontrolled, often violent, behaviors and habits. In describing the patients' violent behaviors, some collocations characterized their habits as insufficiently developed or controlled:

- "vicious and habits"
- "vicious, ugly, and reticent"
- "feeble and melancholic state"
- "filthy in his habits"
- "unclean and twitching"
- "intemperate habits"
- "irritable, will to […], and tremulous"

Again in keeping with prevailing thinking (and recalling characterizations by Aristotle and his ancient colleagues), the patients are disabled by violent and underdeveloped habits, making them appear more like animals, criminals, or savages than fully developed adult humans. Put another way, they cannot be successful because of how they look and move in this categorical society.

Many collocations contain seemingly contradictory terms:

- "reticent and dangerous"
- "steady and excesses"
- "steady, excesses, and spasms"
- "sympathy, melancholic, and agitated"

As the collocations represent them, patient behaviors are extremes rather than balanced means; good habits are never possessed but always treatment goals. But, as the life writing shows, some institutionalized individuals might feel threatened and scared, and act both "reticient and dangerously."

As the individual words, the collocations associate the patients with undesirable social attributions and physical appearances. The argument is clear: the insane are violent, ugly, weak, brutish and out-of-control. Such a motley yet unified group of maladjusted disabled individuals cannot function in society on their own. Conversely, no positive word collocations between the patients' movements and characters are used.

Some collocations are relatively longer phrases. For example, "became irritable, abusive to his family, and finally assaulted his wife" (appears in cases 1, 3, 4, 5; twice in 7-11, 13-15; and four times in 12); and "using profane language and very abusive language, and always required care" (appears in cases 9, 10, 14, and 15, and twice in 12).[29] As the other collocations, these longer phrases characterize the patients in highly negative terms associated with bad behavior.

But, the collocations not only judge the patients negatively; they are also stated with the presumed objectivity and factual nature of medical observation. In fact, the case histories are based on subjective observations that are presented as objective fact. According to Case 14,

> of the twenty-eight deaths among the men, eight were from general paresis. In one instance the disease had been diagnosed five years prior to occurrence of death. The patient was first admitted in 1862, and the history given at that time furnished proof that the disease had been in progress at least one year. After a residence of a few months in the asylum, he was removed by his friends, against our advice, under the impression, on their part, that his recovery was assured. In 1865, he was again committed to our charge for custodial care, as a person "dangerous to be at large." He lived until the spring of the present year. To show the rapidity with which this fatal disease sometimes advances, we note a case in which the patient presented no marked change in either mental or physical condition, or even peculiarity of manner, to his friends, until four weeks before admission, and during two weeks of this period, he pursued his usual avocations. He died the second day after his arrival at the Asylum, in convulsions. (30)

To project objectivity, the passage relies on formal language, clinical terminology, grammatical features such as the collective "we/our," and nominalizations without acknowledging any evaluative aspects they might contain. The content is presented as shared observations of facts; any decisions the "Asylum" makes are unassailable. Conversely, the patient is not only characterized as "peculiar" and "dangerous" but his symptoms also appeared rapidly and without warning, rendering reasoned treatment difficult. This disabled individual dies too quickly for help, manifesting abnormal movements. This objectivity contrasts with the tone in the inmates' life writing and, ironically, supports the situations as they describe them; again, the traces of this irony may be seen in Hay's comments, especially on Bacon.

Finally, the collocations appear verbatim across the corpus, describing different patients in the exact same manner, even in different asylums or states. While they characterize particular patients here, these templates ground arguments which became generalized diagnoses and definitions about the insane through their wide repetition. In addition, through this repetition, medical knowledge was disseminated through teaching practice. In nineteenth century American and European medical schools, students learned by copying lecture notes and case studies by practicing doctors.[30] Benjamin Rush advised his students that note taking should happen after the lecture, to allow students to remember and internalize the material without losing focus on the class.[31] As practiced, lecture notes contained boilerplate language, even over different years and courses of study. This language not only reflects the actual words of teachers but also the form, style, and tone in the case histories.[32] It seems likely that these discursive practices based on copying and resulting in boilerplate helped students become doctors, all of whom constructed and passed on medical meaning through these practices. Thus, these characterizations reached the physicians and staff who worked at the institutions at which the life writers were housed.

Through case histories, practicing physicians and institutional staff created and disseminated normative knowledge about individuals with disabilities; they were disabled and insane when they manifested deviant movements and habits, behaviors which required institutionalizing the insane rather than allowing them to move in public space.

The characterizations offered by medical professionals of the anonymous institutionalized individuals in these case histories conform to prevailing perspectives on mental and physical health and disability. In so doing, they verify the background information discussed above and support the examination of the life writing by institutionalized people below. The environment in which the inmates found themselves is one where the term "love," so prominent in the high medieval life writing in Chapter 3, never appears; it is characterized consistently as harsh, violent, and rigid in ways which looks forward to the kind of categorization that emerges in the appearance of the *Diagnostic Statistical Manual* (*DSM*) in the next century.

The Inmates

As former members of the asylum population, the seven individuals featured in this study write to reform legal, medical, and cultural misperceptions and practices involving insanity.[33] Generally, the individuals acknowledge a set of ongoing personal and health problems which, accentuated by particular life events, lead to their diagnosis and institutionalization as insane. It seems likely that these circumstances are associated with their similar socio-economic class and race. These individuals all exhibit thoughts, movements, and/or expressions which do non-conform to cultural norms, just those characteristics equated with unsoundness of mind and body. Not surprisingly, the individuals question the accuracy of their diagnoses.

In the nineteenth century, religious melancholy was a standard form of insanity; defined as excessive spiritual feelings, it was exhibited, according to contemporary theory, in certain facial expressions and bodily gestures.[34] Although none of the writers self-identifies as a religious melancholic, five of seven associate religion with their institutionalization or vice versa.[35] Reverend Hiram Chase was institutionalized in the Utica Lunatic Asylum from 1863-65 as one those "freaks of insanity."[36] He attributes his institutionalization to melancholy prompted by church politics. Moses Swan spent ten years, 1860-1870, in the Marshall Infirmary or Lunatic Asylum, at Ida Hill, Troy, New York and, prior to that, four months in Brattleboro Asylum, Vermont.[37] Not unlike Chase, he became melancholic a year before his institutionalization; however, he mentions no apparent cause other than a perennially nervous, weak constitution.[38] While he considers religious feeling a sign of strength rather than insanity, spiritual sentiments clearly preoccupy Swan's narrative. He often refers to the guilt and sinfulness he feels and compares his sufferings to those of Paul and Jesus.[39] In addition, he discusses his attempts to convert others, his visions, and his knowledge of plots against him and others.[40] When he comments, "go visitor, go as a patient; you will know but little about the secret workings of these institutions," he certainly seems suspicious; read, however, in light of the entire narrative, his accusations acquire credibility.[41]

Three of the women's narratives mention religion in conjunction with their non-conformist beliefs. Like Swan, Anna Agnew describes a generalized rather than religious melancholy which placed her in the Indiana State Hospital for the Insane from 1876-86; at the same time, her narrative refers regularly to religion. By her own admission, she had always been gloomy, suicidal, and prone to nervous excitability and fixed ideas.[42] Yet this was no one's fault, other than God's; and she lived a happy life with a husband and children until she was overcome in 1876 by nervous prostration and thus disgraced her family.[43]

Born in Vermont, Miss Phebe Davis moved to Syracuse, New York, in 1834 to make a living when her father's farm went under.[44] Considered dangerous, she was confined for two years in the State Lunatic Asylum at Utica, New York, where she received some renown in her own time as a crazy woman.[45] Her narration suggests that asylum staff diagnosed her according to common conventions as disabled: "the doctor first started himself in business by finding fault with my sitting posture, because my feet did not happen to rest on the floor, or else I looked as though I was a little deformed, and the doctor spent much time in endeavoring to regulate my habits in this respect, but to no effect."[46] On her account, she was confined because of her extreme positions for women's rights and against conventional religions, making her "a victim of sectarian circumstances."[47] But, being born "peculiar," and melancholic, she notes, is not a crime. "Why," she asks, "would someone intentionally do this?"[48]

Similarly assertive, Mrs. Packard states that as a "result of Expressing my Obnoxious Views I have been Illinois State's Prisoner three years in Jacksonville Insane Asylum, for simply expressing religious opinions in a community who were unprepared to appreciate and understand them I was incarcerated June 18, 1860, and liberated June 18, 1863."[49] Indeed, prior to her institutionalization she considered herself a functioning member of her family; but her husband, a reverend, felt "my religious views were dangerous to the spiritual interests of his children and community, I feel called upon to present my views, frankly and candidly, that my readers may judge for themselves whether my imprisonment can be justified on this basis."[50]

The last two self-life writers do not mention religious issues but share other features with their fellow writers. Mrs. Olsen characterizes herself as having a troublesome temperament which was grounds for institutionalization, at least from her husband's perspective. And finally, Robert Fuller, the earliest and shortest detained of the writers, tells a story which is most similar to Chase's. A Boston businessman, he was detained after a day of what his business-partners understood as insane, excited, and violent behavior. Fuller was placed in the McLean Asylum in Charlestown, Massachusetts for 65 days (June 24-August 26, 1832). He utterly rejects the diagnosis and links any manifestations with a passing illness.

As a group, then, the self-life writers fit their culture's model of insanity and broader understanding of disability; whether melancholic, excitable, or given to inappropriate thoughts or movements, they are deemed incapable of managing their lives. Being uncooperative or non-conformist, in religious or other matters, is a difficult stance to take in this society, especially for women. Each writes to reform and challenge what they consider a mistaken public perception that asylums are humane and therapeutic.

Medical Abuse

The narratives speak to the arbitrary diagnoses and treatment on which their institutionalization depends. These problems certainly stem from insanity's broad definition. In addition to the sheer numbers in asylums, Chase, Davis, and Swan provide non-scientific descriptions of the wide range of humanity within them (along with personal skepticism that so many would be insane). Demographically, Chase finds inmates from all classes.[51] Moreover, Chase mentions the range of inmates to include "imbeciles."[52] There are also invalids, children, eccentric individuals, and self-abusers.[53] Swan comments on individuals with deformities and neurological conditions such as epilepsy.[54] Variations aside, in nineteenth century parlance, insanity again serves as a catch-all for various kinds of atypicality.

The residents are aware that many elements of their institutionalization are arbitrary yet designed to segregate them, as different, from the normal population. When Chase comments that physicians are empowered to confine anyone considered eccentric, he is no doubt correct.[55] Although Agnew recognizes that, at times, her behavior is difficult, she also knows her treatment is inappropriate for either an insane or a responsible woman—and she "expected a human experience."[56] Despite his melancholy, Chase claims that he showed no signs of "wildness," that is, no lack of self-control.[57] As far as Mrs. Packard is concerned neither she nor any of the wives she met in the asylum is insane.[58] Thus, the writers dispute the broad and arbitrary character of their diagnosis and claim that any difficult behavior on their part is an appropriate response to their situations.

Treatment is similarly skewed in favor of medical authority. Not much care seems to be given to patient perspectives; Davis notes that an attendant answers for the patient to the doctor on rounds.[59] Moreover, inmates claim that the staff presents what are really abuses as treatment by framing abuses as rule-bound therapies. For example, Chase is frequently restrained in a straitjacket.[60] Yet, medical treatments are nearly non-existent. If medication is administered, it is done inconsistently and without patient consent.[61] Fuller is forced to take two pills, but he manages to spit them out in private.[62] Other than medication, no writer mentions any kind of healing therapy—other than restraint as curative.[63]

Their testimonies discuss at length the intimidation and physical abuse they receive, which is administered as therapeutic. The inmates' alleged madness is used as a pretext for helping them manage their thoughts and actions. As Rev. Chase comments, they remain silent, since speaking out is construed as evidence of insanity. In fact, any aversion to institutional practices is read as insanity.[64] For example, employees take Chase's possessions.[65] When he requests their return, the request is deemed a sign of insanity and denied.[66] Similarly, Swan comments that "when I was in the Asylum I saw a concentration of evils in a condensed form; and when I said anything to the doctors about the wrongs of the house, they would tell me that it was my insanity. I told them that a fact was no less a fact because it was told by a crazy person."[67] The writers realize that treatment is not only minimal at best but also inappropriate.

Physical abuse, again presumably meant to enhance inmates' self-control, can be quite extreme. Chase and others are confined in straightjackets, hit, tied with ropes, and strangled.[68] Swan also refers to a man, "much deformed and an object of pity" who is straight-jacketed then allowed to roam.[69] When he kicks objects in his way, because he cannot move them with his hands, he is punished.[70] Based on this bullying and mockery, Swan calls the Marshall Institutions a high school where they tried to teach, or beat, human nature into him. It took him ten years to "graduate."[71] His ironic statement makes its point: this is no teaching or therapeutic environment.

Legal Abuse

According to the law, the individuals are institutionalized to protect themselves and others. But, as the narratives suggest, the laws provide the means to mask and justify intimidation and abuse, rendering the inmates legally powerless. Unable to prevent incarceration, or to attain freedom, they are deprived of any rules or consistency in their asylum lives, and isolated from outside contact.

Each narrator is confined without warning or consultation. On their accounts, Chase, Fuller, Packard, and Swan are simply abducted; despite early attempts to escape, Swan is then held ten years.[72] When Reverend Chase's doctor learns that Chase poisoned himself, he sends Chase to the asylum without any inquiry. To justify such action, Chase comments, some doctors "must think they are doing a service to their country."[73] In reality, this "mode of institutionalization ... can be used by designing people and to speculate and can be used against anyone who has an eccentricity;" without legal recourse, he stays, living like a convict.[74] Chase not only holds that his family institutionalized him because they couldn't put up with him; his experience also indicates this is a common practice: families often place "invalids" in the asylum where they can be taken care of by others.[75] Fuller's experience of abduction is similar, although it is friends rather than family that seem complicit.[76] By all accounts, the individuals are released with similar lack of agency, a circumstance that Rev. Chase resents. When Chase learns that he may be able to leave in two or three months, it is only "if his folks come after him;" if he is free, he wonders, why can't he make his own way home?[77]

The legal system empowers men, husbands in particular, to institutionalize women, according to Miss Davis, Mrs. Olsen, and Mrs. Packard; they are denied their inalienable rights and, in the cases of Olsen and Packard, institutionalized at the behest of their husbands.[78]

According to Mrs. Packard, quoting the Hon. S.S. Jones of St. Charles, Illinois on Illinois law,

> the statute expressly states that the judgment of the medical Superintendent, to whom the husband's request is made, is *all* that is required for him to incarcerate his wife for any indefinite period of time. Neither she, her children, nor her relatives have any voice at all in the matter. Her imprisonment may be life-long, for anything she or her friends can do to prevent it. If the husband has money or influence enough to corrupt the officials, he can carry out his single wishes concerning her life-destiny.[79]

Common law renders the wife a "non-entity" and deprives her of "a legal right to her own identity and individuality."[80] Imprisoned by her husband—"my persecutor"—and his false statements, Packard decries the "cruelty of taking her away from her children."[81] "At the time he forced me from my dear little ones, my daughter was ten years old and my babe eighteen months."[82] Packard also loses her personal papers and marriage money; in essence, she is made homeless by the law for eight years.[83] Indeed, Mrs. Packard remains in her husband's custody after her release.[84] As Mrs. Olsen puts it, the asylum offers "a way of abrogating marriage vows."[85] She believes her husband imprisoned her on the grounds that she might do harm, when, as far as she is concerned, she was not insane but worn out from his abuse.

> This shows the state of feeling existing in consequence of falsely educated public sentiment on this subject. A person is reported insane; the first thing is to deprive him of all proper sympathy and all human rights lest he injure someone ... it is better to examine the facts.... prisons are made for criminals, and not for innocent and feeble women.[86]

Already lacking equal rights based on their gender, these nineteenth-century women suffer additionally because of their perceived mental difference.

Neither law nor rule is applied fairly or consistently within the institution. According to Anna Agnew, "superintendents don't pay attention to what's going on... rules are never shown but change according to the direction of the staff."[87] Thus controlled, Swan is simply judged incurable and moved from the main house to the incurable one in 1861, where he remains for nine years.[88] Some of these practices do not seem entirely unintentional; several writers mention that the first floor of their asylum is well decorated for the public, a ruse to hide the horrible conditions on higher floors.[89]

In addition to the arbitrary, punitive rules, the individuals are isolated from the outside world. None of the inmates has much contact with friends and family, most of whom, apparently, are ashamed of any association with insanity. After admission, Chase has no visitors for ten months.[90] When his daughter visits without notice, he thinks he can be released. However, the doctor won't permit it; as a state officer, he claims, he can't let Chase go. For the rest of his time in the asylum, he has one more letter and one visit from his daughter with his grandchildren, an occasion he finds more cruel than kind.[91] His wife never visits.[92] Although Olsen's doctor promised to let her communicate with husband and friends, she receives no correspondence from the outside world.[93] Agnew receives letters from her husband, but they are cruel and contain "misstatements."[94] In the end, she suffers three years of silence from any loved ones.[95] Fuller is told repeatedly his family will visit but they are denied the opportunity.[96] Finally, because Swan was incurable, his family and friends forsake him.[97] No one speaks for him because of the disgrace. Even within the asylum, he notes, horrible gossip leads many inmates to avoid human contact.[98]

In sum, the asylum controls the inmates within a legal and institutional system that leaves them powerless and isolated, an irony indeed for individuals placed there in part to improve their social conduct. As the narratives emphasize, although the authorities claim the asylums are for the individuals' good, they are in reality prisons, a proper place, the law would claim, for individuals whose condition reflects moral and criminal deviance. In fact, it seems to be the patients who need protection from the very institution that claims to be providing them with that service.

The Real Root of the Problem

Recognizing the tactics the authorities use to justify their asylum practices, the writers present their own understanding of their experiences. From their perspectives, the system causes their problems, not the opposite. According to Davis, staying in the institution aggravates disease rather than helping it, especially when the employees are not qualified.[99] Others confirm that institutionalization makes inmates crazy. Swan comments, "the first night I was locked up in the inner prison or cell heretofore alluded to, and this was enough to make a rational man crazy."[100] Clearly, he comments, education is no "safe-guard to insanity, but sometimes may produce it; it is thought very strange by some, that a man of mind, study, and education, should ever become insane."[101] In the asylum, Agnew experiences new symptoms, such as convulsions, and attempts to poison herself; she notes that she is a difficult patient and has crazy spells.[102] But, this comes, she argues, from years of "mental darkness, degradation and despair."[103] In other words, "it was most unjust; if I was a lunatic it was unjust; if I was not, it was none the less so. Strange, that in a free land, in a thickly settled and civilized community, such barbarous and inhuman acts are allowed by those in authority."[104] As their narratives suggest, reflecting the corpus analysis above, it only makes sense that incarcerated people act as they do.[105] Their reaction might in fact be called sane.

The inmates' experience of cruelty leads them to question who is insane and, like Hay and Husson, characterize their oppressors in their own terms. Swan "thought my attendants were lunatics."[106] Packard contends that it was her husband who was insane as well as cruel. Indeed, when she returns to her husband despite everything, she is imprisoned by him.[107] Packard's narrative indicates that her son is clearly afraid of his father.[108] As Davis comments, the more she "sees of the world the more she thinks three-quarters of it is crazy on some subject or another."[109] Recognizing the ironies in their situations, the writers suggest not only that the employees are insane but that the system's influence also extends beyond the asylum. That is, the system makes its mark on its own arbitrators and society as a whole by constraining other cultural practices. From birth, the system attempts to eradicate difference. For example, standard parenting practices degrade children and "crowd" their brains, energies, imaginations, and thoughts.[110] In so doing, children are conditioned by parents not to be "different." Such practices constrain women especially; they have particularly active minds and thus their tendency to be excited magnifies their peril in this system.[111] In all, those who do not conform in thought, action, and physical appearance are locked away from the world. Because the world is crazy and run by distorted people, the world is a kind of self-perpetuating asylum; everyone is an inmate who abuses those less powerful.

The narrators advocate for dismantling a system that habituates humans to treat each other in insane ways. Yet, the writers are optimistic that "clouds are clearing" because "the world is large enough to hold all the brain that there is in it."[112] By suggesting that the ways in which they have been confined and treated are in fact the ways in which their oppressors have operated, they hope to prompt readers to ask who is insane and who harmful and, with this, prompt action. To that end, they call for reform rather than revenge.

Conclusions

Together, these nineteenth century narratives constitute an historical group within the genre of life writing about disability, one in which middle class, white individuals use their experiences to argue against a system which has denied them legal, medical, and human rights because of their unconventional thoughts, speech, and actions. Although they acknowledge their perceived cognitive differences, they reject the understanding of disability—and treatment of it—which the underlying system of norms imposes on them. As such, their writing speaks to the cultural construction of disability across gender lines; framed as a kind of threat, disability has explicit moral dimensions which lands those thus labeled in a kind of jail. To eradicate the legal-medical system which institutionalizes them as insane because of their apparent mental, cognitive, and physical disabilities, their stories suggest, is to remove the presumed problem it names.

As marginalized people, people considered incapable of social success, the life writers and their stories also raise interesting questions about the character of this group and its relationship to other kinds of disability life writing and life writing more broadly construed. Within its own time period, for example, what can we learn from the relationship between these stories and illness as well as slave narratives, especially as they inform issues of gender, race, and class? With respect to illness narratives, it seems worth investigating the extent to which this disability life writing about mental illness was stimulated and modeled on the writing of other late nineteenth century reform movements, women's rights and abolitionism among them. Similarly, it would be interesting to compare these disability narratives with narratives by slaves. Both kinds of documents expose the incarceration of individuals within then legal institutions, individuals who also had low cultural credibility. While slave narrators were disadvantaged by their race and presumed lack of literacy, those with mental disabilities were hampered by their presumed lack of grip on reality. To vouch for the author's authenticity and veracity, both narrative types contain prefaces and testimonies written by individuals of presumably high repute, for the slave narrative, whites, and lawyers for the mentally disabled.[113] In addition to this difference, slave narratives were written by poor black individuals while the mental disability self-live writers were at least middle-class and white.[114] Given these circumstances, both the narratives under consideration and slave narratives deserve more consideration in light of late nineteenth century mendicancy literature.

These narratives also resonant with more recent stories of individuals constrained within the rigid diagnoses of the *DSM*. In particular, the stories of these nineteenth century authors foretell the struggles of individuals with post-traumatic stress disorder (PTSD). This latter issue returns in Chapter Eight.

---

[1] An abbreviated version of this chapter appeared as "Reports from the Nineteenth Century Asylum" in *The Journal of Literary and Cultural Disability Studies* 5 (2011): 261-278.

[2] Agnew, *From Under the Cloud; or, Personal Reminiscences of Insanity*; Chase, *Two Years and Four Months in A Lunatic Asylum: from August 20th, 1863, to December 20th, 1865*; Davis, *Two years and three months in the New York lunatic asylum, at Utica*; Davis, *The Travels and Experiences of Miss Phebe Davis, of Barnard, Windsor County, VT, being a Sequel to Her Two Years and Three Months in the N.Y. State Lunatic Asylum in Utica N Y*; Fuller, *An Account of the Imprisonment and Sufferings of Robert Fuller of Cambridge*; Olsen, *Mrs. Olsen's Narrative of Her One Year's Imprisonment at Jacksonville Insane Asylum: With the Testimony of Mrs. Minard, Mrs. Shedd, Mrs. Yates, and Mrs. Lake, all corroborated by the Investigating Committee of the Legislature of Illinois*; Packard, *The Prisoners' Hidden Life, Insane Asylums Unveiled;* Packard, *Mrs. Modern Persecution, or Insane Asylums Unveiled*; Swan, *Ten Years and Ten Months in Lunatic Asylums in Different State*; Agnew, *From Under the Cloud; or, Personal Reminiscences of Insanity.*

[3] Davis, *Two years and three months in the New York lunatic asylum, at Utica: together with the outlines of twenty years' peregrinations in Syracuse*, p. 9.

[4] Packard, *The Prisoners' Hidden Life, Insane Asylums Unveiled* (Chicago: J.N. Clarke) 1871, p. iii.

[5] This kind of correlation, however erroneous, is not unique, of course, as in the work of Lombrozo; see Gould, *The Mismeasure of Man*, Chapter Four.

[6] Tuke, *The Insane in the United States and Canada*, p. 48. Life writing about the asylum experience is not limited to the U.S. (see Crowe, *A Letter to Dr. Robert Darling Willis; To Which Are Added Copies of Three Other Letters; Published in the Hope of Rousing A Humane Nation to the Consideration of the Miseries Arising from Private Madhouses*; Haslam, *Illustrations of Madness*. For space limitations, I focus on the American here.

[7] Longrigg, *Greek Medicine, From the Heroic to the Hellenistic Age: A Source Book*, pp. 26-28.

[8] Berkenkotter, *Patient Tales. Case Histories and the Uses of Narrative in Psychiatry*, pp. 80 ff.; Burton, *The Anatomy of Melancholy*; Cheyne, *The English Malady.*

[9] Porter, in Haslam, *Illustrations of Madness*, pp. xii ff.

[10] Newman, "Gestural Enthymemes: Delivering Movement in Eighteenth and Nineteenth Century Medical Images."

[11] Dain, *Concepts of Insanity in the United States, 1789-1865,* pp. 12ff.

[12] Horner, *Notes Physiology including the by Dr. Rush*, p. 255.

[13] The legal definition of insanity also involved "defect" or "deficit"; see Ray, *A Treatise on the Medical Jurisprudence of Insanity*, pp. 58-60.

[14] Crowe, *A Letter to Dr. Robert Darling Willis; To Which Are Added Copies of Three Other Letters; Published in the Hope of Rousing A Humane Nation to the Consideration of the Miseries Arising from Private Madhouses*; Dain, *Concepts of Insanity in the United States, 1789-1865*, pp. 59 ff.; Ray, *A Treatise on the Medical Jurisprudence of Insanity*, pp. 50 ff..

[15] Tuke, *The Insane in the United States and Canada*, p. 47.

[16] Harrison, *Legislation on Insanity. A Collection of all the Lunacy Laws of the State and Territories of the United States*.

[17] Ray, *A Treatise on the Medical Jurisprudence of Insanity, pp.* 58-60.

[18] Mayhew, *London Labour and the London Poor. The Classical Study of the Culture of Poverty and the Criminal Classes in the 19th century*, Vol. 4. .

[19] Davis describes herself as poor, although Utica was a middle-class institution (see *Two years and three months in the New York lunatic asylum, at Utica*, p. 11, for example). Packard resented being put in a lower-class asylum; see Wood, *The Writing on the Wall: Women's Autobiography and the Asylum*, p. 27.

[20] Halttunen, "Gothic Mystery and the Birth of the Asylum: The Cultural Construction of Deviance in Early-Nineteenth-Century America," pp. 41-59; Reiss, *Theatres of Madness: Insane Asylums and Nineteenth Century American Culture*.

[21] Packard is exceptional; she wrote in secret in the asylum; see Wood, *The Writing on the Wall: Women's Autobiography and the Asylum*, p. 28.

[22] The collection is comprised of 25 bound volumes, each containing fifteen to thirty reports from a state asylum, the majority from the latter nineteenth century; one of the case histories I selected came from the Utica facility where Phebe Davis was institutionalized.

[23] See Table 6.1.

[24] See Table 6.2.

[25] Specifically, texts in the Bakken Musuem and Archive, and the Cordell Collection of the Library at Indiana State University.

[26]Goddard, *The Kallikak Family: A Study in the Heredity of Feeblemindedness*.

[27] Schweik, *The Ugly Laws: Disability in Public*, p. vii.

[28] Ibid., p. 67.

[29] Other longer collocations include: "given, was abusive of physicians and attendants, and at" (1, 4, 7, 8 twice, 10 twice, 11 twice, 12, 13, 14 twice, 15 twice); "violent; tore off clothing; was abusive and profane; this was" (1-6, 7-11 twice each, 12 four times, 13-15 twice each).

[30] Berkenkotter, *Patient Tales. Case Histories and the Uses of Narrative in Psychiatry*, p. 23.

[31] Horner, *Notes Physiology including the by Dr Rush*. Eighteenth and nineteenth century teaching practices at the Edinburgh Medical School might be linked to the practice of imitation used in eighteenth century rhetorics; see Berkenkotter, *Patient Tales. Case Histories and the Uses of Narrative in Psychiatry*, pp.20-23.

[32] See, for example, the lecture notes of Archer, *Notes on Dr. Rush's Lectures Vol. 1 on Physiology including the Pulse and Mind*; Horner, *Notes Physiology including the by Dr. Rush*; Rush, *Extracts from His Lectures*.

[33] Luther Benson spends time in the asylum for alcohol abuse; his story mirrors that of the seven individuals featured in this study in as far as he characterizes the asylum as a prison.

[34] Berkenkotter, *Patient Tales. Case Histories and the Uses of Narrative in Psychiatry*, pp. 57-64.

[35] See Wood, *The Writing on the Wall: Women's Autobiography and the Asylum*, p. 28.

[36] Chase, *Two Years and Four Months in A Lunatic Asylum*, pp. 3-4.

[37] Swan, *Ten Years and Ten Months in Lunatic Asylums in Different States*, p.8.

[38] Ibid., p. 43.

[39] Ibid., pp. 56, 82.

[40] Ibid., pp. 61, 67, and 100- 104, 128.

[41] Ibid., p. 13.

[42] Agnew, *From Under the Cloud; or, Personal Reminiscences of Insanity*, pp. 21-5.

[43] Ibid., pp. 11, 18, 20.

[44] Davis, *Two years and three months in the New York lunatic asylum, at Utica*, pp.3-8.

[45] Ibid., p. 19.

[46] Ibid., pp. 26-27.

[47] Ibid., pp. 13-18; Davis, *The Travels and Experiences of Miss Phebe Davis, of Barnard, Windsor County, VT, being a Sequel to Her Two Years and Three Months in the N.Y. State Lunatic Asylum in Utica N Y*, p. 6.

[48] Davis, *The Travels and Experiences of Miss Phebe Davis, of Barnard, Windsor County, VT, being a Sequel to Her Two Years and Three Months in the N.Y. State Lunatic Asylum in Utica N Y*, p. 70; Davis, *Two years and three months in the New York lunatic asylum, at Utica*, pp. 9, 14.

[49] Packard, *The Prisoners' Hidden Life, Insane Asylums Unveiled*, p. 15.

[50] Ibid., pp. 9-10.

[51] Chase, *Two Years and Four Months in A Lunatic Asylum*, 1868, p. 112.

[52] Ibid., pp. 106 ff.

[53] Ibid., pp. 87 ff., pp. 96-97, 112, 116.

[54] Swan, *Ten Years and Ten Months in Lunatic Asylums in Different States*, pp. 84-5.

[55] Ibid., p. 21.

[56] Chase, *Two Years and Four Months in A Lunatic Asylum*, p. 112.

[57] Agnew, *From Under the Cloud*, p. 44.

[58] Chase, *Two Years and Four Months in A Lunatic Asylum*, p. 112.

[59] Packard, *The Prisoners' Hidden Life, Insane Asylums Unveiled*, p. 148.

[60] Davis, *Two Years and Three Months in the New York Lunatic Asylum, at Utica: Together with the Outlines of Twenty Years' Peregrinations in Syracuse*, pp. 145-6.

[61] Chase, *Two Years and Four Months in A Lunatic Asylum*, "Frontispiece."

[62] Ibid., p. 127.

[63]Fuller, *An Account of the Imprisonment and Sufferings of Robert Fuller of Cambridge*, p. 13.

[64] Chase, *Two Years and Four Months in A Lunatic Asylum*, p. 27.

[65] Ibid., pp. 42-5.

[66] Ibid., p. 45.

[67] Ibid., p. 45.

[68] Swan, *Ten Years and Ten Months in Lunatic Asylums in Different States*, p. 59; Chase, *Two Years and Four Months in A Lunatic Asylum*, pp. 8 ff.. 70; cf. Swan, *Ten Years and Ten Months in Lunatic Asylums in Different States* ,p. 59.

[69] Chase, *Two Years and Four Months in A Lunatic Asylum*, p. 85.

[70] Swan, *Ten Years and Ten Months in Lunatic Asylums in Different States*, p. 85.

[71] Ibid., p. 50; cf. p. 81.

[72] Ibid., p. 69.

[73] Chase, *Two Years and Four Months in A Lunatic Asylum*, pp. 8 ff.; Fuller, *An Account of the Imprisonment and Sufferings of Robert Fuller of Cambridge*, pp. 12 ff.; Packard, *The Prisoners' Hidden Life, Insane Asylums Unveiled*, pp. 51 ff.; Swan, *Ten Years and Ten Months in Lunatic Asylums in Different States*, p. 8.

[74] Chase, *Two Years and Four Months in A Lunatic Asylum*, p. 28

[75] Ibid., pp. 11, 29.

[76] Ibid., pp. 11-12.

[77] Fuller, *An Account of the Imprisonment and Sufferings of Robert Fuller of Cambridge*, pp. 12 ff.

[78] Chase, *Two Years and Four Months in A Lunatic Asylum*, p. 35.

[79] Davis, *Two Years and Three Months in the New York Lunatic Asylum, at Utica: Together with the Outlines of Twenty Years' Peregrinations in Syracuse*; Packard, *Modern Persecution, or Insane Asylums Unveiled*, pp. 59-61.

[80] Packard, *Modern Persecution, or Insane Asylums Unveiled*, p.54.

[81] Ibid., p. 54.

[82] Ibid., p. 17.

[83] Ibid., pp. 36; 54-55; 101-102.

[84] Packard, *Mrs. Modern Persecution, or Insane Asylums Unveiled*; Swan, *Ten Years and Ten Months in Lunatic Asylums in Different State* 1874, vol. 2, p. 4.

[85] Ibid., p. 18.

[86] Olsen, *Mrs. Olsen's Narrative of Her One Year's Imprisonment at Jacksonville Insane Asylum*, p. 12.

[87] Agnew, *From Under the Cloud*, p. 17.

[88] Swan, *Ten Years and Ten Months in Lunatic Asylums in Different States*, p.85.

[89] Chase, *Two Years and Four Months in A Lunatic Asylum*, pp. 77, 119; Swan, *Ten Years and Ten Months in Lunatic Asylums in Different States*, p. 60.

[90] Chase, *Two Years and Four Months in A Lunatic Asylum*, pp. 114-7.

[91] Ibid., pp. 128-31.

[92] Ibid., p. 16.

[93] Olsen, *Mrs. Olsen's Narrative of Her One Year's Imprisonment at Jacksonville Insane Asylum*, p. 30.

[94] Agnew, *From Under the Cloud*, p. 58.

[95] Ibid., p. 76.

[96] Fuller, *An Account of the Imprisonment and Sufferings of Robert Fuller of Cambridge*, p. 16.

[97] Swan, *Ten Years and Ten Months in Lunatic Asylums in Different States*, p. 94.

[98] Ibid., pp. 23-4; cf. Agnew, *From Under the Cloud*, p. 33; Davis, *Two Years and Three Months in the New York Lunatic Asylum, at Utica: Together with the Outlines of Twenty Years' Peregrinations in Syracuse*, p. 50; Davis, *The Travels and Experiences of Miss Phebe Davis, of Barnard, Windsor County, VT, being a Sequel to Her Two Years and Three Months in the N.Y. State Lunatic Asylum in Utica NY*, p. 22.

[99] Davis, *Two Years and Three Months in the New York Lunatic Asylum, at Utica: Together with the Outlines of Twenty Years' Peregrinations in Syracuse*, p. 10; cf. p. 17.

[100] Swan, *Ten Years and Ten Months in Lunatic Asylums in Different States*, p. 64.

[101] Ibid., p. 104.

[102] Agnew, *From Under the Cloud*, pp. 22, 68-70.

[103] Ibid., p. 54.

[104] Ibid., pp. 24-25.

[105] Davis, *Two Years and Three Months in the New York Lunatic Asylum, at Utica: Together with the Outlines of Twenty Years' Peregrinations in Syracuse*, p. 45;Fuller, *An Account of the Imprisonment and Sufferings of Robert Fuller of Cambridge*, pp. 20-21.

[106] Swan, *Ten Years and Ten Months in Lunatic Asylums in Different States*, p. 49.

[107] Packard, *The Prisoners' Hidden Life, Insane Asylums Unveiled*, vol. 2, p. 9.

[108] Ibid., p. 11.

[109] Davis, *Two Years and Three Months in the New York Lunatic Asylum, at Utica: Together with the Outlines of Twenty Years' Peregrinations in Syracuse*, p. 17

[110] Ibid., p. 45.

[111] Ibid., p. 45.

[112] Ibid., p. 46. Interestingly, Davis' language mirrors Sojourner Truth's in her 1851 "Ain't I a Woman" speech, given at a Women's rights convention:
"Then they talk about this thing in the head; what's this they call it? [member of audience whispers, 'intellect'] That's it, honey. What's that got to do with women's rights or negroes' rights? If my cup won't hold but a pint, and yours holds a quart, wouldn't you be mean not to let me have my little half measure full?"

[113] For example, these disability self-life writers do not represent all inmates while slaves presumably do; and although slavery has been legally abolished in the U.S., institutionalization for mental illness has not. There is a good deal of interesting material regarding authentication in the documents under consideration, materials involving prefaces and testimonies. A discussion of them, however, is beyond the scope of the present study. Many thanks to G. Thomas Couser for these and other insights.

[114] Schweik, *The Ugly Laws: Disability in Public*, p. 256.

7

The Early Twentieth Century:
Helen Keller and the
Public Reception of Disability

Thus far, my study has considered how individuals have represented themselves as disabled before the 1903 publication of Helen Keller's (1880-1968) autobiography *The Story of My Life*. As many others, I identify her work as a turning point in the history of disability because of its substantive contributions to disability's wider recognition, reception, and representation. Without question, from Keller's work forward, disability has become a more acceptable subject in Western societies; at the same time and by virtue of this acceptance, disability has become more exceptional, that is, more noticed and noticeable. Given her significance and my goals, this chapter considers Keller's early life writing in terms of its profound influence as a communicative act.[1] As I detail below, at the time Keller began to write about her life, the American and European publics were quite familiar with other individuals deemed disabled, among them, the blind and deaf American, Laura Bridgman (1829-1889). While the elder woman was famous in her time, Keller's fame eclipsed hers and has continued to the present. Clearly, Keller had many talents, the literary among them; but, other aspects surrounding Keller's work contributed to her popular success and significance as a life writer. As I argue, these aspects involve her felt sense of writing, a sense she describes in the following excerpt.

> I sometimes wonder if the hand is not more sensitive to the beauties of sculpture than the eye. I should think the wonderful rhythmical flow of lines and curves could be more subtly felt than seen. Be that as it may, I know that I can feel the heart-throbs of the ancient Greeks in their marble gods and goddesses.[2]

That sense she describes is traditionally linked with lack of control and disablement, but no more so than in Keller's print linguistic world. By responding to and overcoming social perceptions that her embodied communicative efforts were deviant, a sense she subtly counters above, she not only facilitated her own acceptance but also that of the disabled more generally.

To demonstrate these points, my analysis considers how Keller's writing embodied her identity, openly integrating various linguistic, emotional, and sensory elements—just those elements which had been suppressed in generations just prior to hers and certainly never so fully and openly integrated in any previous life writing. She was informed by and moved beyond life writers before her. Like the earliest life writers in this study, she represented her identity by means of an embodied, felt sense of it; but, unlike those writers, her representations explicitly acknowledged that sense and intentionally combined it with other sensory and emotional experiences. Like Hay, Husson, and the nineteenth century asylum inmates, Keller adopted and adapted the conventional language and genres of her time to challenge the perception that difference was deviance. But, unlike these predecessors, she did so within an explanatory, assimilative model rather than an ironic attack. This revived, integrative, and very open felt sense of self, addressed in association with the act of writing, involves another forward looking aspect of Keller's work; it was always and openly collaborative, both as crafted and as read on several levels. By using the many material modalities and senses available to her, Keller enjoined her readers to identify with her and to participate in her world as she did in theirs. As a result, Keller inaugurated a new type of life writing about disability, one which represented disability and its writer as very much more human than deviant.

Before discussing Keller's life writing, especially her earlier autobiographical works, and the complex circumstances surrounding their publication, I first provide some context about life writing and disability leading up to Keller's time, focusing on Bridgman.

Disability, Human Nature, and Life Writing Before Helen Keller

In the century or so before Keller's birth, the concept of disability belonged to broader cultural concerns with understanding and categorizing human nature. As the previous two chapters discussed, throughout the eighteenth and nineteenth centuries scientists and educators sought to identify the human body's parts and to standardize their operation. To those ends, they developed categories and taxonomies which separated the normal body from the deviant one in ever more specific ways, leading to investigations concerned with how healthy bodies developed and with fixing them if they did not develop correctly.

Accordingly, intellectuals focused on sense, perception, and language.[3] Cartesians located the will in the mind and detached its rational function from the body; from this perspective, reflected in the development of the print linguistic bias, language, especially the scientific, should be stated in the most logical, unambiguous, and unemotional terms. With respect to this rational mind and the clear language it should craft, Lockean associationists held that the human mind entered the world as a blank slate. To understand how this slate was filled, sensationalists, following Étienne de Condillac, focused on human sensation, suggesting that appropriate mental, emotional, and physical developments depended on socially appropriate sensory stimulation. Because people lacking proper stimuli and/or social settings would be correspondingly impaired, those developmentally inadequate individuals could be advanced by supplying their deficits in measured ways. Physician and educator Philippe Pinel taught students to observe human behaviors, especially those associated with the human potential to develop. All in all, this kind of thinking, although not without detractors or alternative voices, operated in concert with the focus on print linguistic expression evident in the attempt to standardize logic, language, and thinking.[4]

To test these principles on human subjects, scientists often turned to nature's exceptions, the so-called freaks, deformed, and monstrous.[5] When they were still young, wild, or feral, children were especially popular for those efforts; these less than human children provided experimenters with excellent opportunities not simply to study human deficits but also to civilize the underdeveloped to become normal, moral humans. Perhaps most famously, in 1800 Jean Marc Gaspard Itard began working with the wild boy of Aveyron. Unfortunately, he failed, and the child was said to remain an underdeveloped savage.[6]

Individuals with other kinds of abnormal physical attributes were also the objects of educational improvement efforts. Because communication, or language, separated human from beast and animal, the blind and deaf were of considerable interest in these efforts.[7] Beginning in France, deaf educators such as Saboureux De Fontenay, Pierre Desloges, Jean Massieu, and Ferdinand Berthier opened schools and instituted specific pedagogies to help deaf children develop properly and, thus, communicate with and in the world.[8] The work of these individuals was brought to the United States by way of Thomas

Gallaudet, directly influencing the education mission and practices at the Perkins Institute with which Bridgman and Keller were associated.

As part of their efforts, these men wrote educational and personal materials.[9] With respect to the latter, in 1765 de Fontenay's *Autobiography* was published and in 1800 that of Massieu.[10] Following the fashion of the time and reflecting their educational goals, these works, as Husson's, boasted of personal and professional achievements.[11] A certain amount of life writing by blind and/or deaf individuals had appeared by the time Bridgman arrived at the Perkins Institute. But, it was neither particularly well known nor valued beyond the practitioners in the field.

Laura Dewey Bridgman

Bridgman's story has only recently been restored to scholarly and public attention; in her time, however, she was "the most celebrated child in America."[12] Born sickly on December 21, 1829 near Hanover, New Hampshire, she recovered only to contract scarlet fever in 1837 and, at age 7, loose all her senses, other than touch.[13] To help her connect with the world around her, her parents sent her to Boston's Perkins Institution for the Blind to learn from its renowned director, Samuel Gridley Howe. Typical of many nineteenth century disabled individuals, she spent the rest of her life at the institute, dying there in 1889. Also typical of her time, she became an exceptional object of attention, in this case, Howe's educational efforts.

Although his intentions were sincere, Howe also used Bridgman to serve his religious, social, and political agendas. As a Unitarian and supporter of various liberal causes, Howe fought against what he considered were the regressive and rigid standards underpinning Calvinism and traditional classroom practices.[14] His work with the deaf and blind combined his interests in understanding human nature and fulfilling his progressive agenda.

Living primarily through touch, Bridgman was the perfect subject for these efforts. Using his tactile educational method, he claimed, he would help her develop what she lacked in sensory capacities and emerge as an educated and moral example of humanity. Howe did teach Bridgman to read, write, and communicate.[15] But, he failed to produce a perfect moral being. From all accounts, Bridgman was stubborn, eccentric, and prone to bad temper; and she developed a traditional religious attitude that strictly contrasted with Howe's progressive one.[16] In the end, Bridgman was a human being with her own thoughts, needs, and interests which Howe could not entirely shape, no doubt in part because he did not attend to them. But, Howe did not see it that way; to recuperate his effort, he developed a new theory, that her physical deficits had permanently impaired her moral character and mind.[17] By presenting her as both a spectacle and an inferior example of humanity, he ended up placing her in the nineteenth century model he intended to undermine.

In addition to controlling Bridgman's educational, spiritual, and moral development, Howe framed Bridgman's life in another way: he managed all public communication about her.[18] To that end, his reports and letters (at least before his experiment failed) consistently portrayed Bridgman as a blank slate on which he was inscribing humanity. Ironically, Howe taught her to communicate and then communicated for her. Charles Dickens, who visited Boston in 1842, described one of Howe's reports as "an account written by the one man who made her what she is."[19] And, inscribe Howe did. He comments on Bridgman that

> when left alone, she seems very happy if she has her knitting or sewing, and will busy herself for hours: if she has no occupation, she evidently amuses herself by her imaginary dialogues, or by recalling past impressions; she counts with her fingers, or spells out names of things which she has recently learned, in the manual alphabet of the deaf mutes. In this lonely self-communion she seems to reason, reflect, and argue.[20]

Consistent with his experimental perspective, Howe depicts Bridgman as the model and measured student; even in her closed worlds, she is a rational, developed person who reads and reasons.

Following Howe's lead, others communicated about Bridgman in terms celebrating her exceptional nature. Among them, Dickens himself described the blind at Perkins in terms of the visible and manifest as well as the hidden and potential. "It is strange to watch the faces of the blind, and see how free they are from all concealment of what is passing in their thoughts; observing which a, man may blush to contemplate the mask he wears.[21] Their faces, unusual to see en masse, are the *tabula rasa* on which the Perkins educators will write their humanity. On first meeting Bridgman, he comments that

> her face was radiant with intelligence and pleasure. Her hair, braided by her own hands, was bound about a head whose intellectual capacity and development were beautifully expressed in a graceful outline, and its broad open brow; her dress, arranged by herself, was a pattern of neatness and simplicity; her work she had knitted lay beside her; her writing-book was on the desk she leaned upon. From the mournful

ruin of such bereavement, there had slowly risen up this gentle, tender, guileless, grateful-hearted being.[22]

For Dickens, Bridgman is the great accomplishment of Howe's efforts. Rising from the "ruin" of her isolation, implicitly through Howe's efforts, she is intelligent, neat, capable, industrious, gentle, and honest.

Several of Bridgman's teachers at Perkins wrote narratives which reflected Howe's experiment. In 1881, Mary Swift Lamson published such an account. In a prefatory letter, which represents Lamson's work as a whole, Edwards A. Park describes how Bridgman exemplifies true humanity. Perhaps to justify the fact that others wrote for her, he suggests that Bridgman's incomplete overall state of development was reflected specifically in her underdeveloped memory and, thus, her inability to remember her life accurately; but, that circumstance, Park indicates, makes her all the more credible.[23] According to Park, Bridgman is not the purported genius Jean Massieu was, at least as Massieu represented himself in his autobiography; but she is certainly the more authentic human being.[24] In the beginning sentences of the letter's last pages, Park repeats the phrase "the history of Laura Bridgman," four times, connecting her life in each reiteration with the greater history of humanity and its progress: "the history of Laura Bridgman casts some light on the doctrine of intuitions; "the history of Laura Bridgman illustrates the importance of a symmetrical development of the human powers and sensibilities;" "the history of Laura Bridgman suggests a lesson on the importance of early education;" and "the history of Laura Bridgman gives us new suggestions on the worth of human nature."[25] As others, then, Park characterizes Bridgman in typical terms of her exceptional and yet deficient nature.

In fact, Bridgman did write about her life in letters, poems, a journal, and three autobiographical sketches.[26] In places, her account conflicts with what others had written. For example and reflecting the statement quoted above, Howe notes elsewhere that "when left alone, she occupies, and apparently amuses herself, and seems quite contented."[27] But, according to Bridgman, she was often overwhelmed, needed to be alone and inactive and thus shunned social contact.[28] Significantly, it is not simply that conflicts exist between accounts without specific evidence to clarify the situation (Park's statement about her poor memory is neither convincing nor helpful in this regard). Such evaluation is difficult because Bridgman's writing was never published in its entirety and on its own for public consumption. The only contemporaneous publication of her work was an article by psychologist

E. C. Sanford.[29] Although he purports to present her writing objectively, he, too, frames her work within Howe's experimental model. This framing emerges at the outset when he introduces her work in his own words.

> This interest which centered around Laura Bridgman in her early life was two-fold—humanitarian and philosophical. The former has in large measure accomplished its mission and declines. The latter also has in part decline, because Laura's case has not furnished the evidence expected from it, upon certain philosophic questions.[30]

As others, Stanford locates Bridgman within Howe's educational mission as it began and ended. When Bridgman failed, it was her developmental problems not the science which was lacking.

As the article continues, Bridgman continues to speak through Stanford's editorial comments and framing. When Bridgman's writing appears, Stanford uses it to demonstrate particular points he chooses to make about her. To that end, Stanford presents passages from Bridgman in a piecemeal manner; each quotation is removed from its original context, and located in Stanford's account. He neither consistently nor fully indicates where he found the pieces, whether the parts appear together in Bridgman's works, or in what context she happens to be discussing her points.

In addition, he offers bracketed internal comments in response to passages from Bridgman. For example, Stanford often describes how Bridgman's sensory defects have affected her development and, working within the now familiar model, characterizes her as a child or child-like. In the following instance, when describing Howe's methods, Stanford quotes from an unidentified place in Bridgman's writing and offers an explanation of it in brackets.

> Dr. made some signs that brought me up to understanding naturally. He boxed [patted] my head meaning 'right'; he knocked at my elbow for 'wrong.'... [These signs were established, of course, by repetition, in about the same way that a dog is trained to obey his master's word or gesture.][31]

First, Stanford includes Bridgman statements; she notes that Howe used touch to communicate with her. Next, Stanford associates Howe's touch with the treatment and behavior of dogs, suggesting that Bridgman is underdeveloped. But, because touch was her only fully operational sense as well as the foundation of Howe's educational method, it seems to me that Howe would not have contacted her otherwise.

Sanford similarly describes, exemplifies, and explains why Bridgman's writing is impoverished, filled with errors, and hard to understand—i.e., underdeveloped.[32] Bridgman writes, "he was so desirous to sweeten me like sugar," and Sanford comments "[she still retains the fondness of a child for it]."[33] Apparently characterizing her love of sweets, Bridgman personifies herself as a consumable needing to be sweetened; her statement might be read as "sweet" and insightful, if perhaps less than a profound poetic insight. In Stanford's view, that statement simply attests to her underdeveloped state; without any other information about the passage or Bridgman's writing, however, it is hard to evaluate Bridgman's comment.

Elsewhere, Sanford notes that "Laura tells us she used to amuse herself" and among the excerpts includes this example and his comment.[34]

'I recollect most truly that I used to chop some little living things in my Mother's mortar for my own amusement.' [This seems quite improbable, but, if true, it may be taken, perhaps, as showing latent possibilities of cruelty in Laura which, had she remained uneducated, might have developed into that insensibility to suffering in others which is said to be common among untrained deaf-mutes].[35]

Here, Bridgman describes a youthful recollection, mashing insects, most likely, in her mother's kitchen equipment. Stanford dismisses the unsavory actions as unlikely. On the one hand, because she is underdeveloped, he doubts Bridgman's veracity; on the other hand, he suggests that, if true, this practice reveals her underdeveloped state. In either case, her actions are deficient. Still, while no one would condone cruelty to "living things," there is no context in which to understand the brief passage. For one thing, Bridgman seems to be convincing the reader that her memory was accurate. Understood this way, the passage is less about her underdeveloped state than her ability to recall. But, that account also cannot be verified nor would that likely be the whole story either. Anyone who remembers being a child or raising one could probably interpret the account in several ways. Although Stanford again gives the impression that Bridgman was simply underdeveloped, he provides no evidence or context with which to support his interpretation.

Looking back, it is easy to denigrate the motives and methods of Howe and his contemporaries. Despite their shortcomings, those who taught and wrote about Bridgman believed that blind and deaf individuals should be treated and educated at Perkins like any other human.[36] Still, unfortunately and ironically, Howe's progressive efforts had regressive results. In his and others' hands, Bridgman was crafted into a spectacular product of the nineteenth century a "literary artefact" rather than a human being.[37] Marginalized as underdeveloped, Bridgman was not allowed to communicate publicly, presumably because such efforts would be impoverished and deviant.[38]

Bridgman's life provided an immediate backdrop for Keller's life and writing.[39] As Bridgman, Keller was blind and deaf, and lived first through touch; she, too, became the object of public and media attention. Perhaps inevitably, the two exceptional women were compared. For example, the *Boston Globe* reported that Keller took six weeks to master what Laura Bridgman did in three years and claimed that Helen "was already speaking fluently," a skill she never fully learned.[40] Thus, as Bridgman, Keller's story was associated with some exaggeration and reconstruction.[41] Accordingly, as Bridgman, Keller's life was framed as part of the attempt to educate her to communicate and become a fully socialized human.[42] And, as Bridgman, Keller's early life was associated with failure to meet communicative expectations; in Keller's case, the failure involved accusations of copying.

But, here the outright similarities end. While Bridgman was not allowed to communicate openly for herself, Keller wrote, published, and was read. Thus released to speak for herself, as it were, she wrote and reflected on those communicative efforts in ways which helped to overturn those social perceptions which linked disability, deviance, and writing. In great measure, that shift occurred because she returned the felt sense of the body to the act of communicating.

Helen Keller and the Accusations

Born healthy in 1880 in Tuscumbia, Alabama, Keller suffered an illness at 19 months from which she emerged healthy but without her vision and hearing. Because Keller was an unruly and difficult child, her parents sought the advice of Alexander Graham Bell, who had worked with the deaf; he suggested that they contact Howe who then recommended Anne Sullivan as a teacher.[43] In this effort, Howe was entirely successful.

Working with Sullivan, communication and writing became central to Keller's sense of self and identity as well as to the ways in which she engaged with the world. But, as indicated, her writing was not initially received in positive ways; she was accused of various forms of copying. Such accusations, I argue, were based on the social perception that Keller's writing was derivative and deviant, especially because it depended on her highly illogical, embodied sense of touch.

The first accusation happened in 1891, when Keller and Sullivan spent the winter in Boston as guests of the Perkins Institute. At that time, the 11 year old Keller composed a short story, the "Frost King," for Michael Anagnos, director of the Institute. After Anagnos printed it in one of the Perkins publications, he learned that the story repeated parts of a well-known published children's story, *Birdie and His Fairy Friend*, by Margaret Canby.[44] Apparently, Keller had been read the story three years earlier.[45] The incident led to questions about plagiarism as well as Sullivan's role in it. Although a formal hearing absolved Keller and Sullivan, it ruined their relationship with Anagnos. The incident and the failed relationship are no doubt reflected in Anagnos' statement that "Helen Keller is a living lie."[46]

While the details of the scandal are not relevant here, the way it linked Keller's writing and deviance, prompting her reflection on it, are.[47] For my part, the first time I read about the allegations, I found them odd. Plagiarism is a social construct and must, therefore, be learned. Why would anyone think that an 11 year old girl of any ability would intentionally plagiarize (as opposed to accidentally do it)? In part, the initial accusation reflected Anagnos' concerns about his credibility; Keller was his student, represented the Institute, and he published the work. But as mentioned above, in part, the allegation reflected the perception that her writing was derivative and deviant in a culture which privileged the print linguistic medium and insisted on disembodied writing.

However upsetting, the event did not stop Keller from writing. The next text came a year later, in 1894, a short sketch, "My Life," published in *The Youth's Companion*. Accompanying the piece, an editorial note informs the reader that the text was "written wholly without the help of any sort by a deaf and blind girl, twelve years old, and printed without change."[48] Focusing on Keller's individual effort, the editorial remark anticipates the thoughts of a readership familiar with the plagiarism incident.

Suspicions aside, in 1902, as a student at Radcliffe, Keller revised the sketch to appear in six successive numbers of the *Ladies' Home Journal* as "The Story of My Life."[49] The story is introduced by the following descriptive title:

> Helen Keller's Own Story of Her Life Written Entirely by the Wonderful Girl Herself. As the feat may seem almost incredible, it may be in order to sat at the beginning that every word of this story as printed in THE JOURNAL has actually been written by Helen Keller

herself—not dictated, but first written in 'Braille' (raised points): then transferred to the typewriter by this wonderful girl herself.[50]

According to this introductory description, Keller completed the work entirely through her own efforts (no doubt an exaggeration, as I discuss below). Another implicit response to the "Frost King" scandal, the introduction also highlights Keller's exceptional nature; in attempting to deflect suspicion, the statement continues to link her writing and deviance.

Because of its popularity, by the following year, 1903, Keller had revised the serialized version of her story into the well-known book.[51] Once again, questions about authorship and originality arose, in this case, with regard to collaboration. As published, the book contained three sections, each designed to provide information about and perspective on Keller.[52] After all, it was the third published variation of her story. The main feature, Keller's part, appeared in another expanded version, accompanied by several letters. To complement Keller's writing, the book included reflections on teaching Keller by Sullivan and comments on the book's publication by John Macy, Sullivan's future husband, and, at the time, editorial assistant.[53] Perhaps not surprising in this context, readers wondered about this latest collaborative effort.[54] What part was Keller's and what part her collaborators'? Again, these suspicions not only reflected the particular association between Keller and deviant communication but also the general thinking, in recent memory associated with Bridgman, that a disabled woman could not write properly, let alone without help, especially when she relied on her felt sense of touch to do so.

In fact, Keller could not publish her book alone but neither could any of her contemporaries. Then, as now, publishing was a collaborative effort between author, publisher, and editors. In Keller's time, authors often published stories first in serialized form in magazines and then in revised book format. Often, too, the book version changed the content to offer new perspectives, often in response to readers' comments. This is the case with Dickens, among many others; due to reader dissatisfaction with the original ending, *Great Expectations* has a different, happier one in its book version. Even having three authors involved in a work was not unprecedented. As such, the publication of *The Story of My Life* followed common publishing practices and used conventional formats and genres. Nonetheless, the collaborative element attracted attention because of the perception that Keller could not produce acceptable writing alone.

Finally, Keller is accused of plagiarism one last time.[55] At the age of 28, after Keller had graduated from Radcliffe, a letter to an editor complains she presented as her own a passage verbatim from the work of English Unitarian clergyman and philosopher, James Martineau. Again, the issue passes but prompts reflection on Keller's part, as I discuss below.

The various accusations against Keller's originality suggested that she could not write, or write properly, without help.[56] Based on touch and according to popular values, her writing was by nature emotional, subjective, and improper. The attacks reflected the print linguistic bias which insisted that proper writing was disembodied logical discourse. Perhaps it was inevitable that her ability to write was assailed. How could a blind deaf woman, underdeveloped, illogical, and by nature deficient (hadn't Bridgman proven that?) write in the logical disembodied manner of the fully normal person? Hadn't the various versions of her study, each building on the next, indicated the guidance of other, more able individuals. In her responses to the accusations, Keller accepted that embodiment and explained why it was original rather than derivative—not despite but because it proceeded from touch. And, Keller's readers accepted her writing and, over time, abandoned their fears of its inherent improprieties.

Keller Responds: Her Assimilative Model

As indicated, the accusations deeply affected Keller, prompting a series of reflections in her life writing on authorship.[57] In general, her reactions demonstrate her awareness of and response to the implicit characterization of her writing as deviant and merely derivative, particularly in its origins in touch. As she counters, her various communicative acts are assimilative and creative as well as eminently human.

In response to the first accusation in 1891, Keller comments in 1902 that,

> I have read the 'Frost-Fairies' since, also the letters I wrote in which I used other ideas of Miss Canby's. I find in one of them, a letter to Mr. Anagnos, dated September 29, 1891, words and sentiments exactly like those of the book. At this time I was writing, 'The Frost-King,' and this letter, like many others, contains phrases which show that my mind was saturated with the story.... This habit of assimilating what pleases me and giving it out again as my own appears in much of my early correspondence and my first attempts at writing.[58]

After re-reading the Canby, Keller acknowledges that she had used her ideas. But, as she explains, that is hardly plagiarism. Instead, her early references to Canby's work belonged to her youthful writing process. Rather than copying Canby's words, she was using them to develop her own ideas. As she puts it, to learn how to be creative, she assimilated what affected her.

Continuing, Keller explains how this "habit of assimilating" allowed her to acquire more knowledge about the world. To create, she must first be strongly affected by some material object. That affective response, experienced as a felt sensation, or touch, inspires emotions and initiates the creative writing process.

> Yet I cannot think that, because I did not originate the ideas, my little composition is quite devoid of interest, it shows that I could express my appreciation of beautiful and poetic ideas in clear and animated language. Mr. Anagnos seems to ignore the fact that those early compositions are mental gymnastics. I was learning, as all young and inexperienced persons learn, by assimilation and imitation, to put ideas into words. Everything I found in books that pleased me I retained in my memory, consciously or unconsciously, and adapted it.[59]

Keller defends and describes her youthful writing process. Although she did not invent the ideas, her early writing still had value, not because of its originality but because of the clarity and liveliness of her ideas. By characterizing her way of writing as "mental gymnastics," she calls attention to the central and unified role mind and body play in her creativity. Mind and body are also blended by memory, another element of her writing which she evokes.

Next, Keller compares this creative process to making a quilt.

> I am afraid I have not completed this process yet. It is certain that I cannot always distinguish my own thoughts from those I which read, because what I read becomes the very substance and texture of my mind. Consequently, in nearly all that I write I produce something very much like a crazy patchwork.[60]

Like the craft of quilting, her creative process begins seemingly unsystematically with material bits and pieces collected from others, pieces which at first don't adhere. After considering the broader idea into which she wants these pieces to fit, she realigns them until they form that imagined unity. As she puts it, the "odds and ends" eventually come together in a coherent pattern. When the "crazy" pieces coalesce, that unity makes sense and does so in Keller's own terms. Indeed, that seems to have been the case in the writing process which moved from *The Youth Companion Story* to *Ladies Home Journal* to *The Story of My Life*.

As described, arriving at an original creation is a collaborative process on several levels. Of course, it brings together scraps of ideas from various sources. Additionally, as an act uniting mind and body, the process begins in and activates her felt sense and corresponding feelings; as the process continues, she assimilates the "substance and texture" of any pieces which affect her along the way until she completes the quilt, so to speak. Thus, her writing is not stolen, derivative, and deviant but assimilative and creative; because it involves body and mind, it is always an embodied statement of who she is. She embraces that embodiment.

Throughout her early life writing, Keller consistently characterizes her communication processes in terms of an assimilative model which begins with her felt sense of touch; moving from there, she acquires new senses, emotions, and ideas. From them, she eventually forms unified creations or communicative events. By experiencing and using these many experiences, she reveals her inherent humanity. For example, and again responding to accusations of deviance, Keller describes how she thinks of language in human and assimilative terms. As she puts it,

> at first, when my teacher told me about a new thing I asked very few questions. My ideas were vague, and my vocabulary was inadequate; but as my knowledge of things grew, and I learned more and more words, my field of inquiry broadened, and I would return again and again to the same subject, eager for further information. Sometimes a new word revived an image that some earlier experience had engraved in my mind. "I had now the key to language, and I was eager to learn how to use it."[61]

Here, she characterizes her use of language as one which integrates pieces, moving from touch and feeling to ideas, images, and words; with this movement, she links herself with her readers.[62]

Like her understanding of writing and language more generally, Keller reads by moving from ideas she touches to ideas she experiences in other affective, sensory, and imagined ways. When she replies to the last accusation of plagiarism, of the minister's work, she explains that friends often read "interesting fragments" in her writing "in a promiscuous manner;" as she puts it, these fragments are difficult to trace in the "fugitive sentences and paragraphs" because they have been spelled into her hand. As described by others, such reading is deviant.[63] This thinking frustrates her; "sometimes I think I ought to stop writing altogether," she complains, "since I cannot tell surely which of my ideas are borrowed feathers, except for those which I gather from books in raised print."[64] But, she counters, her reading is not deviant but emerges from a process that integrates pieces, first touches then other material bits, from others and leads to her original, if seemingly "borrowed," reading.

More specifically, as Keller suggests, she reads on two levels, one accomplished by herself and one by collaborating with others. On one level, she receives the "generous" touch from others on her hand.[65] On another, she reads alone by feeling the Braille letters on the page. Based in touch rather than sight and hearing, her reading, like her writing, is a creative act which engages and integrates mind and body as well as various senses and feelings. In recognizing these two levels, she acknowledges that reading is a collaborative effort which begins with her own felt sense of touch and links her to other people. As her writing and use of language, her reading is assimilative rather than derivative, creative rather than illegitimate, and altogether human.

So, too, does Keller characterize how she learned to speak within a process that integrates what she knows through touch with what she encounters in the world around her. Once more, she communicates by engaging her mind as well as various senses in order, in this case, to speak.

> It was in the spring of 1890 that I learned to speak. For some time I had known that the people around me used a method of communication different from mine. The impulse to utter audible sounds had always been strong with me. No deaf child who has earnestly tried to speak the words which he has never heard—to come out of the prison of silence, where no tone of loved, no song of bird, no strain of music can pierce the silence—can forget the thrill the surprise, the pathos of pain, the joy of discovery which have come over him when he first learns to utter a words.[66]

From the start, Keller recognized that she communicated differently, though touch, than others. Initially, that difference imprisoned her in a private world. But, by assimilating other senses and experiences within her world, she acquired the ability to speak and hear on her own terms, and to experience corresponding feelings.

> It is an unspeakable boon to me to be able to speak in winged words that need no interpretation. As I talk, happy thoughts flutter up put of my words that might perhaps have struggled in vain to escape the barrier of my fingers. Before I even heard that a deaf child could learn

to speak I was conscious of dissatisfaction with the means of communication I already possessed. One is entirely dependent upon the manual alphabet.[67]

As Keller puts it, acquiring the ability to speak through her sense of touch is an "unspeakable boon;" her description captures how she speaks and hears on her own terms, but she hears nonetheless. Grounded in touch, her speech allows her to participate in more mutual exchange with others, for example, her sister. "'My little sister will understand me now,' was a thought stronger than all obstacles. I used to repeat ecstatically, 'I am not dumb now.'"[68] Again, through assimilation, she combines odds and ends from others within a broader communicative pattern that is neither deviant, nor derivative but creative, collaborative, and human.

Assimilating Senses

In responding to the accusations against her originality, Keller has explained the originality of the assimilative process which allows her to write, read, and speak. Elsewhere, she locates this process with the movement which takes her from her own private sense of touch to appreciate and activate senses to which she would not presumably have access. In so doing, she again links her world and that of her reader as pieces within an overarching quilt.

When Keller describes her world on the day Anne Sullivan entered her life, it is a world in which she knew her own sense of touch alone. She characterizes that private world with frustration; that day it led her to smash a doll. "In the still, dark world in which I lived there was no sentiment, no tenderness."[69] Without the ability to communicate beyond touch, her world was devoid of affect and isolated.

Still, she realized that touch was vital to her and, through that sense, began to escape her private existence. To that end, "my hands felt every object and observed every motion, and in this way, I learned to know many things."[70] Touch, the sense that locked her in isolation, became the means to move beyond it.

Frequently, Keller describes how touch helps her to experience other sensations, emotions, and ideas, and to do so on her terms, although her terms connect her with the world beyond her. Through touch, for example, she feels motion, timing, tension, and textures, these of different degrees and kinds; in turn, she experiences a corresponding series of emotions.[71] She notes,

as I returned to the house every object which I touched seems to quiver
with life. That was because I saw everything with the strange, new
sight which had come to me.... As if it were yesterday, I recall every
incident of the summer of 1887 that followed my soul's awakening. I
did nothing but explore with my hands and learn the name of every
object I touched, and the more I handled things and learned their
names and uses, the more joyous and confident grew my kinship with
the world."[72]

Touching material objects prompts Keller to experience emotions; that
is, touch activates mind and body, allowing her to feel the presence of
life. To know something fully, she must first feel it. As touch engages
her in the world around her during those "incidents," she acquires a
"new sight," or vision. By touching the world, she learns to see it, albeit
on her own terms. In this way, touch releases her from the isolation with
which it was initially associated, and she more fully senses, feels, and
communicates about herself and to others.

Keller often describes this felt sense in terms which call on her
readers to recognize the particular pleasure she experiences in her world.

People who think that all sensations reach us through the eye and the
ear have expressed surprise that I should notice any difference, expect
possibly the absence of pavements, between walking in city streets and
in country roads. They forget that my whole body is alive to the
conditions around me. The rumble and roar of the city smite the nerves
of my face, and I feel the ceaseless tramp of an unseen multitude, and
the dissonant tumult frets my spirit.[73]

As Keller puts it, she can see, hear, and feel with her hands. Thus,
through assimilation, she is as alive as any human to the world around
her.

Keller also makes clear that this felt-sense is not just her own but
available to all humans; all humans use different mediums, modes, and
senses to communicate.

It seems to me that there is in each of us a capacity to comprehend the
impressions and emotions which have been experienced by mankind
from the beginning. Each person has a subconscious memory of the
green earth and murmuring waters, and blindness and deafness cannot
rob him of this gift from past generations. This inherited capacity is a
sort of sixth sense—a soul-sense which sees, hears, feels, all in one.[74]

Keller wants her readers to know that she is not unique. All humans are
born blind, deaf, and speechless; through the process of living, each

individual experiences the world on many levels. Because she uses all the resources available to and in her, Keller's world is just as rich anyone else's—different but valuable. As Keller puts it, she has activated a "sixth sense" with which all humans are born; anyone can activate that sense if s/he uses all the material, sensual, and emotional means available to them.

Conversely, for Keller, situations that do not avail themselves of all resources are unemotional and unaffective; they do not partake in that sixth sense. Thus, she describes a situation that lacks creativity, originality, and community at Radcliffe. "I soon discovered that college was not quite the romantic lyceum I had imagined."[75] As she describes it, this experience is dull because it is mono-modal, as it were, it engages words without feeling and thus mind without body. Communication communicates because it activates mind and body, many modes and mediums, and helps people actualize their shared humanity.

In addition to asking readers to acknowledge how she experiences the world and identify with it, Keller frequently writes in visual language which links her world with her readers'.

> It is very interesting to watch a plant grow, it is like taking part in creation. When all is cold and white, when the little children of the woodland are gone to their nurseries in the warm earth, and the empty nests on the care trees fill with snow, my window-garden glows and smiles, making summer within while it is winter without. It is wonderful to see flowers in bloom in the midst of a snow-storm! I have felt a bud.... Beautiful flower, you have taught me to see a little way into the hidden heart of things. Now I understand that the darkness everywhere may hold possibilities better even than my hopes.[76]

In describing the woodland scene, Keller uses visual language to which she should not be privy; she sees a plant grow as well as a flower bloom. She experiences colors and smiling expressions. But, she does so in her mind's eye. Such sights, aroused through touch, not only allow her to experience vision but also to see things not immediately evident. These sights, she reminds the reader, emerged from darkness. On the one hand, her language and experience are uniquely hers because they begin with touch. On the other hand, what she sees provides a link between her world and the reader's.

Keller not only asks her readers to identify with her world by speaking in visual language but also by speaking directly to their experiences. For example, Keller listens to her audience and connects with them on their terms.

I trust that the readers of THE LADIES' HOME JOURNAL have not concluded from the chapter on books in the preceding number of the magazine that reading is my only pleasure; for my pleasure and amusements are as varied as my moods. More than once in the course of the story I have referred to my love of the country and out-of-door sports.[77]

Using the language and human experiences with which her readers are familiar, Keller enters their world and invites them into her own. Here, her assimilative creativity involves collaborating with her readers. There is no plagiarism evident in such efforts.

Conclusions

Keller arrived in a world which still privileged, disembodied, presumably logical writing and, accordingly, characterized her own communicative efforts as derivative and deviant; that characterization openly validated the long held link between subjective, irrational communication practices—practices often manifested in language associated with the body as well as woman—and disability. In contrast to Bridgman's enforced public silence and Hay's mocking subversion, Keller worked in concert with the world, both in what and how she communicated. Perhaps in reaction to the accusations of plagiarism, she developed and acknowledged her assimilative writing process, assimilative in the ways she collaborated with her own ideas, with the guidance of others, and through the resources of her mind and senses.

By inviting her audience to see her originality and her humanity, Keller overturned prevailing social perceptions and convinced her readers to identify with her. To those ends, she adopted the conventions of her time, writing in the familiar autobiographical form and descriptive style. In using the language of her readers, she taught them about her unique felt sense of the world. By locating a common base for human communication, she linked herself to all humanity and encouraged her readers to join her by activating their felt senses. Ironically, Keller was exceptional in her efforts to be otherwise. Still, she made it easier for others to write about their perceived physical differences. The world had warmed to the prospect of such readings and new technologies in the twentieth and twenty-first centuries would make those efforts easier.

Indeed, Keller's collaboration with and use of all the available experiences marked a moment in Western society when disability was becoming less a physical category than a state of mind.

---

[1] Keller wrote autobiographical accounts throughout her life. Keller *Midstream*; Keller, *Out of the Dark*; Keller, Helen. *The World I Live In*. I will concentrate on the three manifestations in which her story appeared; as discussed below, this include the book-length version, the serialized version which preceded it, and a short sketch which began the process. When I refer to the serialized version I offer part, date and page. When I refer to the book, I use the Shattuck's edition.

[2] Helen Keller, *The Story of My Life*, p. 105.

[3] Berrios and Gili, "Will and Its Disorders: A Conceptual History"; Reed, *From Soul to Mind: The Emergence of Psychology, from Erasmus Darwin to William James.*

[4] For example, materialists and other non-orthodox thinkers were interested in the ways in which entities outside the head could influence though and feelings within the body, making the body the mediating point between the will and the world (see Reed, *From Soul to Mind*).

[5] Leonard J. Davis, "Dr. Johnson, Amelia, and the Discourse of Disability in the Eighteenth Century"; Garland Thomson, *Extraordinary Bodies: Figuring Physical Disability in American Culture and Literature; Jorden, Briefe Discourse of a Disease Called Suffocation of the Mother; Stewart, Some Account of a Boy Born Blind and Deaf, Collected from Authentic Sources of Information With a Few Remarks and Comments*; Gould and Pyle, *Anomalies and Curiosities of Medicine.*

[6] Itard, *De L'education d'un homme sauvage ou de premiers developments physiques et moraux de jeune sauvage de l'Aveyron*; cf. Lane, *The Wild Boy of Aveyron.*

[7] I will not discuss the background and issues involving deaf education and community; see Brueggemann, *Lend Me Your Ear: Rhetorical Constructions of Deafness*; Lane, Ed. *The Deaf Experience. Classics in Language and Education*; Krentz, Ed., *A Mighty Change. An Anthology of Deaf American Writing, 1816-1864*; Lane, *The Wild Boy of Aveyron*; Wheatley, "Blindness, Discipline, and Reward: Louis IX and the Foundation of the Hospice des Quinze-Vingts."

[8] Berthier, *Forging Deaf Education in Nineteenth-Century France. Biographical Sketches of Bébian, Sicard, Massieu, and Clerc*; Lane, Ed. *The Deaf Experience*; Krentz, Ed., *A Mighty Change.*

[9] See Berthier, *Forging Deaf Education in Nineteenth-Century France*; Krentz, Ed., *A Mighty Change. An Anthology of Deaf American Writing, 1816-1864*; Lane, *The Wild Boy of Aveyron.*

[10] See Lane, Ed., *The Deaf Experience*. Interestingly, these sources are available only in archives.

[11] See Husson, Reflections. *The Life and Writings of a Young Blind Woman in Post-Revolutionary France.*

[12] *Boston Transcript*, June 14, 1851; paraphrase in Gitter, *The Imprisoned Guest*, p. 4. In 1869, Adele M. Jewel published an autobiographical pamphlet about her experiences as a deaf, black women. The pamphlet was designed to earn money; see Jewel, Adele M., "A Brief Narrative if the Life of Mrs. Adele M. Jewel (1869)." For other promotional autobiographies by disabled individuals, see Schweik, *The Ugly Laws: Disability in Public.*

[13] Apparently, her taste and smell were compromised; see Ibid., p. 3.

[14] Freeberg, *The Education of Laura Bridgman: First Deaf and Blind person to Learn Language*, p. 5.

[15] Krentz, Ed., *A Mighty Change*, 96 note 3.

[16] See Stanford, *The Writings of Laura Bridgman*, p. 13, for example.

[17] Freeberg, *The Education of Laura Bridgman*, pp. 156, 191; Stanford, *The Writings of Laura Bridgman*, 1887, p. 25.

[18] Ibid., 3.

[19] Dickens, Charles, *American Notes*, 29.

[20] Ibid, p. 33.

[20] Howe and others often use religious conversion language similar to the discourse found in the nineteenth century asylum inmates texts as Chapter Six discusses.

[21] Dickens, Charles, *American Notes*, p. 28

[22] Ibid., p. 29.

[23] Edward A. Park, in Lamson, *Life and Education of Laura Dewey Bridgman, the Deaf, Dumb, and Blind Girl*, p. iv.

[24] Ibid., p. vi.

[25] Ibid., pp. xi, xxv, xxvii.

[26] Stanford, *The Writings of Laura Bridgman*, p. 7.

[27] Dickens, American Notes, p. 36.

[28] See Stanford, *The Writings of Laura Bridgman*, pp. 13 for instance.

[29] Her work is still available only in archives, for example, in The Laura Dewey Bridgman Collection in the Special Collections and University Archives, Leonard H. Axe Library, Pittsburg State University, Pittsburg, KS. This kind of framed narration is evident as well in contemporaneous asylum case histories; see Berkenkotter, *Patient Tales. Case Histories and the Uses of Narrative in Psychiatry*.

[30] Stanford, *The Writings of Laura Bridgman*, p. 25.

[31] Ibid., p. 19.

[32] Ibid., pp. 25 ff.

[33] Ibid., p. 21.

[34] Ibid., p. 10.

[35] Ibid., p. 11.

[36] "We strangely forget that the deaf-mutes and the blind deaf-mutes are human beings and are to be treated as human beings; they are influenced by the same motives which affect the race in general, and are to be educated on the same principles which regulate the education of ordinary scholars. The special difficulty is in opening an avenue to their mind" (Edward A. Park, in Lamson, *Life and Education of Laura Dewey Bridgman, the Deaf, Dumb, and Blind Girl*, p. xi; emphasis in original).

[37] Freeberg, *The Education of Laura Bridgman*, p. 6.

[38] This at a time when disability and deviance, i.e. criminality, were often associated and considered hereditary; see Gould, *The Mismeasure of Man*; Schweik, *The Ugly Laws: Disability in Public*.

[39] The two women met late in Bridgman's life, and Anne Sullivan was a Perkins trained teacher; see Freeberg, *The Education of Laura Bridgman*, pp. 215-217.

[40] Shattuck, "Introduction," in Keller, *The Story of My Life*, p. xiv.

[41] Contemporary readers are likely familiar with the portrayal of Keller as a child wonder as well as her association with her teacher, Anne Sullivan, especially as portrayed in William Gibson's play *The Miracle Worker*. Unfortunately, the play offers an inaccurate representation of her first words; see Herrmann, Helen Keller, A Life, p. xiii.

[42] Shattuck, "Introduction," in Keller, *The Story of My Life*, pp. xi ff.

[43] Part 1/April 1902, 8; Part Third/June 1902, 7.

[44] Part Four/ July 1902, 11-12; cf.; Lash, *Helen and Teacher: The Story of Helen Keller and Anne Sullivan Macy*, p. 140.

[45] Swan, "Touching Words: Helen Keller, Plagiarism, Authorship."

[46] Shattuck, "Introduction," in Keller, The Story of My Life, p. xvii.

[47] See Lash, Helen and Teacher, pp. 140 ff.

[48] Keller, "My Life," Youth's Companion, p. 68.

[49] The issue of her authenticity may be reflected in her application to Radcliffe. For admission, she was subjected to rigorous examinations which other candidates did not have to endure; see Lash, *Helen and Teacher*.

[50] Part 1/April 1902, p. 7.

[51] The differences between the versions are fascinating and would make an interesting study in revision, especially given the other issues of authorship with which Keller is dealing.

[52] Shattuck, "Introduction," in Keller, *The Story of My Life*, p. xvii.

[53] Perhaps an effort on Macy's part to feature his future wife in several ways since his part focuses on Sullivan, see Ibid., pp. xvii.

[54] Lash, Helen and Teacher, pp. 140 ff.

[55] Swan, "Touching Words: Helen Keller, Plagiarism, Authorship," p. 57; Crow, "Helen Keller: Rethinking the Problematic Icon."

[56] In this case, Keller is not allowed to participate in the Romantic tradition of the individual artist working in solitude, although this notion is not entirely accurate.

[57] Not surprisingly, one section of the work is called "Constant Fear of Becoming a Plagiarist (Part Four/ July 1902, p. 12; cf. Chapter Fourteen).

[58] Part Four/July 1902, p. 11.

[59] Part Four/July 1902, pp. 11-12.

[60] Part Four/July 1902, p. 12.

[61] Part Second/May 1902, p. 6.

[62] See also, "I now had the key to all language, and I was eager to learn to use it. Children who hear acquire language without any particular effort; the words that fall from others' lips they catch on the wing, as it were, delightfully, while the little deaf child must trap them by a slow and often painful process. But whatever the process, the result is wonderful. Gradually from naming an object we advance step by step until we have traversed the vast distance between out first stammered syllable and the sweep of thought in a line of Shakespeare" (*The Story of My Life*, p. 31).

[63] Ibid., p. 58.

[64] Joseph P. Lash, *Helen and Teacher*, pp. 342-3.

[65] Jim Swan, "Touching Words: Helen Keller, Plagiarism, Authorship," p. 58.

[66] Part Third/ June 1902, p. 7; cf. *The Story of My Life*, Chapter Thirteen, pp. 53-54.

[67] Ibid., pp. 53-54.

[68] Ibid., p. 54. I grant that Keller uses the negative term "dumb" here, but it was the contemporary parlance with which her readers would be familiar.

[69] Ibid., p. 5.

[70] Part Second/May 1902, p. 6.

[71] Ibid., p. 6.

[72] Part Second/May 1902, p. 5.

[73] *The Story of My Life*, p. 101.

[74] *The Story of My Life*, p. 100; cf. Part Second/May 1902, p. 6; Part 1/April 1902, p. 8.

[75] Part Five/August 1902, p. 13.

[76] *The Story of My Life*, pp. 121-122; Part 1/April 1902, p. 8.

[77] Part Six/September 1902, p. 11; Chapter 22, p. 98.

8

The Twentieth Century: Military, Biomedical, and Personal Perspectives

Part of Helen Keller's legacy was her unique, unapologetic perspective on disability stated within language typically associated with subjectivity and deviance, within a world which still categorized her as exceptional. This perspective resonates in an excerpt from a 1952 essay, in which the anonymous disabled author notes that disability is a matter of perception.

> Disability is mainly in the eye of the beholder. The reflection I see when passing a shop window—the lurching gait, the two sticks, the black eye-shield—is almost unbelievable. In a mirror the stick appears to be being forced on to the ground; it looks tremendously hard work. But in fact it is not. To me, walking on the level is almost always effortless, and I feel I am using my sticks only as many people swing their rolled umbrellas.

> The misconception has a moral. Sometimes I have been disappointed that strangers do not share my enthusiasm for recovery. The mirror has told me why.

> To the fit it is something of a paradox that disability, like war, can bring new and unexpected opportunities for self-development. We see different images of the same object. So it is not surprising that, on first acquaintance, there is a gap between a disabled person's view of his own disability and other people's view of it. The successful disabled person is the one who narrows that gap by developing unsuspected abilities.[1]

As s/he sees it, no difference exists between his/her body and anyone else's; after all, he feels and functions well. But, because his/her body does not represent the norm, the able-bodied see him/her differently, and they measure that difference in terms of war. For them, successful disabled people are equal to the battles they encounter and are all the better for their efforts to regroup and move toward their former normal forms. Significantly, the author notes that the "fit" recognize the paradox in their perspective; they are also unenthusiastic about the disabled person's recovery process. In so doing, the disabled author acknowledges the discrepancy between that "fit" perspective and his own, while championing the latter.

That overt discrepancy, between private/individual and public/collective, is implicitly evident elsewhere in the essay. The piece appears in *Disabilities and How to Live with Them*, a publication of *The Lancet*, an influential British medical journal. As the name they select for the volume indicates, by 1952 disability is the current term for physical differences; and as that name and the publisher's affiliation reveal, the book is framed in the categorical, medical perspective. That perspective is also apparent in the name they select for the author. S/he is "Poliomyelitis," not a person with his own lived perspective but a condition whose apparently objective naming masks any personal experience within the veil of categorical medical diagnosis. Although Poliomyelitis offers the story in his/her own words, that experience is mediated through his/her diagnosis which characterizes his recovery efforts as a discovery of "unsuspected abilities" by an individual who battles with a disabled body.[2] Not surprisingly, Poliomyelitis prefers his/her own "unparadoxical" perspective.

This conflicted thinking—thinking in which the disabled viewpoint is mediated through and against those of the medical community and broader society—recalls how life writers before Keller often represented their bodies in ways which contrasted with their surrounding society's perspective, be the latter constrained by a civic, religious, or medical model. Unlike these previous writers and as Keller, Poliomyelitis openly acknowledges the perspectival rift between his/her sense of disability and the one held by the society around him/her. Thereby, s/he moves beyond the writing of the nineteenth century asylum inmates; deviant rather than disabled, those individuals lived in a world which denied them a presence beyond the walls in which they were held. In contrast, twentieth century disabled life writers, as Poliomyelitis, can openly represent their personal sense of self and recognize it as opposed to how their society medicalizes them, thereby disassociating them from their bodies.

To look more deeply into these matters, without repeating what others have covered, my examination of recent life writing about disability focuses on an underrepresented yet very present topic, at least from a disability studies perspective, the stories of injured soldiers. This topic not only allows me to address a fresh subject but also to return with some expository symmetry to my opening example, the injured Greeks outside Persepolis. My choice also introduces another dimension of disability, since injured veterans have long influenced disability issues as well as the medical and disability models which support these issues. Finally, these recent stories by soldiers allow me to consider acquired disability, a representative disability concern in an increasingly biomedical and electronically-mediated world.

To those ends, my analysis relies on a wealth of scholarship about recent life writing, supplemented by other scholarly inquiries into injured veterans, in particular, into the gendered and technologized aspects of injured veterans' identities, and the history of disability life writing reconstructed in previous chapters. Thus armed, so to speak, I consider how twentieth century soldiers represent their bodies; as Poliomyelitis, and indeed as the Greek soldiers, they are caught between the home to which they return and the military and medical worlds which constrain that effort.

Twentieth Century Medicine and Disability: The Theater of War

When I discussed Helen Keller's writing, crafted at the turn of the twentieth century, the medical model of disability was fully in play. That model, based on the mind/body split, conceptualizes medicine in terms of diseases to cure by means of universalizing criteria rather than patients to treat by considering individual cases.[3] Its biomedical manifestation adds to this categorical understanding the presumably transformative power of medical technologies, for example, scans, prosthetics, and designer surgeries.[4] From this latter twentieth century perspective, diseases are diagnosed and cured by increasingly more specific rubrics and technologies through which physicians see within the living body.[5] With these means, physicians can intervene in the body's operation and develop preventive treatments; these approaches reflect in turn biomedical interest in and ability to eradicate physical problems. By seeking to heal gaps between the disabled and the fit, these transformative medical technologies also detach the disabled person as patient from her/his physician and physical problem. At the same time, the increasing presence of disabled individuals is made present by new informational technologies, as I discuss below.

As indicated, war injuries, wounds of the head and extremities particularly, have long been an impetus to medical developments.[6] Since the American Civil War, these developments have followed a certain arc associated with new technologies. Given that conflict's brutality, a circumstance associated with more sophisticated weapons technologies, the war produced a record number of injuries as well as a record survival rate. These increases also depended on medical technologies. By the Civil War, antiseptics had been discovered, allowing wounds to be decontaminated and treated.[7] Although more soldiers survived, often with amputations, they did so disfigured, both visibly and otherwise. "As far back as the Civil War, American military physicians have recognized and classified combat stress into such categories as 'insanity,' 'nostalgia, and what were called 'soldier's heart,' or 'irritable heart.'"[8] Despite the numbers of affected, post-war treatment was at best minimal (as this was the era of the asylum).

Battlefield medical practices remained limited during World War I, as post-deployment treatments expanded. To treat physical wounds, World War I physicians developed technologies which focused on reconstructive surgery and prosthetics. Presumably, these rehabilitative efforts helped disfigured individuals close the gap between their disabled and former fit states. Interestingly, Henry Tonks created photographic and drawn portraits of the war injured in WWI, along with plaster casts by sculptor Lt. J. Edwards "for the direct purpose of showing the injuries in various stages of repair and also to reconstruct the features before the actual operation was performed."[9] In using art works, visual representations of the injured, he anticipated recent imagining technologies. Although mental trauma was widespread (the term "shell shock" was first defined during this war in *The Lancet* in February 1915),[10] it was often taken as an unfortunate consequence of war.

From World War II to Vietnam, military medicine focused on onsite treatment. Mobile army surgical hospitals (MASH units) used triage to determine which patients to treat and where best to do so. Once deployed, these units responded to gun shot and bomb wounds efficiently and effectively; but, "brain injuries of any kind in [World War II and] Vietnam were universally fatal."[11] Shell shock was increasingly common; eventually, it received a clinical name, PTSD, and a place and pathology in the *DSM*; those individuals thus labeled began receiving treatment in veteran's hospitals.[12]

From the mid-1990s to the present, the US and allied involvement in middle eastern conflicts (the Gulf War, Afghanistan, Iraq) has resulted in numerous casualties. At the time of this writing, there have been 1.9 million soldiers and marines deployed to Afghanistan and Iraq over the last decade, with over 5,000 killed, some 300,000 with traumatic brain or concussive central nervous system injuries, along with amputees approaching levels not seen since our Civil War. These are by any measurement or comparison truly enormous numbers.[13]

Increased survival rates depend on developments in medical technology. Protective Kevlar vests, for instance, help solders survive roadside and suicide bombs. Yet, these preventive measures result in "polytraumas" of the brain, muscle, skin, and extremity injuries.[14]

To deal with these conditions, civilian trauma medicine continues to be brought to the battlefield, as these efforts are coordinated with remote treatment sites.[15] Most military units have x-rays to scan injuries and, if necessary, to send elsewhere electronically for consultation.[16] New battlefield surgical techniques, for amputations especially, allow for greater post-deployment options, options which provide patients with increased comfort and a greater range of post-surgical function.[17] Overall, treatment aims at healing the gap between military and civilian life and between the duties and functions associated with each.

Obviously, the number and presence of disabled soldiers has increased.[18] By and large, the public sees these soldiers within the biomedical model and its concerns with transformation and rehabilitation rather than spectacle or cure. Success in this society, as Poliomyelitis suggested, involves maintaining fitness and, for the disabled, closing the gap between that fitness and one's sense of self. Although the fit may never see the disabled as whole, the disabled are always aware of the gap they seek to fill and increasingly interested in defending their own experience of disability.[19]

Disabled veterans face additional societal constraints; these constraints are based on Western values about the military and masculinity. The military, of course, is a hierarchical structure which depends on and enforces conventional, structured, and rule-bound conduct. Such conduct also conforms to deeply held Western values about masculinity.[20]

> The greatest challenge for many returning veterans is not just dealing with PTSD but also trying to manage their suffering striving for a normative life in America society. As is the case throughout the world, trying to create a 'successful' life in the United States in a heavily gendered task, and gender proves to a piece of the puzzle here as well.[21]

As noted, acquired disability challenges veterans' male identities, not only as military members but as individuals who have civilian expectations to uphold.[22] These duties, associated with courage, resolve, and brotherhood, also reflect their masculine identities.

Military and masculinist identities are developed and maintained in the military community and applied on the battlefield. Within this realm,

> war represents the ultimate danger to identity (both personal and national). This danger comes not from any quality of war that makes it an aberration of culture, but rather because war exists at the boundary between primal human behaviors and the 'constructed' norms of a larger society that can function only with prohibitions" and thus shifts identities … it is this shared (or communal) quality of the self that is endangered by war."[23]

War in and of itself affects soldiers deeply, pitting their individual duties against their national ones.[24] Acquired disabilities place veterans in a more complicated position.[25] Those affected face the competing demands of their masculinity, their family, and their military status, all against the unavoidable presence of their bodies.[26] Finally, increased media coverage of the wars increases the likelihood that disabled soldiers will confront these expectations regularly.[27]

Since the Civil War, then, combat injuries have transformed medical practices and the treatment of the injured. As medical practices have developed on the battlefield, in the civilian hospital, and between them, soldiers have survived in greater numbers and with a greater societal presence. Once disabled, veterans are rehabilitated within the biomedical model yet must reckon with their private identities, often hidden beneath their collective representation. These conflicted and deeply felt senses of self are reflected in the fact that survivors of war have always had difficulty discussing their experiences. By and large, World War II veterans wanted to move on from the horror; for Vietnam vets, discussing the war was difficult in a country which rejected their efforts.[28] Fortunately, as I discuss below, life writing has become a means for disabled veterans to close the gap between their perspective and that of the society to which they return.

Life Writing in the Twentieth Century

As previous chapters have demonstrated, technologies have long influenced the design, production, and dissemination of the cultural materials which shape social values and, in particular, life writing. In the latter half of the twentieth century, these literacy technologies have been the source of new communicative mediums, genres, and modes. An increasingly broad spectrum of individuals and groups can communicate in more complex ways: with words, images (still or moving), and sound on computer screens, tablets, hand held devises, and so forth. More individuals are writing, and writing about themselves, including individuals with disabilities. This latter life writing has been interestingly examined in terms of its structures, genres, and connections with social contexts. These efforts also demonstrate how recent disability writing can be located in the longer history I have begun to reconstruct.

Arthur Frank is interested in the narratives ill individuals, or people who acquire disabilities, write to represent their personal sense of that changed embodiment; that is, they tell tales "not just about the body but through it."[29] To those ends, their narratives necessarily rely on "culturally conventional rhetorics of self-change."[30] To unpack this reliance, Frank identities four longstanding narrative types which appear in recent illness narratives.[31] First, disabled individuals craft narratives that represent their identities as self-change either as epiphany; as "who I have always been;" as "who I might become;" and as cumulative epiphanies and reluctant phoenixes.[32] As Frank suggests, by telling their own stories, or reclaiming them, these authors reflect postmodern thinking. And, by appropriating these tried and true strategies to those personal ends, the narrators use their oppressors' language, manifesting a post-colonialist perspective.[33] In using these strategies, I would add, the writers recall the writing of previous authors in this study.[34] Earlier disability life writers, from the Greek soldiers to Helen Keller, reappropriated the language of their oppressors yet reclaimed that language in their own terms. But, previous writers conceptualized those uses within their own cultural contexts without any explicit intent to "reclaim." As such, the recent disability narratives are not new in using conventional strategies as the basis for describing their own senses of their bodies, although understanding them as post-modern and as post-colonial is only recently possible.

Turning from narrative structure to genre, G. Thomas Couser rightly calls autobiography "a threshold genre for marginalized people."[35] In contrast to recent life writing by the able-bodied, he suggests, disabled autobiographers engage the body in new ways.[36] As Couser puts it, "perhaps what distinguishes life writing in contemporary America is that individuals with such bodies are choosing to signify *on* their own bodies, rather than to allow their signification to be determined by others."[37]

In addition to identifying sub-genres of disability autobiography, Couser describes a type he sees as genuinely original, the new disability memoir, exemplified by the works of Stephen Kuusisto and Nancy Mairs, among others.[38] Their novelty lies not in form but "in an aspect of their content: their disability consciousness…. These are some body memoirs with (an) attitude … in large part a function of their focus on disability rather than impairment."[39] To that end, the new disability memoir often evokes passing; this concern links disability with discussions of race, class, and sexual orientation. Moreover, these characteristics link the new disability memoir, again implicitly, with earlier life writers in this study. Although Hay, for instance, knew nothing of the difference between illness and disability, he certainly used lamentation and irony to discuss his body with "attitude."[40] Similarly, Trapnel's performative efforts and some of the nineteenth century asylum inmates' ironic language were literally "in your face."

In addition to identifying and characterizing this genre, Couser validates its literary and cultural contributions, in part to counter those who call recent disability memoirs bad writing.[41] For some critics, these memoirs are too literary, for others too sentimental, and for others, about nobodies; typically, the disabled cannot win for losing. But, as Couser points out, disability memoirs acknowledge the presence of disabled bodies, a topic previously found only in works by well-known athletes and movie stars. As such, the new disability memoir is valuable for its content, perspective, and numbers.[42] That is, because of their numbers, the disability memoirs confront the fit with their bodily presence; and because they assert the validity of the disabled body and associated perspective, they foster more accurate perceptions of disability status.

In addition to structure and genre, scholars have considered how the internet has influenced life writing, disability life writing specifically. Initially, many heralded the prospect that virtual spaces would utterly revolutionize and democratize communication; more recently, that vision has been complicated. True, new media promote access and a voice for many (if not all), for the disabled through remote and assistive technologies; but such access and the education to use those technologies are not always distributed equally.[43] Far from being untethered by rules, online communicators are subject to the conventions and values which reflect the larger culture and specific contexts; again and typically, the disadvantaged are most likely to be negatively affected by these constraints.[44]

In all, the internet is a mediated technology; that is, no one can use it entirely alone.[45] All e-users experience tensions between personal autonomy and the control imposed on them by the groups in which they participate as well as by the gatekeepers overseeing the technology. Accordingly, the internet can be used for collective civic engagement, at the same time that the structure of virtual communities emphasizes individual rather than collective identities.[46] This conflict is especially salient for the disabled; although the internet provides them with enhanced ability and opportunity to communicate with others, it nonetheless constrains them within its normative practices and communities which might not adopt a disability-friendly perspective. Still, the internet has increased the presence of disabled writers and, within certain venues, that of disabled soldiers.[47] As this study's previous chapters have shown, all communication is on some level socially mediated; on the internet, however, the mediation is seemingly more obvious and thus more noted.

To recapitulate, the wealth of recent disability life writing appears in a world in which disability is a named and visible condition associated with transformative rehabilitation and passing. Enhanced by the equally transformative capacities of the internet, life writing is helping to heal the gap between the writer's perspective on his/her body and that of the surrounding world. In so doing, the disabled call attention to their efforts and perspectives. Within this disabled presence, wounded veterans form a significant subset.

The Soldiers: World War II

To begin, I offer another story framed within *The Lancet*'s previously mentioned volume, one written by a World War II veteran, matter-of-factly and anonymously named "Loss of a Leg." After sustaining injuries from German bombs in Italy, he undergoes a treatment and recovery process in a Neapolitan military hospital; initially, everything goes wrong. As he relates his story, Lost a Leg discusses his physical and mental pains in ways which contrast his public and personal identities; the conflict is situated within and revolves around two perspectives on his body. He represents this conflict by means of language which contrasts first a medical perspective and next a military one with his personal understanding of his body.

To describe his injuries, he adopts clinical medical language; he refers, for example, to his "leg ankylosed at the knee with a foot-drop" and to "a pyarthrosis of the knee."[48] This presumably objective discussion reflects the world of the hospital and staff around him; constrained by its terminology when discussing the wounds, he represents them from a detached medicalized perspective. Thus described, he does not feel the injuries but allows others to deal with them as separate entities, entities from which he is thereby disassociated.

His own perspective, the way he sees the situation in his mind's eye, emerges when he turns to the personal issues with which he must contend. To discuss this private self, Lost a Leg uses emotional language which represents the changes he is undergoing. These feelings appear when he recounts the story of his injury.

> At about midnight four and a half years ago the blast of a German Schu mine took my right leg off. I knew what had happened—it was not necessary to soldier in Italy long to encounter this situation pretty often in others—and my mental condition was not improved by my thinking that I had been blinded, for I could see nothing and could not feel my hands. At that moment I felt so unutterably lonely that my instinct of self-preservation fled entirely, and a vivid memory is of me head falling to the ground in helpless despair.[49]

Here and without clinical terminology, Lost a Leg describes the bombing in subjective phrases such as "unutterably lonely, "vivid memory," and "helpless despair." Continuing in similar language, he characterizes the horrendous complications he endured for three months, stuck in a bed with one leg up, a bone sticking out of the other.[50] Understandably, his personal experience cannot be contained in, and conflicts with, the clinical language the staff has imposed on his wounds. While the clinical language distances him from the injuries, the personal words allow him to confront and embody the changes he is experiencing and fears.

In truth, he is less interested in treatment than in going home to his wife.[51] Anticipating that event terrifies him. Fortunately,

> here I had a first sight of my wife. And my secret fear that she would be repelled by a limbless man was soon dissipated. Self-confidence began to grow as my family came down from the north to visit me, and when friends made arduous war-time journeys to spend an hour with me.[52]

His worst nightmare, being rejected by his wife because she finds him repulsive, does not materialize. His friends also accept him as he is. Not surprisingly, the experience is represented in emotional and embodied language; as he puts it, "I did not see that pity in their eyes which I had dreaded."[53] Acceptance revives his personal sense of self. Again, that personal success is unmediated by clinical language.

Despite familial acceptance, his problems continue within the broader military society. In this venue, his fears are actualized when the army rejects him because of his wounds; from their perspective, his injuries render him unfit to serve his country.

> A red-tabbed Army colonel who gave me a medical board, announced that I was not further use to the Army, graded me category E, asked what my plans were, and suggested the 'psychiatry racket.' His idea was that I should be carried in on a stretcher to learn about it at psychiatry clinics. This was rehabilitation on the grade scale, especially as I had estimated that I would be another year in hospital. Being graded category E was really bad news, for it meant that I must henceforth exist on a disability pension.[54]

Because he lacks a limb, the army categorizes him as physically disabled; thus "downgraded," he cannot work and is referred to a psychiatrist. By military and medical standards, his mind and body are compromised and unfit. He loathes the prospect of living within and depending on the broader society and, thus, unable to fulfill his civic role.

> Fortunately, "with the aid of my friends I was given a respite and my discharge was cancelled."[55] From this point, he appropriates the language of the hero quest narrative. Now, he describes each "milestone" for which he has to work; in these efforts, "will-power alone was ... sufficient ... to make progress."[56] He focuses on receiving an artificial leg and walking.

> This was the day I dreamed of. It was an erratic, wavering, shaky walk, but I was proud of it. Several weeks later I was offered a job doing medical boards, when I was out of the Army. Accordingly I traveled to London, was boarded out, shaved off my mustache, and danced at one of the more fashionable hotels. This was a huge success, for I was not the complete social outcast I had anticipated. I started doing medical boards and felt that for the first time in 18 months my existence was justified. I was actually doing something to keep my place in society.... Later I was appointed to the permanent pensionable staff of this Ministry, where I am working alongside fit men and not in any sense a passenger.[57]

Receiving and using the prosthetic leg, a significant personal accomplishment, improves his ability to "pass" as fit and, thus, to close the gap between the two perceptions of his bodily state. For him, walking makes him whole, justifies his existence, and allows him to pass in society.

Although he resolves many problems and returns to society, Lost a Leg remains conflicted about what he and his body represent; he also knows he does not fully fit into society. As he realizes, his compromised, imposed public identity does not match his personal experience. He ends his story by acknowledging the conflict between his personal perceptions and those of the military, the medical establishment, and the public.

> I still feel sure that had the surgeons yielded to my please to amputate this limb, life would have been more comfortable, and I still would have walked without sticks. However, there is still the chance of arthroplasty when the results are a little better. I have patches of depression and frustration three or four times a year, but fortunately both my wife and I recognize them for what they are and take the necessary steps. Altogether life is a great improvement on what I had anticipated four years ago, but nothing will ever convince me that an ankylosed or arthrodesed knee is a good thing to have. Of the things that irritate me, one is being called a cripple as opposed to disabled, and another is having an amputation referred to as a stump.[58]

Here and like Poliomyelitis, Lost a Leg acknowledges the conflict between his sense of self and society's perception of him, a conflict manifested in his certainty that he, not the doctors, knew the proper, though unused, procedure for his amputation. This conflict is evident as well in his statements on the words others use to describe him. For example, he objects to being called "crippled" rather than "disabled," a difference which reflects in part his desire for society to validate his experience even if it means using its own official terminology to do so. Similarly, when he refers to his distaste for the term "stump," he rejects its characterization of him as only part of a whole; again, he would rather the fit use validating rather than distancing terminology. As he reflects on the two worlds with which he identifies, he ends with a significant assertion: he knows his own experience and perspective are accurate; no imposed military detached perspective will convince him otherwise.

In several ways, his story recalls the early Greeks who deliberated about their bodies and their civic reception and duties. Although Lost a Leg is an individual and the Greeks a group, each is caught between conflicting perceptions of their bodies. For the Greeks, public deliberation renders a decision; they recognize they no longer belong in Greece and stay in Persepolis. In Lost a Leg's case, the deliberation is private; he recognizes he has returned to a society which does not accept his representation of who he is. Neither the Greeks nor Lost a Leg fully belong in their homeland; but both decide for themselves whose perspective to accept about their very visible physical problems.

More Soldiers: The Gulf War, Afghanistan, and Iraq

Fast forward fifty years. By the time of the conflicts in the Middle East, communicative and medical practices and technologies have changed across the board. More soldiers survive with different kinds of disabilities. Although veterans, especially disabled ones, still tend not to write about these experiences in traditional mediums, they do so increasing on the internet. In this venue, Lost a Leg's perspective develops in concert with the norms of the internet, which allow for a mediated interplay between individual and collective perspectives. To demonstrate how this interplay facilitates the telling and acceptance of soldiers' experiences, I examine the website of The Wounded Warrior Project, a non-profit organization which supports injured veterans as they recuperate, in part by offering their stories.[59] By providing the soldiers with a venue to speak, and one which acknowledges their disability on their own terms, this site has begun to break a deadlock on personal representations of war injuries and, in so doing, educated its audience about disability issues.

At the time I examined it, the site presented 13 stories by veterans with disabilities, 12 men and one woman, who experienced the typical range of injuries, TBI, PTSD, amputations, and burns.[60] As the soldiers tell their stories, their representations are mediated by the site and its mission. The site moves back and forth between their stories and the broader mission, each supporting the other; in so doing, the site plays out the conflicts between the soldiers' personal sense of self and family, and their collective, masculine duties as soldiers. Through this mediated interplay, the gap between the audience's and soldiers' perspectives on identity (rather than the gap between the soldiers' former and present bodies) mends. Significantly, the site allows the soldiers' personal voices to be primary, to be heard, as it were, over the voices of the biomedical and military perspectives. This approach allows the audience to accept the soldiers' representation of their disabilities.

The Wounded Warrior Project began after 9/11; it is widely publicized on television, internet, and radio, and, for all intents and purpose, well received for its efforts. On its homepage, the Wounded Warrior Project announces its mission, "to honor and empower wounded warriors."[61] More specifically, the project aims "to foster the most successful, well-adjusted generation of wounded warriors in this nation's history."[62] To those ends, the organization sells merchandise, provides services, and solicits donations.[63] Naturally, language plays a significant role in those marketing efforts. Also not surprisingly, that language locates the site's mission and the soldiers' stories within a traditional narrative of self-change, the hero quest; in its mission statement, the site characterizes the wounded soldiers as "successful," "well-adjusted, and empower[ed]," that is, as individuals who have overcome the obstacles they have faced.

The language of the modern military hero quest continues when the site introduces the soldiers and contextualizes their stories.

> The Sacrifice Center is designed to tell the stories of America's injured service members, starting with the decision to serve and continuing on through injuries to triumphs and empowerment after their injuries. These stories are shared through our programs, which are structured to nurture the mind and body, and encourage economic empowerment and engagement.[64]

Here, the stories are further characterized in terms of survival, victory, and balance, evident in such words as "triumph" and "empowerment." In this way, the site reinforces the understanding that the veterans are well-adjusted, successful individuals. The notion of "sacrifice" adds a traditional Judeo-Christian element to the hero quest, one which would be familiar to the audience. Thus framed, the soldiers' stories provide a window into their own successful experiences with a difficult foe.

Elsewhere, the site returns to and notes the individuality of the stories, while speaking to the injuries sustained and their aftermath in relatively personalized terms.

> All stories shared in the Sacrifice Center are told through the warriors' eyes. These are their words and their experiences. There are a few stories that go a little more in depth into the serious issues facing our warriors and their families today, including combat stress post-traumatic stress disorder (PTSD) and those who become full-time caregivers for their loved ones; which WWP remains diligently focused on for the long term.[65]

Again, the site stresses that the stories are represented from the soldiers' own perspective. In support of this perspective, the site refers to other personal matters, notably, the soldiers' relationship with their families. By emphasizing the personal side, the site elevates the soldiers' perspective.

In addition to introducing the stories, the site offers some context about how the injuries occurred and were treated.

Also on display is some of the actual body armor which keeps these men and women alive; many of whom would have died in previous conflict without the advancements in body armor. There's a full combat uniform from the day one of our warriors suffered an IED blast and lived to tell about it. The uniform was donated to Wounded Warrior Project™ (WWP) to aid in sharing the story of these brave men and women.[66]

To better understand the soldiers' experience, the site mentions the life-saving technologies that, perhaps ironically, made the Project possible. In so doing, the site recognizes the biomedical perspective associated with the soldiers' survival but subordinates that perspective to their personal experiences.[67]

And it's not just the body armor, but the medical technologies which are helping to save and then enrich the lives of our warriors. You'll see several prostetics [sic] including a prostetic [sic] eye donated by one of our warriors.[68]

In addition to saving their lives, technology (and the generosity of the soldiers) supports their quest to survive successfully. As sponsor of the stories, The Wounded Warrior Project locates the soldiers' personal tales within the typical hero narrative. Although the site acknowledges the biomedical perspective, it downplays the role of technology in the recovery process; as a result, that perspective is subordinated to the soldiers' personal experiences. Thus framed, the wounded soldiers are individual heroes who have overcome incredible obstacles to survive rather than conditions, detached from their bodies and the world (and not likely to overcome that essential naming).

Mediated by hero quest, the writers express their stories in terms which recount their journeys to successful survival. As Chad Brumpton puts it,

I won't let anything hold me down, especially my disability. After the explosion, doctors told me I'd never walk again, but on the day I was discharged from the hospital, I walked out.... There was no way I was going to let anything stop me. I've recently received a pair of running legs. It was the first time I was able to run in five years. I have been able to be more active with my amputation than I was when I was going through limb salvage. I'll never quit. To the end I'll fight or find a way to fix it.[69]

Chad's identity as a soldier assists him in accommodating to his changed bodily state. Because of his sense of duty, he asserts, he will not give up.

In this case, the macho-attitude fits the goals he is undertaking and bridges the gap between military and personal identities. This perspective allows him to remain true to his former sense of self yet discuss his wounded body positively. By blending personal and public identities, with the personal the primary one, he can accept the shift in his bodily condition and implicitly prompts his audience to do so, too.

Other soldiers describe their injuries in highly personal language. While such non-clinical language allows them to acknowledge the medical practices that were vital to their recovery, it also helps the soldiers connect with their wounds and thus accept them. In Anthony Villarreal's terms,

> 'My recovery and rehab was long and painful,' says Anthony. 'Having skin grafts, where they take a piece of your good skin and place it on an area that was burned, is physically and emotionally stressful. But my family helped me through it all.'

> 'My wife and my family were there at my side. But I had had surgery to replace my eyelids, so it was hard for me to look. I was just trying to remember all the faces and recognize everyone's voice.[70]

Thus described, Anthony's personal experience is a tale of recovery, facilitated by family support rather than a detached medical and technology-driven process. It is also a story which connects emotionally with the audience.

Relationships with military "brothers" are especially important to the veterans in their attempts to make sense of their experiences. Interestingly, the soldiers characterize these intensely male relationships, and their role in their recoveries, in emotional language. For Mike Heller,

> perhaps his most dominant emotion, the loss of a friend he couldn't save.

> 'Right there in that garage,' Mike recalls, 'staring at that gear shift, coping with the pain, guilt, and memories, was a turning point for me. I broke down and sought help. I was determined to ensure one thing: I would never put my daughter through an experience like that ever again.'

> And the incessant question in his mind remained: 'What could I have done to change things so Joey could live?'

Mike continues to manage his back pain and his mood swings. He says he'll occasionally go through old photos to remember the good times and he'll reflect on Joey and all the funny things he used to do. It's Mike's silent way to honor Joey.[71]

As Mike relates, his PTSD is linked with and triggered by memories of a friend, Joey, who did not survive. When he is reminded of Joey, Mike does not wonder why he survived and his friend did not (a common reaction to such tragedies), only how he could have been a better soldier. Mike's perspective is extremely personal yet reflects the masculine identity he shared with Joey as members of the military family.

Similarly, Justin Constantine is not afraid to reveal his feelings. "'Even though I try not to,' admits Justin Constantine, 'I still feel embarrassed and guilty about my injury.' A heartfelt confession like.... A heartfelt confession like that can be difficult for a civilian to understand, especially coming from a Marine Corps major who's talking about being shot in the head."[72] Justin's emotional statement about his wounds contrasts starkly with Lost a Leg's clinical description of his amputation. Within this, the site's mediating comment calls attention to the soldier's perspective rather than to the medical model. Justin does not distance himself from the wound; instead, his personal experience takes precedence over more public perspectives on his identity. His display of emotions also connects Justin and his audience.

A similar kind of integration is evident in Anthony's discussion of his very visible skin wounds.

I spent two years at BAMC. When I got out, I struggled with the looks I'd get from everybody. You know, people staring. Sometimes children would see me – this person who'd been burned – and they would get scared. Getting over the fear of people's reaction to me was a big thing for me going back into civilian life.... I want to help wounded warriors in their recovery process. And I want to give insight to civilians that these warriors are out there. Ask us and we'll tell you our story. We're so much more than something to stare at.'[73]

On the one hand, Anthony accepts the visibility of his wounds; on the other hand, he seeks to educate the public to look beyond that surface appearance. His statement, as the ones above, demonstrates a shift in perspective from the one offered by *The Lancet*'s editors. Once more, a soldier represents himself associated with his injuries. Interestingly too, to demonstrate how he musters up his courage, Anthony refers to a play by William Shakespeare, *Henry V*; such a personal and literary reference is a far cry from the medical language found elsewhere in typical combat discussions.[74] Once more, the show of emotions helps the soldier connect with the audience—and not as an object of pity but of praise.

Although the Wounded Warrior Project site offers both the soldiers' perspective and that of the broader military-medical complex, the soldiers' experience is primary. Thus mediated, this online venue allows the soldiers to speak for themselves. True, the transformative capacities of medical technologies underpin the soldiers' success, but that objectifying perspective no longer detaches the patients from their physicians, physical problems, and audiences. In this venue, tensions between autonomy and control are made real in the interplay between site/mission and soldiers/stories. As such, the site's presentation recalls how Anna Trapnel embodied her story in writing and in process for her audience. And, as opposed to Poliomyelitis' situation, here the "fit" feel enthusiastic about the disabled experience, recognize and value their perspective, and, ideally, will make it their own.

Conclusions

Wars often lead to new medical developments, though perhaps no more so than since the American Civil War. Recent life writing about disability by wounded soldiers reflects all the ironies of a world transformed by biomedical classification and global communication practices. Medical technology saves soldiers while leaving them to make sense of acquired disabilities. Technology helps them communicate locally and remotely to those who might better understand the soldiers' injuries from those communicative efforts.

These circumstances have, again ironically, increased the presence and awareness of disability while changing how late twentieth and early twentieth first-century individuals are perceived, treated, and write about those experiences. For many, the ability to express themselves has been enhanced by the availability of personal computers and computerized devices, devises which not only facilitate written communication but also incorporate sound, images, color, and motion (through streaming video) and distribute these stories to a global array of audiences.[75] By bridging the gap between medical technologies and physical problems, online communication is also helping to destigmatize disability. Perhaps, too, these changes will help to dismantle the association between embodied communication and deviant, irrational disabled bodies.

Because the veterans belong to many classes and ethnicities, their stories also represent a space where class, ethnicity and gender (though not gender preference or orientation) merge and work with disability issues. In this venue, disabled soldiers are no longer nobodies with "no body" but somebodies within a long tradition of such bodies.

---

[1] Poliomyelitis, in *Disabilities and How To Live with Them*.

[2] As the editor states in the "Foreword," continuing to offer this perspective, "this book is a collection of true stories written by patients, or former patients, for publication in *The Lancet*. We began to collect them because we knew that people who lose a limb, or become blind of deaf, or have to put up with some chronic illness, often find ingenuous ways of reducing their handicap. We thought that, if a number of such people would tell us how they cope with their different kinds of disability, the information might help our medical readers to foresee and forestall more of the difficulties of their own patients…. Disaster, as everyone knows, is often the means of evoking a person's finest qualities; and this book proves yet again the spirit is more than the flesh, and that a disability is largely what you make of it." Disabilities and How To Live with Them, iii.

[3] See Chapter Nine, p. and Foucault, *The Birth of the Clinic: An Archaeology of Medical Perception*.

[4] Clarke et. al., "Biomedicalization: A Theoretical and Substantive Introduction."

[5] Newman, "Gestural Enthymemes: Delivering Movement in Eighteenth and Nineteenth Century Medical Images."

[6] For example, in 1527, during a battle between the France and the Holy Roman Empire, famed surgeon Ambroise Paré developed the tourniquet. Prior to this invention, wounded limbs were cauterized boiling oil over wounds; the new practice was probably less painful and also allowed the surgical amputation to be more precisely rendered, albeit surgery at the time was a very specialized practice which fell to the speedy and strong. Still, until antibiotics and anesthesia, surgical procedures were dicey at best

[7] Antiseptics were discovered in 1848 by Joseph Lister; see Ellis, *The Cambridge Illustrated History of Surgery*, pp. 63-64.

[8] Finley, *Fields of Combat: Understanding PTSD Among Veterans of Iraq and Afghanistan*, p. 89.

[9] Bennett, "Henry Tonks and His Contemporaries," p. 13.

[10] Alexander, "The Shock of War," p. 59.

[11] Glasser, *Broken Bodies Shattered Minds: A Medical Odyssey From Vietnam to Afghanistan*, p. 21.

[12] Tick, *War and the Soul: Healing Our Nation's Veterans from Post-traumatic Stress Disorder*, p. 2; Lorenz, *Narratives of Rehabilitation and Healing*.

[13] Glasser, *Broken Bodies Shattered Minds: A Medical Odyssey From Vietnam to Afghanistan*, p. 11.

[14] Ibid., p. 21. Research, prompted by the growing numbers of affected, confirms the connection between TBI and PTSD. Both are diagnosed by the following symptoms: concentrating, sleep disturbances, altered moods. Thus far, studies have estimated that about 20 percent of soldiers returning from Iraq and Afghanistan have suffered a mild traumatic brain injury while deployed. Of those, anywhere between 5 percent to nearly 50 percent may suffer both PTSD

and lingering problems from traumatic brain injuries; see Miller, "Healing the Brain, Healing the Mind," p. 515.

[15] Glasser, *Broken Bodies Shattered Minds: A Medical Odyssey From Vietnam to Afghanistan*, p. 31.

[16] Finley, *Fields of Combat: Understanding PTSD Among Veterans of Iraq and Afghanistan*, p. 89.

[17] Ibid., pp. 34-35.

[18] No day passes, it seems, without TV, radio, and online news coverage of these individuals from both sides of the political spectrum. For example, on September 30, 2011, the following report on Wounded Warrior battalion was aired: http://www.cbsnews.com/video/ watch/?id=7382995n.

[19] These characteristics of the disability perspectives not only depend on and mirror medical developments, but social reform. Legislation aimed at education, jobs, and civil rights has helped individuals close the gap but not often be seen as equal , for example, in the United States, Rehabilitation Act of 1973; Individuals with Disabilities Education Act of 1975; Americans with Disabilities Act of 1990; the Independent Living Movement; and in England, The Disabled Persons Act and the new National Assistance Act.

[20] These values affect all soldiers, male and female alike. Because masculinity is a symbolic notion and based on a spectrum, and because women in the military are on some level enculturated into that world, they too can and are affected by these perceptions of disability. Other factors will also affect them based on gender and personal identity issues.

[21] Finley, *Fields of Combat: Understanding PTSD Among Veterans of Iraq and Afghanistan*, pp. 7-8.

[22] Ibid., p. 100.

[22] Ibid., p. 89.

[23] D.C. Gill, *How We Are Changed by War: A Study of Letters and Diaries from Colonial Conflicts to Operation Iraqi Freedom*, p. 3.

[24] Ibid., p. 2.

[25] Glasser, *Broken Bodies Shattered Minds: A Medical Odyssey From Vietnam to Afghanistan*, pp. 183-5.

[26] Gerschick and Miller, "Coming to Terms: Masculinity and Physical Disability," pp. 183-204.

[27] Ibid., p. 160.

[28] Clark, *Wounded Soldier, Healing Warrior: A Personal Story of a Vietnam Veteran Who Lost His Kegs but Found His Soul*, wrote on in 2007 and Dole, *A Soldier's Story: A Memoir*, in 2005 and as a well-known politician.

[29] Frank, "The Rhetoric of Self-Change: Illness Experience as Narrative," and *The Wounded Storyteller: Body, Illness, and Ethics*.

[30] Frank, *The Wounded Storyteller: Body, Illness, and Ethics*, p. 48.

[31] In the Western tradition, these narratives go back at least to Homer and appear in texts from that time till the present.

[32] Frank, *The Wounded Storyteller: Body, Illness, and Ethics*, pp. 41-45; Ibid., p. 45.

[33] Ibid., p. 13.

[34] Ibid., p. 7.

[35] Couser, "Introduction: The Empire of the 'Normal': A Forum on Disability and Self-Representation," p. 305.

[36] Couser, "Autopathography: Women, Illness, and Lifewriting," p. 165.

[37] Couser, G. Thomas, *Recovering Bodies: Illness, Disability, and Life Writing*, p. 11.

[38] Kuuisisto, *Planet of the Blind*; Mairs, *Waist-High in the World. A Life Among the Disabled*.

[39] Couser, "Autopathography: Women, Illness, and Lifewriting," p. 165.

[40] Ibid., p. 175.

[41] Couser, *Recovering Bodies: Illness, Disability, and Life Writing*, p. 288.

[42] Ibid, p. 8.

[43] See Jaeger, *Disability and the Internet*; "'This Stuff Doesn't Change the World'": Disability and Steve Jobs' Legacy," http://www.wired.com/epicenter/2011/10/steve-jobs-disability/

[44] See Chapter 9, p. 221, for example.

[45] Song, Virtual Communities: Bowling Alone, Online Together, chapter 5.

[46] Ibid.; Jaeger, *Disability and the Internet*.

[47] According to Patrick Thomas, soldiers are not yet blogging about their disabilities, a circumstance that heightens the importance of the sites I discuss below.

[48] *Disabilities and How To Live with Them*, p. 141.

[49] Ibid., p. 141.

[50] Ibid., p. 141.

[51] Ibid. ,p. 142.

[52] Ibid., p. 143.

[53] Ibid., p. 143.

[54] Ibid., p. 143.

[55] Ibid., p. 143.

[56] Ibid., p. 144.

[57] Ibid., p. 144.

[58] Ibid., pp. 144-5.

[59] For various reasons, I am not focusing on other intentions the site's sponsors may have in downplaying certain aspects of the military perspective. My purpose here is not overtly political but rather designed to examine how the disabled soldiers represent their identities. If anything, this study shows how, till the present, the disabled have never been able to represent themselves unmediated by cultural context. Necessarily, too, I focus on the words alone. The site is filled with visuals and videos which support the language and add to it, too.

[60] These 13 include: Claude Boushey, Justin Constantine, Roberto Cruz, Paul De La Cerda, Harold Freeman, David Guzman, Mike Heller, Severa Rodriguez, Deron Santiny, Mike Smee, Anthony Villarreal, and Brent Whitten.

[61] http://www.woundedwarriorproject.org/

[62] http://www.woundedwarriorproject.org/mission/who-we-serve.aspx

[63] The project supports television ads, too. As I am suggesting, despite the military nature of the site, it has indeed received wide and universal acceptance.

[64] http://www.woundedwarriorproject.org/mission/sacrifice-center.aspx

[65] http://www.woundedwarriorproject.org/mission/sacrifice-center.aspx

[66] http://www.woundedwarriorproject.org/mission/sacrifice-center.aspx

[67] This subordination conforms to the hierarchical operations of the military establishment.

[68] http://www.woundedwarriorproject.org/mission/sacrifice-center.aspx

[69]http://www.woundedwarriorproject.org/mission/meet-a-warrior/chad-brumpton.aspx

[70] http://www.woundedwarriorproject.org/mission/meet-a-warrior/anthony-villarreal.aspx

[71]   http://www.woundedwarriorproject.org/mission/meet-a-warrior/mike-heller.aspx

[72]   http://www.woundedwarriorproject.org/mission/meet-a-warrior/justin-constantine.aspx

[73] http://www.woundedwarriorproject.org/mission/meet-a-warrior/anthony-villarreal.aspx

[74] Ibid.

[75] Jaeger, *Disability and the Internet*.

9

Into the Twenty-First Century: Presence in the Digital Age

As with many proverbial projects, this one began with an instinct and an ambitious goal. That aim: to recover a history of life writing about disability prior to the twentieth century and Keller's work. Also typical of such projects, this one developed into more than originally conceived. The unexpected wealth of untapped, original materials I unearthed required me to select and frame the study in particular ways. Accordingly, I characterized literary genres as social practices and analyzed them based on a composite methodology, one which recognized texts in their originating cultures and as those perspectives informed contemporary ones as reappropriations. Together, this framing and these many materials have allowed me to overturn my initial assumption while examining how conceptions of disability and representations of it by those thus marked, have developed and shifted over many centuries, millennia in fact.

Although the sources discussed in this study are diverse, certain core themes have emerged, themes associated with the portrayal and acceptance of disability as visible and as felt, or embodied. To conclude, I return to these themes in their historical contexts and as reappropriated into the present, offering some final thoughts on how individuals have and can identify as disabled and complicating the notion that past perspectives on disability are simply outdated and have little to offer the present.

Presence as Perspective

My inquiry has embraced Western concepts of disability in terms of its presence, that is, the inevitable presence of human physical variations as well as the human propensity, seemingly inevitable, to regulate perceptions of that presence and thus construct notions of disability. The earliest recorded Western notions of disability I examined reflect a simple but significant practical circumstance: the public landscape in ancient societies was populated with people manifesting many physical variations, congenital and acquired, permanent and temporary. Few among us today have witnessed the incredible variety of differences that were publicly visible in the ancient world. Based on their cultural resources, particularly their civic ideals of a successful life and their abstract, humoral, relatively rudimentary knowledge of the body, ancient Greece and Rome societies made sense of that physical variety not by focusing on visible categories but by concentrating on how those attributes affected civic success. To that end, citizens considered physical differences as either cosmetic or functional, the latter in association with what we now call disability. As the stories of Lahda and Isocrates' pensioner in Chapter Two indicated, physical problems were considered cosmetic if individuals could fulfill their civic responsibilities regardless of their specific physical attributes; despite being lame, Lahda could reproduce and the pensioner could travel by horse. Certainly, what were perceived as cosmetic physical differences had important consequences in their lives; looking less than the proportional ideal of beauty reflected poorly on these individuals in aesthetic, economic, and moral terms. Nonetheless, their cosmetic difference did not render those persons disabled. That status was associated with individuals whose physical differences prevented them from being successful, that is, from performing their civic functions. Because of their severe injuries, the Greek soldiers at Persepolis could no longer pursue their role as warriors. Effectively disabled, they stayed as a group in Persepolis where they had developed new civic bonds. Similarly, Aristides could not orate when disabled by pain nor could Seneca fully participate as Roman citizen when overtaken by age. Accordingly, these disabled Greeks and Romans felt and represented their identity in ways reflecting their diminished civic functions and, with that, correspondingly diminished social bonds.

Broadly speaking, this perspective on disability continued through the high medieval period. Despite a shift in the governing body from city-state to Church, physical variations remained a non-categorical presence, a presence experienced and represented within a felt sense of social obligations; this sense was still based on the humoral correspondence between outer physicality and inner spirituality. Given that society's concerns with achieving salvation, the high medieval women visionaries in the study used their disabled earthly state as a location, a mediating point, from which to move towards the perfection of body and soul necessary for them to arrive in heaven. As such, their disablement was manifested and represented through their bodies in a felt sense of physical difference; that felt sense, associated with pain and love, was particularly salient for women whose bodies were considered by nature deficient.

In the Greek, Roman and high medieval life writing texts, then, physical variation became disability when it interfered with an individual's ability to fulfill her/his social expectations; framed in this way, the life writers represented disability through their particular bodies as a felt rather than visible, categorical presence. These characteristics reflected the cultural conflation of bodily impropriety and disability along lines of medical and communication practices especially.

As chapters five through seven detailed, from the early modern period onward, increasing standardization in virtually all aspects of Western society undermined the non-categorical, openly felt conception of disability. Specific standards began to matter. Although these concerns led to medical practices which eased the burdens of many problematic conditions, quality of life issues as we now call it, these standards rendered physical differences, in all their ability to be observed, an easy target for classification and in turn for marginalization. In such an environment, individuals with physical differences were classified as abnormal or deviant. Such difference became a complex, categorical, and visible presence rather a felt public one, as well as the disabling basis on which abnormal individuals were first identified by observation and then hidden within institutions or exhibited as spectacles.

Printing helped to distribute these norms, aid standardization, and enable the individual to read and write on his/her own rather than as part of a group. Such standardization also affected medical categorization, diagnosis, and treatment; with this focus on the specific, disability was increasingly a heightened, dependent presence and one not always welcome in public. The works of Hay, Husson, and Keller all respond to these developments involving individual, categorical, and exceptional differences. While Hay and Husson each wrote ironically to overturn the norms within which they had to contend, Keller challenged those norms with openness rather than irony.

As Chapter Eight emphasized, the categorical presence of disability is very much alive in the twenty-first century as conceptualized in the latest version of the medical model. As world population increases, humans live longer, despite a multitude of increasingly more specifically categorized congenital and acquired physical differences. These differences, too often the outcome of war, previously compromised life and life span before they could emerge as disabilities. At present, then, disability is a potential threat to everyone and hardly a simple presence in the everyday environment.[1] These circumstances depend in part on developing technologies. Assistive technologies, power-chairs, for example, help people pursue proper lives in urban, industrialized environments. Sonar sensors now offer the blind the opportunity to ride bicycles.[2] So, too, do medical technologies and surgical procedures, for example, prosthetics and transplants, enable individuals with physical differences to participate with and in the world in more seemingly transparent ways. And, computer and informational technologies, voice recognition among many others, facilitate human interaction and communication asynchronically and remotely, mobility or communication differences aside.[3] These technologies have been a boon to communication on many levels; in particular, they have provided material support for the recent surge of life writing about disability which forms the backdrop for this study.

In addition to their benefits, these technologies create new, problematic hierarchies of impairments while complicating existing ones, these by and large associated with visibility as well as with such categories as gender, sexual orientation, class, and ethnicity. For one thing, to know about and access technology requires education, opportunity, and income, commodities not equally available to all humans worldwide.[4] For another, individuals who acquire disabilities in their life course must adapt to shifting identities in association with technologies which call attention to their similarly shifting bodily status. As the previous chapter discussed, an injured male war veteran returning to civilian life in a power-chair may confront complex issues involving his masculinity and/or his class.[5] The process of adjusting to physical change is hardly new; but the context, with its very visible technologies, expansive categories, and threatening potential to affect all human lives, changes the nature of the shift and the identities involved.

Finally, although many of these technologies are designed to offer individuals more healthcare options and more freedom to choose them, they promote physical normalization.[6] By reifying the perfect body as normal and opposing it to a broader range of defective conditions, medical procedures, reconstructive surgeries most obviously but numerous designer subspecialties as well, encourage an "aestheticizing" approach to the body; this approach places an undue burden on all members of society to be physically normal, especially those not considered normal to start.[7] As Couser points out, "The surgeries that are increasing in frequency serve not to efface ethnicity—as the nose job historically has done—but to forestall or reverse the effects of ageing; rather than disguising our different origins, plastic surgery today tends to deny our common destiny."[8] By making physical variations and disability more visible rather than more transparent, these technologies undermine what they presumably set out to accomplish. This contemporary focus on appearance also recalls the ancient notion of cosmetic difference but locates it within the domain of disability with all of its additional intolerances.

It is time to consider what pre-twentieth century life writers can contribute to these current complexities involving disability, on the one hand and categories, visibility, and technologies, on the other. As I have framed it, earlier cultures did not consider physical variations as disabling per se; instead, disability was felt, or embodied, when it prevented people from living successfully. Of course, these values fostered horrendous intolerance towards those deemed unsuccessful, i.e., outsiders; what the ancient and medieval societies lacked in rigid medical categories they more than made up for in rigid social notions of belonging. Still, a measure of this kind of acceptance, this looking past difference per se, could counter the increasing emphasis on visible and categorical normality in a world in which the specter of acquired disability is always present. This reappropriated perspective on physical difference allows technologies their assistive but not their visible normalizing roles; this is already the case with certain technologies, eyeglasses, for example, which are no longer a visible sign of disability. Reappropriating this non-categorical presence of disability also requires adjusting other social norms involving success. Whatever they might be, these standards must look beyond the ancient intolerance for outsiders as well as the more recent tragic and miracle models which conjure up the unfortunate notions of spectacle or pity.[9]

This approach is beautifully illustrated in an event which Tobin Siebers discusses, involving a confrontation between legal, social, and ability issues.[10] In 2000, a lodge in New Hampshire was mandated by the ADA to install expensive ramps, even though, the owners argued, the lodge was quite remote.

> Jill Gravink, the director of Northeast Passage, led a group of three hikers in wheelchairs and two on crutches on a twelve-hour climb to the lodge, at the end of which they rolled happily up the ramp to its front door. A local television reporter on the scene asked why, if people in wheelchairs could drag themselves up the trail, they could not drag themselves up the steps into the hut, implying that the ramp was a waste of money. Gravink responded, "Why bother putting steps on the hut at all? Why not drag yourself in through a window?"[11]

Although Siebers uses the incident to demonstrate a key point about the socially constructed nature of disability vis-à-vis ability and identity, in this context, the event illuminates how accepting disability's presence as non-categorical might be linked with constructive standards of success. Or, as the life writers in this study might put it, it is not what we see and not how we get it done that matters. No body and nobody are inherently disabled.

In theory, this approach would eventually obliterate the notion of disability. And, it would obviate the need to write about disability as I have defined it, since, from my perspective, individuals must perceive themselves as disabled (though not necessarily accept that perception) to write about that status. In reality, this disappearance is not likely to happen soon; it is clear from this study's long historical view that ways of marginalizing have always managed to reproduce themselves on some level. But, it is as good a time as ever to shift the burden, or body, of proof, so to speak.

Writing and the Body: Form, Function, and Felt Experience

In conjunction with its long perspective on the presence of disability, my study has also focused on how individuals who identify as disabled represent that identity not only in terms of content but also of genres and style. As a group, the authors in this study used cultural conventions to represent their felt, embodied sense of self. Although this embodied sense of self has long been associated with figurative language and irrational and hence improper disabled thinking, these authors provide a means of dismantling that thinking. They demonstrate that writing is a meaningful act, that is, a process that requires the entire human, body and mind. Using all materials and senses available to them, their writing heals the mind-body gap; by breaking down the normative assumption that only clear, rational words communicate logical, substantive content, they break down the implicit divide it sets up between presumably normal and deviant bodies, and their public presences.

In part because disability was such an everyday presence, this study's earlier authors manifested this embodied, felt sense openly. They had no choice, because disability was so often on public display. Although the life writers I examined were writers (except for the Greek soldiers), they communicated by representing their felt, embodied sense of self in ways which explicitly manifested their marginalized status. In that earliest text examined in this study, from the predominantly oral Greek world, communication involved actual physical, aural exchange; the medium and message were felt and embodied simultaneously and publicly. Thus, each bodily act engendered a reaction from the interlocutor. Through such ongoing deliberation, between men in the case of the Greek soldiers and between man and god in Aristides' case, ideas could be worked out as an embodied interchange of ideas, an interchange which integrated body and mind.[12]

The oral performative element remained, though often submerged, in subsequent life writing. In the high medieval and early modern texts, bodies became the mediating point around which the visionary women represented their felt sense of disablement. In this case, the embodied representation united bodies and souls. Although their stories now survive in print, they began as bodily actions and spoken words preserved through dictation; these complex acts reproduced actual feelings and responses exchanged between several individuals, mediums and modes, that is, in several material forms and formats. That personal, implicit sense of embodiment was fully represented when Trapnel went public with her bodily communication; by embodying her actions in her actual presentations of them, she adds explicitly interactive aural and gestural elements.

From the mid-sixteenth century, this open felt sense was marginalized; limiting communicative options reflected the demands of social standardization, also manifested in the rise of the medical model, mass printing and the developing individual sense of self. Because the printed text relied on standardized arbitrary conventions (letters) rather than natural movements and lines (rendered by the body), it became the culturally primary form of communication. From this perspective, logical, disembodied printed discourse was superior to emotional, subjective images and movements. To communicate appropriately in this realm, individuals necessarily wrote within the prevailing disembodied conventions. Disabled individuals such as Hay and Husson discussed their embodied physical difference by subverting their felt sense of body within ironic, emotional, turns of argument and speech; in so doing, they advocated for difference and challenged the conventions that effectively disabled their bodies. Necessarily, then, Hay and Husson adapted the disembodied print medium and its conventions and the disablement it represented; accordingly, they embodied their unconventional identity in the ironic, figural language of the conventional satire. Similarly, and despite their overt use of conventional terminology, the nineteenth century asylum inmates represented their felt sense of self in part by means of style and arrangement rather than presumably logical arguments. Finally, by openly acknowledging and integrating the various feelings, senses, and modes of communication available to her, Keller helped her readers collaborate and identify with her. She opened up a comfort zone of difference in which Wounded Warriors currently write blogs and other online materials. Because their stories combine so many media and modes, they embody many possibilities for rethinking what disability is and how and what it communicates.

Thus, each of the life writers represented her/his sense of self and identity by communicating with, through, and about the body. Doing so undermines the prevailing sense that logic resides only in numbers and clear, rational, non-figurative or non-embodied words. Instead, as the authors demonstrate, the mind and body participate together in meaning making. Their work calls attention to how writing, i.e. communication, is vital to articulating one's identity and sense of self as disabled or otherwise; it also reiterates and reinforces the value of human communication in private as well as public forms and forums.

By offering their felt, accepted experiences of the body, these stories offer a perspective on a contemporary dilemma about communicative technologies and practice in a multimodal environment. The print linguistic bias towards expression in logical words rather subjective images, sounds, and movements still retains its strength in many contemporary circles. Its supporters contend that computers and touch screens, avatars and animation, are game-like diversions that dumb down communication.[13] In essence, this position is an expression of fear, fear of the body's return to communication practices. More specifically, this fear involves the disabled body, the body long associated with irrationality, underdevelopment, and deviance, and the body now visible in greater threatening numbers in contemporary publics.

But, as this study has certainly shown, print linguistic literacy is a relatively recent phenomenon; for the better part of our existence, humans have not communicated primarily in print but in many modes and media.[14] Most extant ancient and medieval sources were not written on paper or parchment but manifested visually and materially in sculpture, architecture, and the like. And many more sources, now lost, were temporal public performances.

Thus, the print linguistic perspective is not only misguided as a social practice but also as a historical phenomenon. Accordingly, many twenty-first century citizens support new communication practices, and interdisciplinary researchers attempt to better understand how human interact and communicate on many complex levels reaching beyond the printed word on the page. As George Lakoff and Mark Johnson have demonstrated, the language we use embodies the world we inhabit.[15] When English speakers feel "up," they are conceptualizing in words a prevailing Judeo-Christian sense, a sense felt both metaphorically and physically, of what "good" means—it resides above us in heaven. In contrast, in the earth-centered Hmong culture, the correlate phrase represents happy individuals as feeling "down," where their spiritual beings reside. In additional to demonstrating the physically and culturally constructed nature of words, scholars have shown how writing itself, is an embodied act involving movement and gesture.[16] Other scholars have considered the materials out of which these acts are made, investigating how images, movements, and sounds function in contemporary documents. According to The New London Group, there are six modes with which we communicate (the linguistic, visual, audio, gestural, spatial and multimodal patterns of meaning). And, other scholars examine how bodily and facial movement, thought, and speech contribute as a unit to the communicative act.[17]

Such research confirms that human bodies belong to and inform how we understand, make sense of, and communicate in our world. By demonstrating how movement, rhythm, and timing belong to human interaction, these efforts also confirm that writing is an embodied action, involving a felt presence, more than one sense, and more than one mode and medium of representation. From this perspective, one supported by this study's life writers, it is impossible to communicate without using our minds and our bodies.[18] From this perspective, too, the split between the mind as rational and body as deviant is entirely invalid. No language, figurative embodied, for example, is inherently subjective, irrational, and deviant. As Mark Johnson puts it,

> There is a nonlinguistic dimension ... that gets its fulfillment in and through the words we try out as candidates to complete the line. This felt sense of the situation is not the words of forms alone. Yet neither is this felt sense of the situation utterly distinct or separate from the words or forms or distinctions ... they [the felt sense and the formal expression] are two dimensions of a simple ongoing activity of meaning-making, each one intrinsically related to the other.[19]

When the life writers in this study challenge cultural norms by representing their identities through embodied and metaphorical language, they implicitly recognized and confirmed that human communication best engages all parts of the human rather than hiding the body to favor the mind. In so doing, their stories show us that neither the mind and body nor reason and emotion are ever entirely disengaged from each other. Reappropriated, their felt senses of representation can reinvigorate, without negating, the print linguistic heritage that has preserved them and help integrate print linguistic and multi-modal means of communication. Such reinvigoration will also break done assumptions that disability is irrational and communicated in a like manner.

I intended and intend this book as a start, a provocation, and a prompt to study a neglected and important topic. To that end, I have necessarily taken both a broad and a narrow path, looking across categories and historical periods as well as into particular stories. In this way, I hope to have practiced the kind of acceptance I have found so compelling in the accounts I have examined as well as to have offered my own felt sense of their meaning (constrained though it is by the academic printed page).

As I pointed out in Chapter One, life writing's current popularity is due, in part, to a world in which people communicate often and with more material means than ever before. This study has allowed some marginalized voices to speak for themselves and correct or complicate some misconceptions. Their work not only demonstrates that the current popularity of life writing about disability has a long history; these authors also teach us that knowing what it means to be human also means learning from those often considered to be less human.

---

[1] At present, scholars and advocates, have developed models which recognize and integrate current issues of life course and acquired disability. Darling and Heckert ("Orientations toward Disability: Difference over the Lifecourse") introduced the concept of the disability orientation, while Swain and French counter those who focus on the problem by offering the non-tragic model which looks to the individual. Although these efforts complicate the social model, they do not address the visibility issues mentioned above.

[2] For a national Public Radio account on this issue, aired on March 13, 2011, see http://www.npr.org/2011/03/13/134425825/human-echolocation-using-sound-to-see.

[3] Despite technology, studies show that disabled people are still more often excluded from employment in the informational sector; this fact may effect current welfare provisions; see Sapey, "Disablement in the Informational Age," p. 619.

[4] Jaeger, *Disability and the Internet*.

[5] Gerschick and Miller, "Coming to Terms: Masculinity and Physical Disability," pp. 183-204; Baker, *The Politics of Neurodiversity*.

[6] Hughes, "Medicine and the Aesthetic Validation of Disabled People," p. 563.

[7] Ibid., p. 561.

[8] Couser, *Recovering Bodies: Illness, Disability, and Life Writing*, p. 10.

[9] See Swain and French, "Towards an Affirmation Model of Disability"; Baker, *The Politics of Neurodiversity*.

[10] Siebers, *Disability Theory*.

[11] Ibid., pp. 30-31.

[12] Hawhee, *Bodily Arts: Rhetoric and Athletics in Ancient Greece*.

[13] Stafford, *Artful Science: Enlightenment Entertainment and the Eclipse of Visual Education,* "Introduction."

[14] Ibid., p. xxvii.

[15] Lakoff and Johnson, *Metaphors We Live By.*

[16] Haas and Witte, "Writing as an Embodied Practice: The Case of Engineering Standards; Sigrid Streit, *Gesture and Rhetorical Delivery: The Transmission of Knowledge in Complex Situations.*

[17] Ekman and Rosenberg, Eds. *What the Face Reveals: Basic and Applied Studies of Spontaneous Expression using the Facial Action Coding System* (FACS); Goldin-Meadow, *Hearing Gesture: How Our Hands Help Us Think*; Kendon, *Gesture: Visible Action as Utterance*; McNeil, *Gesture and Thought.*

[18] Johnson, *The Meaning of the Body: Aesthetics of Human Understanding.*

[19] Ibid., pp. 80-81.

Bibliography

Agnew, Anna. *From Under the Cloud; or, Personal Reminiscences of Insanity.* Cincinnati: Robert Clarke and Co., 1887.

Alexander, Sally Hobart and Robert Alexander. *She Touched the World: Laura Bridgman, Deaf-Blind Pioneer.* NY: Clarion Books, 2008.

Allen, Hannah. *A Narrative of God's Gracious Dealings. With that Choice Christian Mrs. Hannah Allen.* London: John Wallis, 1683.

American Psychiatric Association. *Diagnostic Statistic Manual of Mental Disorders (DSM-IV).* 4th ed. Rev.ed. Washington, D.C.: American Psychiatric Association, 1994.

American Psychiatric Association. *Diagnostic Statistic Manual of Mental Disorders. (DSM-III-R).* 3rd ed. Rev.ed. Washington, D.C.: American Psychiatric Association, 1986.

Aristides, Aelius. *Aristides.* 4 vols. Charles Behr, Transl. Cambridge: Harvard University Press, 1973.

Aristotle. *The Complete Works.* 2 vols. Jonathan Barnes, Transl. Oxford: Oxford University Press, 1982.

Aronowitz, Robert. *A. Making Sense of Illness: Science, Society, and Disease.* Cambridge: Cambridge University Press, 1998.

Aterman, Kurt. "From Horus the Child to Hephaestus Who Limps: A Romp Through History." *American Journal of Medical Genetics* 83 (1999): 53-63.

Audelay, John. *The Poems.* London: The Early English Text Society/Humphrey Milford, Oxford University Press, 1931.

Augustine. *The Confessions of St. Augustine.* E. B. Pusey, Transl. NY: J. B. Alden, 1892.

Augustine. *The City of God.* In *Nicene and Post-Nicene Fathers.* Vol. 2 Philip Schaff, Ed. Peabody, MA: Henrickson Publishers, 1995. 1-511.

Bacon, Francis. "Of Deformity." 1625. In *Francis Bacon: The Major Words.* Ed. Brian Vickers. Oxford: Oxford University Press, 1996: 426-427.

Bacon, Francis. *The Advancement of Learning.* 1640. Alburgh: Archival Facsimiles, 1987.

Baker, Dana Lee. *The Politics of Neurodiversity: Why Public Policy Matters.* (Disability in Society Series) Boulder, CO: Lynne Rienner Publishers, 2011.

Baird Joseph, Ed. *The Personal Correspondence of Hildegard of Bingen.* Oxford: Oxford University Press, 2006.

Baird, Joseph and Radd Ehrman. Trans. *The Letters of Hildegard of Bingen.* Vol. 1. NY: Oxford University Press, 1994.

Barros, Carolyn A. and Johanna M. Smith. *Life-Writings by British Women 1660-1850: An Anthology.* Boston: Northeastern University Press, 2000.

Bauby, Jean-Dominique. *The Diving Bell and the Butterfly.* NY: Random House, 1997.

Behr, Charles. Aelius Aristides. *The Complete Works.* Vol 1. Leiden: E.J. Brill, 1986.

Behr, Charles. *Aelius Aristides and The Sacred Tales.* Amsterdam: Adolf M. Hakkert, 1968.

Benson, Luther. *Fifteen Years in Hell. An Autobiography.* Indianapolis, IN: Carlon and Hollenbeck, 1881.

Berrios, G. and M. Gili. "Will and its Disorders: a Conceptual History." *History of Psychiatry* 6 (1995): 87-104.

Berkenkotter, Carol. *Patient Tales. Case Histories and the Uses of Narrative in Psychiatry.* Columbia, SC: University of South Carolina Press, 2008.

Berthier, Ferdinand. *Forging Deaf Education in Nineteenth-Century France. Biographical Sketches of Bébian, Sicard, Massieu, and Clerc.* Freeman G. Henry, Transl. and Ed. Washington D.C.: Gallaudet University Press, 2009.

Boaistuau, Pierre. *Histoires Prodigeuses.* Paris: Vincent Sertenas Libraire, 1560.

Bogusslavsky, Julien. and Francois Boller, Eds. *Neurological Disorders in Famous Artists.* Part 1. London: Karger, 2005.

Bogusslavsky, Julien. and Michael Hennerici, Eds. *Neurological Disorders in Famous Artists.* Part 2. London: Karger, 2007.

Boissier de Sauvages. *Nosologie Méthodique: ou Distribution des Maladies en Classes, en Genres et en Espèces, Suivant L'esprit de Sydenham, & la Methode des Botanistes.* M. Gouvion, Transl. Lyon: Jean-Marie Bruyset, 1772.

Boswell, James. *Boswell's Life of Johnson.* Volume I. G.B. Hill Ed. Oxford: Clarendon Press, 1934/1791.

Bright, Timothy. *A Treatise of Melancholie.* 1586. NY: Facsimile Text Society: Columbia University Press, 1940.

Brisenden, Simon, "Independent Living and the Medical Model of Disability." *Disability, Handicap and* Society 1 (1986): 173-8.

Brody, Howard. *Stories of Sickness.* New Haven, CT: Yale University Press, 1987.

Brueggemann, Brenda Jo. *Lend Me Your Ear: Rhetorical Constructions of Deafness.* Washington, D.C.: Gallaudet University Press, 1999.

Bucknill, John Charles. *Notes on Asylums for the Insane in America.* Reprint, NY: Arno Press, 1973/1876.

Burr, George Lincoln. *Narratives of the Witchcraft Cases. 1648-1706.* NY: George Scribner's Sons, 1914.

Burton, Robert. *The Anatomy of Melancholy.* Floyd Dell and Paul Jordan-Smith, Eds. New York: Tudor Publishing Co, 1927/1651.

Butler, Cuthbert. *Western Mysticism.* London: Constable, 1922.

Bynum, Caroline Walker. *Holy Feast and Holy Fast: The Religious Significance of Food to Medieval Women.* Berkeley: University of California Press, 1987.

Caciola, Nancy. *Discerning Spirits. Divine and Demonic Possession in the Middle Ages*. Ithaca, NY: Cornell University Press, 2003.

Caciola, Nancy. "Mystics, Demoniacs, and the Physiology of Spirit Possession in Medieval Europe." *Comparative Studies in Society and History* 42/2 (April 2000): 296-306.

Cartwright, Lisa. *Screening the Body. Tracing Medicine's Visual Culture*. Minneapolis, MN: University of Minnesota Press, 1995.

Caterina da Siena. *Saint Catherine of Siena as Seen in Her Letters*. Vida D. Scudder, Transl., Ed. London: J.M. Dent and Sons, Ltd. 1911.

Channel, Elinor. "A Message from God, by a Dumb Woman. 1653/4. Microfilm. BL, G. 16132: 1-7.

Charon, Rita. *Narrative Medicine: Honoring the Stories of Illness*. NY: Oxford University Press, 2009.

Chase, Hiram. *Two years and four months in a lunatic asylum: from August 20th, 1863, to December 20th, 1865*. Saratoga Springs: Van Benthuysen and Son's, 1868.

Cheyne, George. The English Malady. NY: Scholars Facsimiles and reprints, 1976/1733.

Cicero, *De Inventione*. H.M. Hubbell, Transl. Cambridge: Harvard University Press, 1949.

Clarke, Adele E. et. al., "Biomedicalization: A Theoretical and Substantive Introduction." In *Biomedicalization: Technoscience, Health, and Illness in the U.S.*, Adele, E Clarke, et. al., Eds. Durham NC: Duke 2010:1-46.

Cohen, Beth. Ed. *Not the Classical Ideal: Athens and the Construction of the Other in Greek Art*. Leiden: Brill, 2000.

Cohen, Edward H. "An Uncollected Hospital Essay by W.E. Henley." *Prose Studies* 28/3 (December 2006): 258-266.

Cohen, Jeffrey Jerome. *Hybridity, Identity, and Monstrosity in Medieval Britain: On Difficult Middles*. Hampshire, England: Palgrave Macmillan, 2006.

Coleman, Patrick. "Introduction: life-writing and the legitimation of the modern self." In *Representations of the Self from the Renaissance to Romanticism*. P. Coleman, J. Lewis, and J. Kowalik, Eds. NY: Cambridge University Press, 2002: 1-16.

Corbeill, Anthony. *Controlling Laughter: Political Humor in the Late Roman Republic*. Princeton, N.J.: Princeton University Press, 1996.

Couser, G.Thomas. "Conflicting Paradigms: The Rhetoric of Disability Memoirs." In *Embodied Rhetorics: Disability in Language and Culture*. J.C. Wilson and C. Lewiecki-Wilson, Eds. Carbondale, IL: Southern Illinois University Press, 2001: 78-91.

Couser, G. Thomas. *Recovering Bodies: Illness, Disability, and Life Writing*. Madison: University of Wisconsin Press, 1994.

Couser, G. Thomas. "Autopathography: Women, Illness, and Lifewriting." In *Women and Autobiography*. M. W. Brownley and A. B. Kimmich, Eds. Wilmington, DE: Scholarly Resources Books, 1999:163-175.

Couser, G. Thomas. *Signifying Bodies: Disability in Contemporary Life Writing*. Ann Arbor, MI: University of Michigan Press, 2009.

Couser, G. Thomas, Ed. "Special Issue on Disability and Life Writing." *Journal of Cultural and Disability Studies*, 5. Spring 2011.

Covey, Herbert. *Social Perceptions of People with Disabilities in History*. Springfield, IL: Charles C. Thomas, 1998.

Crow, Liz. "Helen Keller: Rethinking the Problematic Icon." *Disability and Society* 15/6 (2000): 845-859.

Crowe, Ann Mary. "*A Letter to Dr. Robert Darling Willis; To Which Are Added Copies of Three Other Letters; Published in the Hope of Rousing A Humane Nation to the Consideration of the Miseries Arising from Private Madhouses*." London: R. Ryan, 1811.

Cullen, William. *First Lines of the Practice of Physic*. 4th edition. Edinburgh: C. Elliot. 1784.

Cullen, William. *A Synopsis of Methodical Nosology: in which the Genera of Disorders are Particularly Defined, and the Species Added with the Synonimous of those from Sauvages.* Philadelphia: Parry Hall,1793.

Dain, Norman. *Concepts of Insanity in the United States, 1789-1865*. Brunswick, NJ: Rutgers University Press, 1964.

Darling, Rosalyn B. and D. Alex Heckert. "Orientations Toward Disability: Difference over the Lifecourse." *International Journal of Disability, Development and Education,* 57/2 (June 2010): 131-143.

Dasen, Véronique. *Dwarfs in Ancient Egypt and Greece*. Oxford: Clarendon Press, 1993.

Davies, Eleanor. *Prophetic Writings of Lady Eleanor Davies*. Ester S. Cope, Ed. NY: Oxford University Press, 1995.

Davis, Leonard J. "Constructing Normalcy: The Bell Curve, the Novel, and the Invention of the Disabled Body in the Nineteenth Century." In *The Disability Studies Reader.* Davis, L.J. Ed. New York: Routledge/Taylor and Francis Group, 2006: 3-16.

Davis, Leonard J. "The End of Identity Politics and the Beginning of Dismodernism. On Disability as an Unstable Category." In *The Disability Studies Reader*. Davis, L.J. Ed. New York: Routledge/Taylor and Francis Group, 2006: 231-242.

Davis, Leonard J. Ed. *The Disability Studies Reader*. NY: Routledge/Taylor and Francis Group, 2006.

Davis, Leonard J. "Dr. Johnson, Amelia, and the Discourse of Disability in the Eighteenth Century." In *Defects: Engendering the Modern Body*. E. Deutsch and F. Nussbaum, Eds. Ann Arbor, MI: University of Michigan Press, 2000. 54-74.

Davis, Phebe B. *The Travels and Experiences of Miss Phebe Davis, of Barnard, Windsor County, VT, Being a Sequel to Her Two Years and Three Months in the N.Y. State Lunatic Asylum in Utica N Y*. Syracuse, NY: J. G. K. Truair and Co., 1860.

Davis, Phebe B., *Two Years and Three Months in the New York Lunatic Asylum, at Utica: Together with the Outlines of Twenty Years' Peregrinations in Syracuse*. Syracuse, NY: by the author, 1855.

Descartes, René. *Discours de la Méthode et Première Meditation.* 1637/1641. Paris: Hachette, 1881.

Dickens, Charles. *American Notes*. NY: St. Martin's Press, 1985/1892.

Diodorus. *Diodorus of Sicily*. Vol. 8. C. Bradford Welles, Transl. Cambridge: Harvard University Press: 1933.

Edelstein, Emma J. and Ludwig Edelstein. *Asclepius: A Collection and Interpretation of the Testimonies. Vol. 1: Collection of the Testimonies*. Baltimore: The Johns Hopkins University Press, 1945.

Edwards, Catharine. "The Suffering Body: Philosophy and Pain in Seneca's Letters." In *Constructions of the Classical Body*. J. Porter, Ed. Ann Arbor, MI: University of Michigan Press, 1999: 252-268.

Edwards, Catharine. "Self-Scrutiny and Self-Transformation in Seneca's Letters." *Greece and Rome* xliv/1 (April 1997): 23-39.

Ehrman, Brad D. *Didymus the Blind and the Text of the Gospels*. Atlanta, GA: Scholars Press, 1986.

Ekman, Paul and Erika L. Rosenberg, Eds. *What the Face Reveals: Basic and Applied Studies of Spontaneous Expression Using the Facial Action Coding System* (FACS). NY: Oxford University Press, 1997.

Epstein, Julia. *Altered Conditions: Disease, Medicine, and Storytelling*. London: Routledge, 1995.

Eyler, Joshua, Ed. *Disability in the Middle Ages: Reconsiderations and Reverberations*. Farnham, Surrey; Burlington, VT: Ashgate, 2010.

Fahnestock, Jeanne. *Rhetorical Figures in Science*. NY: Oxford University Press, 1999.

Farmer, Sharon. *Surviving Poverty in Medieval Paris: Gender, Ideology, and the Daily Lives of the Poor*. Ithaca, NY: Cornell University Press, 2002.

Ferngren, Gary B. *Medicine and Health-Care in Early Christianity*. Baltimore, MD: Johns Hopkins University Press, 2009.

Finkelstein, Vic. *Attitudes and Disabled People: Issues for Discussion*. NY: World Rehabilitation Fund,1980.

Fontenrose, Joseph. *The Delphic Oracle. Its Responses and Operations*. Berkeley: University of California Press, 1978.

Flanagan, Sabrina. *Hildegard of Bingen, 1098-1179. A Visionary Life*. London: Routledge, 1989.

Foucault, Michel. *Madness and Civilization: a History of Insanity in the Age of Reason*. Richard Howard, Transl., NY: Pantheon Books, 1965.

Foucault, Michel. *The Birth of the Clinic: an Archaeology of Medical Perception*. A. M. Sheridan Smith, Transl., NY: Vintage Books, 1974/1994.

Frank, Arthur W. *The Wounded Storyteller: Body, Illness, and Ethics*. Chicago: Chicago University Press, 1995.

Freeberg, Ernest. *The Education of Laura Bridgman: First Deaf and Blind Person to Learn Language*. Cambridge: Harvard University Press, 2001.

Fuller, Robert. *An Account of the Imprisonment and Sufferings of Robert Fuller of Cambridge*. Boston: Robert Fuller, 1853.

Galvani, Luigi. (1791/1953). *The Effect of Electricity on Muscular Motion*. Robert Montraville Green Trans. Cambridge, MA: Elizabeth Licht, Publisher.

Garland, Robert. *The Eye of the Beholder: Deformity and Disability on the Graeco-Roman World*. Ithaca, NY: Cornell University Press, 1995.

Garland Thomson, Rosemarie. *Extraordinary Bodies: Figuring Physical Disability in American Culture and Literature*. NY: Columbia University Press, 1997.

Gibson, William. *The Miracle Worker.* NY: Bantam Books, 1962.

Gitter, Elizabeth. *The Imprisoned Guest*. NY: Picador, 2001.

Givens, Reed Touwaide 2006. Givens, J. A. K., M. Reed, and A. Touwaide. (2006). *Visualizing medicine and natural history, 1200-1550*. Hampshire England: Ashgate Publishing.

Goldin-Meadow. *Hearing Gesture: How Our Hands Help Us Think*. NY: Belknap Press, 2005.

Goring, Paul. *The Rhetoric of Sensibility in Eighteenth-Century Culture*. Cambridge: Cambridge University Press, 2005.

Gould, George M. and Walter L. Pyle. *Anomalies and Curiosities of Medicine*. NY: Bell Publishing, 1956/1871.

Gould, Steven Jay. *The Mismeasure of Man*. NY: W. W. Norton & Company, 1996.

Grandin, Temple and Margaret M. Scariano. *Emergence: Labeled Autistic*. NY: Warner Books, 1996.

Griffin, Miriam. *Seneca: A Philosopher in Politics*. Oxford: Clarendon Press, 1976.

Gygax, Franziska. "Life Writing and Illness: Auto/Bio/Theory by Eve Sedgwick, Jackie Stacey, and Jill Bolte Taylor." *Prose Studies* 31/3 (December 2009): 291-299.

Haas, Christina and S. P. Witte, "Writing as an Embodied Practice: The Case of Engineering Standards." *Journal of Business and Technical Communication* 15/4 (2001): 413-457.

Hadewijch. *Hadewijch. The Complete Works*. Mother Columbia Hart, Transl., Ed. NY: Paulist Press, 1980.

Halttunen, Karen. "Gothic Mystery and the Birth of the Asylum: The Cultural Construction of Deviance in Early-Nineteenth-Century America." In *Moral Problems in American Life*. Karen Halttunen and Lewis Perry, Eds. Ithaca, NY: Cornell University Press, 1998: 41-59.

Hanson, Craig Ashley. *The English Virtuoso: Art, Medicine, and Antiquarianism in the Age of Empiricism*. Chicago: University of Chicago Press, 2009.

Harrison, George L. *Legislation on Insanity. A Collection of all the Lunacy Laws of the State and Territories of the United States*. Privately printed: Philadelphia, 1884.

Harvey, William. *De motu cordis et sanguinis./An anatomical disquisition on the motion of the heart and blood in animals*. London: J.M. Dent, 1628/1923.

Hawhee, Debra. *Bodily Arts: Rhetoric and Athletics in Ancient Greece*. Austin, TX: University of Texas Press, 2004.

Hawkins, Anne Hunsaker. *Reconstructing Illness: Studies in Pathography*. 2nd ed. West Lafayette, Indiana: Purdue University Press, 1999.

Haslam, John. *Illustrations of Madness....* London: printed by G. Hayden. Reprint Edition, Roy Porter, Ed. Tavistock Classics in the History of Psychiatry. London: Routledge, 1988.

Hay, William. *Deformity: An Essay*. Kathleen James-Cavan, Ed. Victoria, B.C.: English Literary Studies, University of Victoria, 1754/2004.

Henley, William Ernest. "In Hospital." In *Poems*. NY: Charles Scribner's Sons, 1898/1920: 3-44.

Herrmann, Dorothy. *Helen Keller, A Life*. NY: Knopf, 1998.

Hinds, Hilary. *God's Englishwomen: Seventeenth-Century Radical Sectarian Writing and Feminist Criticism*. NY: St. Martin's Press, 1996.

Hippocrates. *Hippocrates*. Vol II. W.H.S. Jones, Transl. Cambridge: Harvard University Press, 1923.

Hippocrates. *Hippocrates*. Vols V. and VI. Paul Potter, Transl. Cambridge: Harvard University Press, 1988.

Hobby, Elaine. "The Politics of Women's Prophecy in The English Revolution." In *Sacred and Profane: Secular and Devotional Interplay in Early Modern British Literature*, Helen Wilcox, Richard Todd, and Alasdair MacDonald, Eds. Amsterdam: VU University Press, 1995: 295-306.

Hoby, Margaret. *The Private Life of an Elizabeth Lady: The Diary of Lady Margaret Hoby. 1599-1605*. J. Moody, Ed. Gloucestershire: Sutton Publishing, 1998.

Hockenberry, John. *Moving Violations. A Memoir. War Zones, Wheelchairs, and Declarations of Independence*. NY: Hyperion, 1995.

Hodgson-Wright, Stephanie. Ed. *Women's Writing of the Early Modern Period 1588-1688*. An Anthology. NY: Columbia University Press, 2002.

Horwitz, Allan V. *Creating Mental Illness*. Chicago: University of Chicago Press, 2002.

Hughes, Bill. "Medicine and the Aesthetic Validation of Disabled People." *Disability and Society* 15/5 (2000): 555-568.

Husson, Thérèse-Adéle. *Reflections. The Life and Writings of a Young Blind Woman in Post-Revolutionary France*. Catherine J. Kudlick and Zina Weygand, Trans. NY: New York University Press, 2001.

Isocrates. *Isocrates I*. David Mirady and Yun Lee Too. Transl. Austin, TX: University of Texas Press, 2000.

Itard, Jean Marc Gaspard. *De L'education d'un Homme Sauvage ou de Premiers Developments Physiques et Moraux de Jeune Sauvage de l'Aveyron*. Paris, Gouyon, 1801.

Jaeger, Paul T. *Disability and the Internet: Confronting a Digital Divide*. (Disability in Society Series) Boulder, CO: Lynne Rienner Publishers, 2012.

Jamison, Kay Redford. *An Unquiet Mind: A Memoir of Moods and Madness*. NY: Vintage, 1997.

Jay, Mike. *The Air Loom Gang. The Strange and True Story of James Tilly Matthews and his Visionary Madness*. NY: Four Walls Eight Windows, 2003.

Johnson, Mark. *The Body in the Mind: the Bodily Basis of Meaning, Imagination, and Reason*. Chicago: University of Chicago Press, 1987

Johnson, Mark. *The Meaning of the Body: Aesthetics of Human Understanding*. Chicago: University of Chicago Press, 2007.

Johnson, Samuel. *Dictionary of the English Language*, 2 vols. London: Thomas Tegg, 1831.

Jorden, Edward. *Briefe Discourse of a Disease called Suffocation of the Mother*. London: Underwood, 1603.

Julian of Norwich. *Showings*. Edmund Colledge and James Walsh, Transl. Edited by Richard J. Payne. NY: Paulist Press, 1978.

Karp, Andrew "Prophecy and Divination in Archaic Greek Literature." In *Mediators of the Divine*. Robert Berchman, Ed. Atlanta, GA: Scholars Press, 1998: 9-41.

Keller, Helen. "My Story." *The Youth's Companion* (January 4, 1894): 3-4.

Keller, Helen. "The Story of My Life." *The Ladies Home Journal* (April 1902): 7-8; (May 1902): 5-6; (June 1902): 7-8; (July 1902): 11, 32; (August 1902): 13-14, 28-29; (September 1902): 11-12, 38.

Keller, Helen. *The Story of My Life*, 1903. Roger Shattuck, Dorothy Herrmann, and Anne Sullivan, Eds. NY: W. W. Norton & Company, 2003.

Keller, Helen. *The World I Live In*. NY: The Century Co, 1908.

Keller, Helen. *Out of the Dark*. NY: Doubleday: Page & Company, Inc., 1913.

Keller, Helen. "To Senator Robert M. La Follette." In *Helen Keller: Her Socialist Years*, P. Foner, Ed. NY: International Publishers, 1924, 113-116.

Keller, Helen. *Midstream*. NY: Doubleday: Doran & Company, Inc., 1929.

Kempe, Margery. *The Book of Margery Kempe*. Lynn Staley, Ed. Kalamazoo, MI: Consortium for the Teaching of the Middle Ages/University of Rochester by Medieval Institute Publications, Western Michigan University, 1996.

Kendon, Adam. *Gesture: Visible Action as Utterance*. Cambridge: Cambridge University Press, 2004.

King, Helen. "Chronic Pain and the Creation of Narrative." In *Constructions of the Classical Body*. J. Porter. Ann Arbor, MI: University of Michigan Press, 1999: 269-286.

Kleege, Georgina. "Readings A Life Between the Lines: Thérèse-Adéle Husson's Reflections on Blindness." *Prose Studies* 27/1-2 (April-August 2005): 72-79.

Kleinman, Arthur. *The Illness Narratives*. NY: Basic Books, Inc., 1989.

Kors, Alan Charles and Edward Peters. *Witchcraft in Europe, 400-1700: A Documentary History*. Philadelphia: University of Pennsylvania Press, 2001.

Krentz, Christopher, Ed. *A Mighty Change. An Anthology of Deaf American Writing, 1816-1864*. Washington D.C.: Gallaudet University Press, 2002.

Kris, Ernst. "A Psychotic Artist of the Middle Ages." In *Psychoanalytic Explorations of Art*. Ernst Kris. NY: International Universities Press, Inc., 1952: 118-27.

Kuuisisto, Stephen. *Planet of the Blind*. NY: Delta Dimensions Paperbacks, 1998.

Lamson, Mary Swift. *Life and Education of Laura Dewey Bridgman, the Deaf, Dumb, and Blind Girl*. NY: Arnos Press, 1975. Reprint of Edi Boston: Houghton, Mifflin and Company, 1881.

Lakoff, George and Mark Johnson. *Metaphors We Live By*. Chicago: University of Chicago Press, 1980.

Lane, Harlan. *The Wild Boy of Aveyron*. Cambridge: Harvard University Press, 1976.

Lane, Harlan. Ed. *The Deaf Experience. Classics in Language and Education*. Franklin Philip, Transl. Cambridge: Cambridge University Press, 1984.

Lash, Joseph P. *Helen and Teacher: The Story of Helen Keller and Anne Sullivan Macy*. NY: Dell Publishing Co, Inc., 1980.

Lavater, J. C. *Essays in Physiognomy: Designed to Promote Knowledge and Love of Mankind. London*: J. Murphy, 1789.

Linton, Simi. *Claiming Disability: Knowledge and Identity*. NY: New York University Press, 1998.

Linton, Simi. "Reassigning Meaning." In *The Disability Studies Reader*. Davis, L.J. Ed. New York: Routledge/Taylor and Francis Group, 2006: 161-172.

Locke, John. Locke, John. (1690). *An Essay Concerning Human Understanding*. http://socserv.mcmaster. ca/~econ/ugcm/3ll3/locke /Essay.htm.

Longmore, Paul K. and Lauri Umanski, Eds. *The New Disability History: American Perspectives*. New York and London: New York University Press, 2001.

Longrigg, James. *Greek Medicine. From the Heroic to the Hellenistic Age: A Source Book*. New York: Routledge, 1998.

Lorenz, Laura S. *Brain Injury Survivors: Narratives of Rehabilitation and Healing*. (Disability in Society Series) Boulder, CO: Lynne Rienner Publishers, 2010.

Lunt, Mrs. George. *Behind the Bars*. Boston: Lee and Shepard, 1871.

Lysias. 24 "On the Refusal of a Pension." W. R. M. Lamb, Transl. http://classics.mit.edu/Lysias/lys.24.html.

Mack, Phyllis. "The Prophet and Her Audience: Gender and Knowledge in the World Turned Upside Down." *In Reviving the English Revolution: Reflections and Elaborations on the Work of Christopher Hill*. Eley, G. and Hunt W., Eds. London: Verso, 1988: 139-152.

Mairs, Nancy. *Waist-High in the World. A Life Among the Disabled*. Boston: Beacon Press, 1996.

Majno, Guido. *The Healing Hand: Man and Wound in the Ancient World*. Cambridge: Harvard University Press, 1975.

Malaval, François. *A Simple Method of Raising the Soul to Contemplation in the Form of a Dialogue*. 1670. L. Menzies, Transl. London: J.M Dent and Sons, Ltd., 1931.

Maurizio, Lisa. "Delphic Oracles as Oral Performances: Authenticity and Historical Evidence." *Classical Antiquity* 16/2 (Oct. 1997): 308-334.

Mayhew, Henry. *London Labour and the London Poor. The Classical Study of the Culture of Poverty and the Criminal Classes in the 19th century*. 1861-2. 4 vols. NY: Dover Publications 1968.

McHenry, L.C., Jr. "Samuel Johnson's Tics and Gesticulations." *Journal of the History of Medicine* 22 (1967): 152-168.

McNeil, David. *Gesture and Thought*. Chicago: University of Chicago Press, 2007.

Metzler, Irina. *Disability in the Middle Ages: Thinking about Physical Impairment during the High Middle Ages, c. 1100-1400*. New York and London: Routledge, 2006.

Micale, Mark S. *Approaching Hysteria: Disease and Its Interpretations*. Princeton: Princeton University Press, 1995.

Midelfort, H.C. Erik. *A History of Madness in Sixteenth-Century Germany*. Stanford CA: Stanford University Press, 1999.

Miles, M. "'Segregated We Stand? The Mutilated Greeks' Debate at Persepois, 330 BC," *Disability & Society* 18/7 (2003): 865-879.

Miller, Carolyn R. "Rhetoric as Social Action." In *Genre and the New Rhetoric*. Aviva Freedman and Peter Medway, Eds. London; Bristol: Taylor and Francis, 1994, 23-43.

Misch, Georg. *A History of Autobiography in Antiquity*. 2 vols. Cambridge: Harvard University Press, 1951.

Mitchell, David T. and Sharon Snyder. *The Body and Physical Differences: Discourses of Disability.* Ann Arbor, MI: University of Michigan Press, 1997.

Mitchell, David T. and Sharon Snyder. *Narrative Prosthesis: Disability and the Dependencies of Discourse.* Ann Arbor, MI: University of Michigan Press, 2000.

Mitchell, David T. and Sharon Mitchell. *Cultural Locations of Disability.* Chicago: University of Chicago Press, 2006.

Montgomery, Kathryn. *How Doctors Think: Clinical Judgment and the Practice of Medicine.* Oxford: Oxford University Press, 2005.

New London Group. (Cazden, Courtney; Cope, Bill; Fairclough, Norman; Gee, Jim;et al) "A pedagogy of multiliteracies: Designing social futures." *Harvard Educational Review*; Cambridge; Spring 1996: (http://www-personal.umich.edu/~jaylemke/courses/HistLit/New-London-multiliteracies. htm).

Newman, Barbara. "Possessed by the Spirit: Devout Women, Demoniacs, and the Apostolic Life in the Thirteenth Century." *Speculum* 73/3 (July 1998): 733-770.

Newman, Sara. "Gestural Enthymemes: Delivering Movement in Eighteenth and Nineteenth Century Medical Images." *Written Communication* 26/3 (July 2009): 273-294.

Newman, Sara. "J.M. Itard's 1825 Study: Movement and the Science of the Human Mind." *History of Psychiatry* 21/1 (March 2010): 1-12.

Newman, Sara. Classic Text 67: "Study of several involuntary functions of the apparatus of movement, gripping, and voice," Itard, J. M. G. "Memoire sur Quelques Fonctions Involuntaires des Appareils de la Locomotion, de la Prehension et de la Voix." *Archives Generales de Medicine* 8 (1825): 385-407, *History of Psychiatry* 17/3 (September 2006): 333-351.

Ogden, Daniel. *The Crooked Kings of Ancient Greece.* London: Duckworth, 1997.

Oliver, Michael. *The Politics of Disablement: a Sociological Approach.* NY: St. Martin's Press, 1990.

Olsen, Sophia N.B., *Mrs. Olsen's Narrative of Her One Year's Imprisonment at Jacksonville Insane Asylum: With the Testimony of Mrs. Minard, Mrs. Shedd, Mrs. Yates, and Mrs. Lake, all corroborated by the Investigating Committee of the Legislature of Illinois.* Collected and Published by E.P. W. Packard, Chicago: J.N. Clarke, 1871.

Ong, Walter. *Orality and Literacy: the Technologizing of the Word.* New York: Methuen, 1982.

Opicinus de Canistris. *Ananymi Ticinensis Liber de Laudibus Civitatis Ticinesis.* Cod.Vat.lat. 6435. c. 1340.

Ostovich, Helen and Elizabeth Sauer, Eds. *Reading Early Modern Women. An Anthology of Texts in Manuscript and Print, 1550-1700.* New York: Routledge, 2004.

"Our Country and the London Fair." *Boston Evening Transcript* June 14, 1851.

Packard, E.P.W., Mrs. *Modern Persecution, or Insane Asylums Unveiled,* Hartford: Case, Lockwood and Brainard, 1874.

Packard, E.P.W. Mrs., *The Prisoners' Hidden Life, Insane Asylums Unveiled,* Chicago: J.N. Clarke, 1871.

Panofsky, Erwin. *Early Netherlandish Painting*. Vol 1. NY: Harper and Row, 1971.

Paré, Ambroise. *Des Monstres et Prodiges*. 1573. Paris: Éditions L'Oeil D' Or, 2003/1840.

Parke, H.W. and D.E.W. Wormell. *The Dephic Oracle*. Oxford: Basil Blackwell, 1956.

Pearman, Tory Vandeventer. "'O Sweete Venym Queynte!': Pregnancy and the Disabled Female Body in the *Merchant's Tale*." In *Disability in the Middle Ages: Reconsiderations and Reverberations.* Joshua Eyler, Ed.Farnham, Surrey; Burlington, VT: Ashgate, 2010: 25-39.

Poslusney, Venard. Trans. and Ed. *Prayer, Aspiration and Contemplation: From the Writings of John of St. Samson, O. Carm., Mystic and Charismatic*. NY: Alba House, 1975.

Porter, James I. *Constructions of the Classical Body*. Ann Arbor: University of Michigan Press, 1999.

Porter, Roy. *Flesh in the Age of Reason*. NY: W.W. Norton, 2003.

Purkiss, Diane. "Producing the Voice, Consuming the Body: Women Prophet of the Seventeenth Century." In *Women, Writing, History 1640-1740*. Grundy, I. and Wiseman, S., Eds. London: Batsford, 1992: 139-158.

Putnam, Michelle. "Conceptualizing Disability: Developing a Framework for Political Disability Identity." *Journal of Disability Policy Studies* 16/3 (2005): 188–198.

Rapp. Emily. *Poster Child. A Memoir*. NY: Bloomsbury, 2007.

Ray, Isaac. *A Treatise on the MedicalJurisprudence of Insanity*. Boston: Charles C. Little and James Brown, 1838.

Reed, Edwin. *From Soul to Mind: The Emergence of Psychology, from Erasmus Darwin to William James*. New Haven, CT: Yale University Press, 1997.

Reiss, Benjamin. *Theatres of Madness: Insane Asylums and Nineteenth Century American Culture*. Chicago: University of Chicago Press, 2008.

Riu, Xavier. *Dionysism and Comedy*. Lanham, MD: Rowan and Littlefield, 1999.

Robertson, Lisa Ann. "'Sensible' Slavery: Pleasure, Bain and the Body in Matthew Lewis' Journal of a West India Proprietor." *Prose Studies* 29/2 (August 2007): 220-237.

Rodenbach, Alexandre. *Lettre Sur les Aveugles Faisant Suite à Celle de Diderot, ou Considérations sure Leur Etat Moral, Comment on les Instruit, Comment ile Jusent des Couleurs, de la Beauté, ainsi que leur Méthode pur Conserser avec les Sourd-muets, Suivies de Notices Biographiques sure les Aveugles les plus Remarquables*. Brussels: Imprimeris de J Sacré, 1828.

Rose (Edwards), Martha L. *The Staff of Oedipus: Transforming Disability in Ancient Greece*. Ann Arbor: University of Michigan Press, 2003.

Rose (Edwards), Martha L. "Women and Disability in Ancient Greece." *Ancient World* 29/1 (1998): 3-9.

Rose (Edwards), Martha L. "Construction of Physical Disability in the Ancient Greek World: The Community Concept." In *The Body and Physical Difference: Discourses of Disability*. D. Mitchell and S. Snyder, Eds. Ann Arbor, MI: University of Michigan Press, 1997: 35-50.

Roux, Guy and Muriel Laharie. *Art et Folie au Moyen Age. Aventures et Enigmes d'Opicinus de Canistris* (1296-vers 1351). Paris: Editions Le Leopard d'Or, 1997.

Ruys, Juanita Feros. "Medieval Latin Meditations on Old Age: Rhetoric, Autobiography, and Experience." In *Old Age in the Middle Ages and the Renaissance: Interdisciplinary Approaches to a Neglected Topic*. Albrecht Classen, Ed. Berlin: Walter de Gruyter, 2007: 171-200.

Salomon, Richard G. "Aftermath to Opicinus de Canistris." *Journal of the Warburg and Courtauld Institute*, 25/1-2 (1962): 137-146

Salomon, Richard G. "A Newly Discovered Manuscript of Opicinus de Canistris: A Preliminary Report." *Journal of the Warburg and Courtauld Institute*. 16/1-2 (1953): 45-57.

Salomon, Richard G. *Opicinus de Canistris. Weltbild und Bekenntnisse Eines Avignonesishen Klerikers des. 14*. Jahrhunderts. London: The Warburg Institute: 1936.

Samson, Jean de. *Directions Pour la Vie Intérieure*.1648 S.M. Bouchereaux, Ed. Paris: Aux Éditions du Seuil, 1947.

Samson, Jean de. *La Vie, les Maximes et Partie des Oeuvres du. Fr. Jean de St. Samson*. 1651. F.P. Donatien De S. Nicolas, Ed. Paris: Denis Thierry, 1954

Samson, Jean de. *Le Cabinet Mystique*. Rennes: Vensue Yvon, 1955.

Samson, Jean de. *Le Vrai Esprit du Carmel*. Rennes: Jean Durand, 1965.

Samson, Jean de. *Les Contemplations et les Divers Soliloques du Venerable F. Jean de Samson*. 1651. Paris: Denis Thierry, 1964.

Sapey, Bob. "Disablement in the Informational Age." *Disability and Society* 15/4 (2000): 619-636.

Schiappa, Edward. *Defining Reality: Definitions and the Politics of Meaning*. Carbondale: Southern Illinois University Press, 2003.

Schiappa, Edward. *Protagoros and Logos: A Study in Greek Philosophy and Rhetoric*,1990.

Schweik, Susan. *The Ugly Laws: Disability in Public*. NY: New York University Press, 2009.

Segal, Judy Z. *Health and the Rhetoric of Medicine*. Carbondale, IL: Southern Illinois UP, 2005.

Seneca. *Ad Lucilium. Epistulae Morales*. Vol. 1. Richard Gummere, Transl. Cambridge: Harvard University Press, 1917.

Seneca. *Ad Lucilium. Epistulae Morales*. Vol. 2. Richard Gummere, Transl. Cambridge: Harvard University Press,1917.

Seneca. *Ad Lucilium. Epistulae Morales*. Vol. 3. Richard Gummere, Transl. Cambridge: Harvard University Press, 1943.

Seneca. *Moral Essays*. John Basore, Transl. London: William Heinemann, 1928.

Shakespeare, Tom. "The Social Model of Disability." In *The Disability Studies Reader*. Davis, L.J. Ed. NY: Routledge/Taylor and Francis Group, 2006: 197-206.

Siebers, Tobin Anthony. *Disability Theory*. Ann Arbor, MI: University of Michigan Press, 2008.

Siebers, Tobin Anthony. "Disability Theory. From Social Constructionism to the New Realism of the Body." In *The Disability Studies Reader*. Davis, L.J. Ed. NY: Routledge/Taylor and Francis Group, 2006: 173-183.

Simkin, A. "Mozart's Scatological Disorder." *British Medical Journal* CCCV (1992): 1563-7.

Skerpan-Wheeler, Elizabeth, Travitsky Betty, and Cullen, Patrick, Eds. *The Early Modern Englishwoman: A Facsimile Library of Essential Works*. Part

1. Printed Writings, 1641-1700. Aldershot, Essex: Ashgate Publishing Company, 2001.

Smith, Lydia A. *Behind the Scenes, or, Life in an Insane Asylum*. Chicago, Printed for the author by Culver, Page, Hoyne & Co., 1879.

Smith, Sidonie and Julia Watson, *Reading Autobiography: A Guide for Reading Life Narratives*. Minneapolis: University of Minnesota Press, 2001.

Smith, Sidonie. *A Poetics of Women's Autobiography*. Purdue: Indiana University Press, 1997.

Snyder, Sharon L. Brenda Jo Brueggemann and Rosemarie Garland-Thomson, Eds. *Disability Studies: Enabling the Humanities*. NY: Modern Language Association of America, 2002. *The Spectator* of March 20, 1711 #17.

Spender, Stephen. "In the Bodyshop: Human Exhibition in Early Modern England. In *Defects: Engendering the Modern Body*. E. Deutsch and F. Nussbaum, Eds. Ann Arbor, MI: University of Michigan Press, 2000.

Sprat, Thomas. *The History of the Royal-Society of London for the Improving of Natural Knowledge*. London: J. Martyn. 1667.

Sprenger, Jacobus and Henricus Institoris. *Malleus Maleficarum. Christopher S. Mackay*, Trans. Cambridge: Cambridge University Press, 2006.

Stafford, Barbara Maria. *Artful Science: Enlightenment Entertainment and the Eclipse of Visual Education*. Cambridge: Massachusetts Institute of Technology Press, 1996.

Stanford, E.C. *The Writings of Laura Bridgman*. San Francisco: Overland Monthly Publishing Co., 1887.

Stewart, Dugald. *Some Account of a Boy Born Blind and Deaf, Collected from Authentic Sources of Information With a Few Remarks and Comments*.

Stiker, Henri-Jacques. *A History of Disability*. W. Sayers. Transl. University of Michigan Press, 1999.

Stoddard Holmes, Martha. "Working (with) the Rhetoric of Affliction: Autobiographical Narratives of Victorians with Physical Disabilities." In *Embodied Rhetorics: Disability in Language and Culture*. J.C. Wilson and C. Lewiecki-Wilson, Eds. Carbondale: Southern Illinois University Press, 2001: 27-44.

Strong, Elizabeth Stone. *A sketch of the life of Elizabeth T. Stone, and of her persecutions, with an appendix of her treatment and sufferings while in the Charlestown McLean Assylum [sic] where she was confined under the pretense of insanity*.

Streit, Sigrid. *Gesture and Rhetorical delivery: the Transmission of Knowledge in Complex Situations* Kent, OH: Kent State University, 2011.

Swain, John and Sally French. "Towards an Affirmation Model of Disability." *Disability and Society* 15/5 (2000): 569-582.

Swan, Jim. "Touching Words: Helen Keller, Plagiarism, Authorship." In *The Construction of Authorship. Textual Appropriation in law and Literature*. M. Woodmansee and P. Jaszi, Eds. Durham, NC: Duke University Press, 1994: 57-100.

Swan, Moses. *Ten Years and Ten Months in Lunatic Asylums in Different States*. Hoosick Falls, NY, 1874.

Thiher, Allen. *Revels in Madness: Insanity in Medicine and Literature*. Ann Arbor, MI: The University of Michigan Press, 1999.

Trapnel, Anna. *Anna Trapnel's Report*. 1654. London: Brewster, 1954.

Trapnel, Anna. *The Cry of a Stone*. 1654. H. Hinds, Ed. Tempe, AZ: Arizona Center for Medieval and Renaissance Studies, 2000.

Trapnel, Anna. *Strange and Wonderfull Newes from White-Hall: or the Mighty Visions ... to diverse Colonels, Ladies and gentlewomen, concerning the government of the common wealth of England, Scotland, and Ireland; and her revelations touching his highness the Lord Protector, and the army. With her Declaration touching the state affairs of Great Britain even from the death of the late King Charles, to the dissolution of the late King Charles*. 1654.

Tuke, Daniel Hake. *The Insane in the United States and Canada*. 1885. Reprint, New York: Arno Press, 1973.

Van Gogh, Vincent. *The Letters of Vincent Van Gogh*. Ronald de Leeuw, Ed. Arnold Pomerans, Transl. London: Penguin Press, 1996.

Vesalius, Andreas. (1949/1543). *De humani corporis fabrica liborum epitome /The epitome of Andreas Vesalius*. New York: Macmillian, 1949/1543.

Vlahogiannis, Nicholas. "Disabling Bodies." In *Changing Bodies, Changing Meanings: Studies on the Human Body in Antiquity*. D. Montserrat, Ed. NY: Routledge, 1998: 13-37.

Voaden, Rosalynn. *God's Words, Women's Voices: The Discernment of Spirits in the Writing of Late-Medieval Women Visionaries*. York: York Medieval Press, 1999.

Walsh, Lynda. "The Rhetoric of Oracles." *Rhetoric Society Quarterly* 33/3 (Summer 2003): 55-78.

Walters, Jonathan. "Making a Spectacle: Deviant Men, Invectice, and Pleasure." *Arethusa* 31/3 (1998): 355-367.

Whittaker, C.R. "The Delphic Oracle: Belief and Behaviour in Ancient Greece: And Africa." *The Harvard Theological Review* 58/1 (Jan. 1965): 21-47.

Weygand, Zina. *The Blind in French Society from the Middle Ages to the Century of Louis Braille*. E.J. Cohen, Trans. Stanford: Stanford University Press, 2009.

Wheatley, Edward. *Stumbling Blocks Before the Blind: Medieval Constructions of a Disability*. Ann Arbor, MI: University of Michigan Press, 2010.

Wheatley, Edward. "Blindness, Discipline, and Reward: Louis IX and the Foundation of the Hospice des Quinze-Vingts." *Disability Studies Quarterly* 22 (2002): 194-212.

Wickkiser, Bronwen Lara. *Asklepios, Medicine, and the Politics of Healing in Fifth Century Greece: Between Craft and Cult*. Baltimore: The Johns Hopkins University Press, 2008.

Wilson, James and Cynthia Lewiecki-Wilson. Eds. *Embodied Rhetorics: Disability in Language and Culture*. Carbondale, IL: Southern Illinois University Press, 2001.

Wilson Logan, Shirley. *We Are Coming: The Persuasive Discourse of Nineteenth-Century Black Women*. Carbondale, IL: Southern Illinois University Press, 1999.

Wood, Mary Elene. *The Writing on the Wall: Women's Autobiography and the Asylum*. Urbana and Chicago: University of Illinois Press, 1994.

Woodmansee, Martha and Peter Jaszi. "Introduction." In *The Construction of Authorship. Textual Appropriation in Law and Literature*. M. Woodmansee and P. Jaszi, Eds. Durham, NC: Duke University Press, 1994: 1-13.

Index

About the Book

What accounts for the differing ways that individuals and cultures have tried to make sense of mental and physical disabilities? Can we see a pattern of change over time? Sara Newman examines personal narratives across a broad sweep of history—from ancient Greece to the present day—to reveal the interplay of dynamics that have shaped both personal and societal conceptions of mental and physical difference.

Sara Newman is professor of English at Kent State University.